DISRUPTIVE ARCHIVES

DISSIDENT FEMINISMS

Elora Halim Chowdhury, Editor

A list of books in the series appears at the end of this book.

DISRUPTIVE ARCHIVES

Feminist Memories of Resistance in Latin America's Dirty Wars

VIVIANA BEATRIZ MACMANUS

UNIVERSITY OF ILLINOIS PRESS
Urbana, Chicago, and Springfield

© 2020 by the Board of Trustees
of the University of Illinois
All rights reserved
Manufactured in the United States of America
1 2 3 4 5 C P 5 4 3 2 1
♾ This book is printed on acid-free paper.

Library of Congress Cataloging-in-Publication Data
Names: MacManus, Viviana Beatriz, 1981– author.
Title: Disruptive archives: feminist memories of resistance in
   Latin America's dirty wars / Viviana Beatriz MacManus.
Description: Urbana: University of Illinois Press, [2020] | Series:
   Dissident feminisms | Includes bibliographical references and
   index. |
Identifiers: LCCN 2020030516 (print) | LCCN 2020030517
   (ebook) | ISBN 9780252043536 (cloth; alk. paper) |
   ISBN 9780252085437 (paperback; alk. paper) | ISBN
   9780252052415 (ebook)
Subjects: LCSH: Feminism—Latin America—History—20th
   century. | State-sponsored terrorism—Latin America—
   History—20th century. | Women—Violence against—Latin
   America—History—20th century. | Women—Political
   activity—Latin America—History—20th century. | Political
   violence—Latin America—History—20th century. | Latin
   America—Politics and government—20th century.
Classification: LCC HQ1460.5 .M32 2020 (print) | LCC HQ1460.5
   (ebook) | DDC 305.42098/0904—dc23
LC record available at https://lccn.loc.gov/2020030516
LC ebook record available at https://lccn.loc.gov/2020030517

For my parents,
Eduardo MacManus and Susanna Robertson

We are not victims, we are protagonists of this history . . . we were not uncritical victims, because above all we were politically militant.

—*Margarita Cruz, survivor of the Argentinean repression who was detained at the Escuelita de Famaillá in Tucumán, Argentina*

There are many brave women, but they are anonymous . . . there are many women who don't speak of this. . . . Many people never spoke of this again. Many people were scared. And I understand them . . . there are many women who were protagonists of this history, and who form part of this memory and who have not spoken of this again. And they do not want to, and I respect that . . . and well, before only the men narrated these histories until we women began to speak . . . women participated in social movements, in the Communist movement, but women's participation in political struggles were not visible.

—*Ana Ignacia Rodríguez Márquez, survivor of the 1968 Mexico City massacre and former political prisoner*

Contents

Acknowledgments xi

Introduction. "All of Latin America Is Sown with the Bones of [Its] Forgotten Youth": Hemispheric State Terror and Latin American Feminist Theories of Justice 1

1 Critical Latin American Feminist Perspectives and the Limits and Possibilities of Human Rights Reports 26

2 Sexual Necropolitics, Survival, and the Gender of Betrayal 61

3 "Ghosts of Another Era": Gendered Haunting and the Legacy of Women's Armed Resistance 99

4 Gendered Memories, Collective Subjectivity, and Solidarity Practices in Women's Oral Histories 133

Epilogue. The Legacy of State-Sanctioned Violence and Specters of the Dirty Wars' Radical Women 162

Notes 169

Bibliography 181

Index 191

Acknowledgments

This book is a labor of love shaped by the generosity of family, friends, mentors, colleagues, activists, and many other people in the United States, Mexico, and Argentina. I would like to first thank the women I interviewed in Argentina and Mexico between 2009 and 2014 whose stories form the narrative arc of this book. In Mexico, I would like to thank "Alejandra," Bertha Lilia Gutiérrez Campos, Ana Ignacia Rodríguez Márquez, Maricela Balderas Silva, and Luz Aguilar Terrés. In Argentina, many thanks to Margarita Cruz, Marta Díaz, Nilda Eloy, Lelia Ferrarese, Liliana Forchetti, Mirta Sgro, and Silvia Yáñez for sharing their stories with me. They welcomed me into their lives and shared intimate, harrowing, and inspiring stories of survival and resistance to state terror. Their stories of *lucha por la justicia* kept me afloat during the hardest moments of writing this book, and turning to their words reinvigorated me with the passion for justice and storytelling that helped to create this project.

Storytelling as a form of resistance is something I learned from members of my family, particularly my maternal grandparents. My investment in the construction and recovery of a feminist historical archive in Latin America is a notion that was inculcated by my great-grandmother and grandmother, Aurora and Ana Guerrero, who immigrated from Zacatecas, Mexico, to Los Angeles in the 1920s. They would often share stories of the hardships they experienced as immigrant women in Los Angeles, but they always emphasized the importance of love, family, and giving back to the community. Their bravery has taught me the importance of storytelling as a form of Latin American feminist resistance, and legacies of Latin American women's survival serve as the foundation to this book.

This book is also inspired by my grandfather, Luis Robertson, whose stories of surviving extreme poverty during pre-Revolution era Cuba left an indelible mark on my young mind. His passion for history, justice, leftist politics, as well as his unwavering support of the Cuban Revolution, profoundly shaped my political consciousness. This book is a product of his love for his grandchildren, but also his love for justice.

As for my parents, Eduardo MacManus and Susanna Robertson, there are truly no words to capture the love, appreciation, and admiration I have for you both. You taught me the value of an education as well as the importance of politics and justice for all marginalized communities. Thank you for providing your children with the support, love, and encouragement necessary to thrive and feel nurtured. This book is truly written in your honor, and I cannot express to you here the profound love I have for you both. *Los quiero tanto, tanto.*

I would also like to convey deep gratitude and love for the rest of my family members—my brother Carlos, my Tía Betty, and all *mis primas queridas*—who provided me with constant and unconditional love and support. *A mi suegra, Carmen Velázquez y toda la familia Velázquez en Carolina del norte, gracias por dejarme ser parte de tu familia tan linda.*

The fieldwork I conducted in Argentina and Mexico would not have been possible without the generosity of various human rights groups, civic organizations, and individuals who went above and beyond to support me during my research process. It is through these organizations that I was able to connect with the women I interviewed for this project, and I am indebted to their kindness and generosity. In Mexico City, I want to specifically thank Romeo Cartagena of El Comité '68 for his friendship and also his overwhelming support when I conducted fieldwork in Mexico. I would also like to thank colleagues Adela Cedillo, Fernando Calderón, and Alex Aviña for their support of my project and for connecting me with folks in Mexico. In Argentina, many thanks to Veronica Jeria of La Asociación de Ex-Detenidos Desaparecidos for allowing me to work with their organization and to interview various members. To my friend Sara Kozameh, thank you for your friendship, but also, thank you for connecting me to the incredible activists and survivors in Argentina. The tireless advocacy and justice-focused projects of these organizations and survivors keep the historical memory of the Dirty Wars alive in Mexico and Argentina.

I would be remiss not to acknowledge the various fellowships and grants that funded the research for this book. As a graduate student at UC San Diego,

I received generous grants and fellowships from the Department of Literature, the Center for Iberian and Latin American Studies, and the Institute for International, Comparative, and Area Studies. Through the UC Human Rights Fellowship, I was able to spend the summer of 2009 in Argentina working closely with La Asociación de Ex-Detenidos Desaparecidos. I am also thankful for my experience as a graduate student fellow of UCSD's Audiovisual Archive of the Spanish Civil War/Francoist Dictatorship in 2008. A deep, heartfelt thank-you to my mentors at UCSD—Luis Martín-Cabrera, Jaime Concha, Rosaura Sánchez, Rosemary George, and Lisa Lowe—for helping me with the initial ideas that inspired this book.

While at the University of Maryland, Baltimore County, I received immense support from colleagues, fellowships, grants, and mentors. As a postdoctoral fellow for faculty diversity, I was able to conduct additional research in Mexico in the summer of 2012. UMBC also granted me Summer Research Fellowships in 2012 and 2014, allowing me to complete essential research in Argentina and Mexico. In 2015, UMBC's Office of the Provost funded an Eminent Scholar Mentor Program, where I worked closely with Rosa-Linda Fregoso. This mentorship and friendship continued during my time as a Woodrow Wilson Career Enhancement Fellow in 2016. During this time, Rosa-Linda Fregoso provided invaluable feedback and support throughout various stages of this book. I cannot thank Rosa-Linda enough for the mentorship she has provided me over the years and to the wonderful friendship we have now established: she is truly my academic role model!

To Carole McCann, I am indebted to your mentorship and everything you have done to support me and nurture my academic career. UMBC's Department of Gender and Women's Studies was the ideal place for a first job out of graduate school, and Dr. McCann ensured that my transition from graduate student to junior faculty was as seamless as possible. Carole, thank you from the bottom of my heart for all that you've done, and for the invaluable advice you offered on this book. A warm and loving thank you to Kate Drabinski, Amy Bhatt, and Mejdulene Shomali for being such wonderful friends, colleagues, and sources of support during my time at UMBC.

Sylvanna Falcón and Pascha Bueno-Hansen, you took me under your wing and have been wonderful role models and mentors to me. Thank you for believing in the essence of my project, and I look forward to continuing our friendship and to having more conversations on Latin American feminisms.

At Occidental College, I thank Mary Christianakis for welcoming me into the Department of Critical Theory and Social Justice and for letting me teach what I love in the city that I love. Salvador Fernández, you have been a wonderful friend and mentor since my undergraduate days at Oxy and to this day, you still selflessly support me in my professional endeavors. I can only aspire to be as giving and as supportive of a mentor-friend as you! I would also like to extend my gratitude to Oxy's dean of faculty and the dean of the college for supporting the final stages of publication. I look forward to continuing projects on Latin American feminisms and cultural studies as a faculty member of the Spanish and French studies department at Oxy.

I would also like to thank the editors at the University of Illinois Press—Dawn Durante and Elora Chowdhury—as well as the anonymous reviewers for their thoughtful and critical feedback on my manuscript. Their reviews helped me articulate my argument in new ways and their feedback has been invaluable in strengthening the overall manuscript, and for that I am very grateful.

This book is a result of the hours of labor and love selflessly offered by writing groups, friends, and colleagues who provided welcome feedback. To my DC writing group—Dixa Ramírez, Fan Yang, and Chelsea Stieber—this book would not be what it is today without the thoughtful and critical feedback you provided on various drafts.

To my chosen family and my dearest friends, Megha Shah, Leila Roumani, Susan Ayoob, and Liz Andrews: thank you for the love you've shown me over the years and for believing in this project. To my graduate school friends, and now family: Sean Dinces, Jodi Eisenberg, Dixa Ramírez, Caralyn Bialo, Chase Smith, Yumi Pak, Bernadine Hernández, and Lauren Heintz, I would not have survived graduate school or any part of academia without your ridiculous jokes, endless laughter, work dates, and most importantly, the constant love you've shown me. This book is dedicated to you all and the love and bond we share for life. Even during the most difficult stages of writing, my friends gently encouraged me to carry on as they all believed in the importance of this project.

And finally, I dedicate this book to my little family: my beautiful partner and love, David Velázquez, *nuestra perrhija* BonBon, and our beautiful new son, Leonardo. David, thank you for being so loving, patient, kind, and supportive throughout these years as I completed my book. I am always in awe of your beautiful heart and your commitment to social justice and your tireless efforts to advocate for those in our community and beyond. Your beautiful heart and soul are a constant source of inspiration, and you make me want to learn and grow in every way. I cannot wait to raise Leo with you to be a beautiful little human and future social justice advocate. *Gracias, mi corazón de melón, mi vida. Te quiero mucho.*

Portions of chapters 1 and 3 appeared in earlier publications. Chapter 1 features selections from my previously published article with the *International*

Feminist Journal of Politics, "'We Are Not Victims, We Are Protagonists of This History': Latin American Gender Violence and the Limits of Women's Rights as Human Rights." A portion of my article with the *Journal of Latin American Cultural Studies*, "'Ghosts of Another Era': Gender and Haunting in Visual Cultural Narratives of Mexico's Dirty War," appears in chapter 3.

DISRUPTIVE ARCHIVES

INTRODUCTION

"All of Latin America Is Sown with the Bones of [Its] Forgotten Youth"

Hemispheric State Terror and Latin American Feminist Theories of Justice

In July 2012, I met ex-guerrillera, "Alejandra," a former member of the Guadalajara-based armed organizations the People's Revolutionary Armed Forces (FRAP), the 23rd of September Communist League (Liga), and the People's Union. Over café con leche in the quiet lobby of the Hotel de Mendoza in downtown Guadalajara, Mexico, Alejandra shared memories of her political awakening as a student at the University of Guadalajara in the early 1970s.[1] As a student there, she became involved with the Student Revolutionary Front (FER), but she joined the armed insurgency after witnessing the repression of FER members by the conservative, state-backed Student Federation of Guadalajara (FEG).[2] A jovial, middle-aged woman, Alejandra discussed the illegal war the Mexican government waged against armed and unarmed organizations, enthusiastically describing witnessing the shoot-out by the anticommunist student group the FEG, being on the run from the White Brigade (Brigada Blanca) antiguerrilla task force, and surviving the murder, torture, disappearances, and gendered violence of many of her compañeros.

I was introduced to Alejandra through my contacts at the Mexico City–based historical memory group, the Committee for Democratic Liberties (Comité '68), while I was conducting research on women participants in armed and unarmed organizations during the "Dirty War" in Mexico (1960–1980s).[3] In July 2012 I had the opportunity to interview Alejandra and Bertha Lilia Gutiérrez Campos in Guadalajara, both friends and compañeras in the University of Guadalajara's

FER and in the urban guerrilla, the Liga. In the early 1970s, both women bore witness to egregious acts of violence sponsored by the Mexican state and survived counterinsurgency plans that sought to eradicate armed and unarmed leftist movements in the country. Alejandra was a respected figure in Guadalajara's armed movements in the 1970s, and her tenacity, outspokenness, and political resolve led to positions of leadership within the People's Union guerrilla organization, which was uncommon for women members of the time. While some women rose to positions of leadership in various urban and rural guerrillas in Mexico, most of these women were assassinated by the state or are still missing; very few leaders of the movements are alive to tell us their stories.

Toward the end of our interview, I asked Alejandra about her involvement in feminist movements in Guadalajara. I turned to this question in order to explore the histories of women political militants of 1960s and 1970s Mexico and to learn more about how Alejandra positioned her feminist and revolutionary politics in relation to the legacy of the armed insurgencies in Mexico. She stated the following: "I joined a feminist organization later after my participation in the guerrilla; first, what we had to do was fight against inequality, since there couldn't be democracy with inequality even in the guerrilla groups, and wherever there was inequality, there could not be democracy. You want to democratize society but you don't democratize your home, and then I realized that men and groups like the Church, the governments, are bothered more by a feminist than [a guerrillero] who is armed." Alejandra's response articulates a rich, complex theory of feminism that evinces the hierarchization that was found in both the state and leftist organizations during this time.

Alejandra's interview, along with the eleven other interviews I conducted with survivors of political violence during Mexico and Argentina's so-called Dirty Wars (1960–80s), unearth women's submerged histories of resistance to oppressive political systems of power in Latin America, in both right-wing military states such as Argentina's Process for National Reorganization (1976–84) and nominally democratic states, as in the case of the Institutional Revolutionary Party's (PRI) seventy-one-year-reign in Mexico (1929–2000). *Disruptive Archives: Feminist Memories of Resistance in Latin America's Dirty Wars* examines parallel histories of gendered and political forms of state violence that emerged in Argentina and Mexico during the Cold War, focusing on the origins of the systematic, organized repressive apparatuses that were in place across the Americas from 1960 until the early 1980s. The women I interviewed survived harrowing forms of state-sponsored terrorism that operated transnationally at the height of the Cold War era in Mexico and Argentina. Indeed, while many scholars have produced important, pathbreaking literature on the histories of

Latin America's state-sponsored terrorism during the Cold War era particularly in relation to the Southern Cone dictatorships, these scholarly conversations exclude Mexico's history of state violence.[4] It is imperative that we study the normalization of state-sanctioned violence of the Southern Cone alongside the lesser-known history of state-sponsored repression in Mexico in order to examine the hemispheric patterns of extralegal, gendered state violence during the height of the Cold War.

While one aim of this book is to illuminate the parallel forms of gendered state violence that undergirded the nascent, neoliberal modernist projects of Argentina and Mexico, *Disruptive Archives* is at its core a project that highlights women's resistance to authoritarian state projects and the dominant narratives espoused by male leaders of leftist organizations. This book examines cultural productions and oral histories that challenge dominant, masculinist discourses that have positioned the women political activists on the periphery, and/or have criminalized and erased their agency from this history. As Ana Ignacia Rodríguez Márquez asserted in the epigraph to this book, many women were protagonists who participated in anticapitalist, antiauthoritarian, and revolutionary political organizations, yet many of their narratives remain unknown. *Disruptive Archives* examines women's histories of struggle against state violence and trauma and encourages us to consider how they form new feminist knowledge on Latin America's Dirty Wars. We find multiple articulations of resistance in the cultural texts and the voices of survivors create imagined communities that foment expressions of solidarity and resistance, transcending nation-states and temporal boundaries.

This book asks readers to consider the following: How does the memory work of women survivors of state violence intervene into assumed epistemological reference points on the Dirty Wars? What knowledge and feminist theory is produced in women's narratives of struggle against abusive political and institutional systems of power, and leftist male-centered accounts of Latin America's Dirty Wars? What is unique and particular to these women's narratives, and how does the *form* of the oral histories and cultural texts illuminate embodied feminist knowledge of the gendered history of the Dirty Wars? And most importantly, what can we learn from these women's histories of bravery and resistance?

Illuminating the little-known histories of Mexico's and Argentina's gendered opposition to the masculinist discourses of the Dirty Wars, *Disruptive Archives* pieces together narratives of struggle from oral histories, human rights reports, testimonial literature, cinematic and literary fiction, and documentary film. Rather than merely recovering unearthed histories of women involved in resistance movements and historical memory projects, the cultural works I examine here reflect tensions and contradictions of particular historical junctures, events, and social structures that characterized this period in Latin American history. The cultural texts, particularly the oral histories, operate as theory and knowledge producers; they not only destabilize the hegemonic, masculinist histories that have decentered their presences and delegitimized their voices, but they also function as critical feminist articulations of new social justice projects that weave together transnational histories of violence and legacies of Latin American women's resistance to repression.

In essence, *Disruptive Archives* examines the heterogeneity of form and content found in the cultural productions and works to uncover the feminist genealogies buried in the Dirty War archives. This book argues that new epistemological framings of the Dirty War emerge in the gaps, silences, hauntings, and embodied expressions found in these cultural texts and offer us new Latin American feminist theories of justice. Although some of the women I interviewed would not consider themselves feminist, their activism and involvement in historical memory projects evoke a feminist ethos of revolutionary politics that unites women in imagined communities of struggle in the Americas, refusing to forget the state crimes of the past and the present as they work towards a vision of what Wendy Brown terms "comprehensive justice." Brown's concept of comprehensive justice challenges dominant paradigms of human rights that center on suffering and victimization rather than radical change that leads to justice for those affected by human rights violence. This notion of human rights with comprehensive justice centers the subjects of human rights not as mere victims of violence, but rather as arbiters of justice and agents of social change.[5] In this vein, the women in my project demand to be read as "protagonists of this history," as they survived violence of the patriarchal, nascent neoliberal state and defied cultural and gendered expectations of the time.

Mexico's Secret Dirty War and Argentina's Process for National Reorganization

During the early 1960s until the 1980s, Mexico's Revolutionary Institutional Party (PRI) and Argentina's Process for National Reorganization (Proceso) coordinated exhaustive, organized plans to dismantle armed and unarmed leftist organizations. Despite the difference in the magnitude of repression in both nations, the so-called Dirty Wars refer to the organized forms of violence that these authoritarian regimes waged against political resistance and mobilization efforts during the height of the Cold War. In order to stymie growing international socialist resistance efforts, the Mexican and Argentinean governments—with the military and financial assistance of the US government—waged Dirty Wars against so-called subversive political dissidents who were perceived to be threats to the social, national, patriarchal, and neoliberal capitalist order. The success of the Cuban Revolution in 1959, as well as the thwarted US attempts to overthrow Fidel Castro, inspired activists in Mexico and Argentina to organize against the governments that colluded with foreign interests at the expense of their own nation's social welfare. With the financial and military aid of the United States, these Latin American governments developed elaborate plans to obliterate dissenting bodies who intervened in the creation of a communist-free Latin America and who threatened their economic interests.[6]

Under the guise of national security, the Argentinean and Mexican states committed acts of terrorism that included the torture, enforced disappearance, theft and kidnapping of babies, and murder of thousands of people, many of whom were of university age. *Dirty War* itself is a contested term that has been debated among academics, activists, and survivors, primarily due to the implication that "war" erroneously suggests that there was a political, armed conflict between two factions of equal power: the government and leftist political dissidents. Some activists, scholars, and survivors, however, refer to this term in order to debunk the myth that the leftist social movements and the authoritarian governments had equal power. Thus, I invoke the term *Dirty War* throughout this book in order to shed light on the unjust war the governments waged against a segment of the population that was no match, militarily, to the repressive apparatus of the state. As Alejandra aptly declared, "they [the state] just abused, destroyed, and killed young people, and for that reason, this should be known." To this end, the title of this introductory chapter alludes to the "forgotten bones" of Latin America's youths who had participated in revolutionary movements during the Dirty War era.

The term *Dirty War* is generally associated with the military regimes of the Southern Cone and is not typically used in reference to Mexico's Cold War history. In general, the history of Mexico's systemic, state-sanctioned violence is absent from the overall history of Cold War Latin America. This erasure is a form of discursive violence that has silenced the lived histories of state terror and repression that many Mexicans endured during the Dirty War era. Recently, however, more scholarship has centered on Mexico's unknown history of the Dirty War and how its legacy has shaped the current political landscape, particularly as it has ties to contemporary narco-trafficking violence in Mexico.[7] As critical as this scholarship is, few of these historiographical works use a gender analytic to assess Mexico's Dirty War violence.[8]

During the Cold War, Mexico promoted a national narrative that *appeared* to be more tolerant of political dissent than Southern Cone nations, yet the PRI covertly sanctioned the same violent tactics against political dissidents. Since the PRI had historical ties to the Mexican Revolution as being the party of the Revolution, it was preoccupied with its image, and therefore leaders approached their "problem" of leftist political movements in a secretive and contradictory manner. Thus, the PRI lauded itself as a democratic, modern nation-state, which stood in contrast to other Latin American nations experiencing political and economic turmoil, such as Chile and Argentina. As Calderon and Cedillo note, "the PRI claimed its revolutionary nationalism to be the ideal alternative to left- and right-wing authoritarianism and projected itself as progressive but not radical."[9] Despite the government's attempt to quietly mitigate social activism, political unrest exploded during President Gustavo Díaz Ordaz's term (1964–70) as social movements across the nation gained momentum. During his term, armed guerrillas formed in the rural regions of Guerrero and Chihuahua, and the student movement in Mexico City gained more international visibility. In response to the student movement, the Mexican military occupied the National Polytechnic Institute and the National University of Mexico (UNAM). The presence of the Mexican military in universities led students to organize more demonstrations and soon the movement grew to include 300,000 supporters (including medical professionals, railroad workers, and electrical workers).[10] Such solidarity movements threatened the PRI's political power, and a national narrative was invented to justify extreme forms of state violence. As historian Renata Keller notes, "Mexico's Cold War escalated into a vicious cycle in which the government's treatment of its own citizens prompted them to participate in domestic opposition groups and international solidarity efforts, which in turn inspired authorities to resort to further acts of repression and violence."[11] This extreme state violence culminated in the Tlatelolco massacre on October 2, 1968, when paramilitary forces entered the Plaza de las Tres Culturas in the Tlatelolco area of Mexico City and opened fire on three thousand peaceful protestors.

While Luis Echeverría (1970–76) proclaimed to be more progressive than his predecessor Díaz Ordaz, he continued similar repressive measures against dissidents, including the 1971 Corpus Christi massacre of student protestors, the murders of guerrilla leaders Lucío Cabañas in 1974 and Genaro Vásquez in 1972, the terrorizing and murders of guerrilla members and their sympathizers in the state of Guerrero, and the torture and systematic disappearance of suspected members of armed organizations. Echeverría sanctioned these forms of state terrorism, yet in a contradictory turn, the PRI provided amnesty to political exiles from Chile and Argentina. By welcoming exiles from the Dirty Wars in other Latin American nations, the PRI was able to situate itself as a liberal democratic haven in a Latin America plagued by political and economic unrest. Due to this duplicity on the part of the PRI government, the harrowing acts of violence were not made visible to many international human rights entities and remained invisible until the PRI lost power in 2001. As such, Mexico's position during the Cold War in Latin America was unique. During Mexico's secret Dirty War, three thousand activists, guerrilla members, family members, and sympathizers were murdered by the state, another seven thousand people were tortured, and three thousand remain missing to this day.[12]

While Mexico's PRI covertly sanctioned state violence against its political dissidents, the Argentinean military regime overtly declared a war against communism during their Dirty War period. Argentina experienced many years of political turmoil prior to the 1976 coup d'état. Prior to the 1976 coup d'état that overthrew Isabel Martínez de Perón and installed Jorge Rafael Videla as dictator, the nation experienced a series of violent episodes; the military coup d'état of 1976 was the apex of the previous military coups d'état.[13] What demarcates the 1976–83 military regime as unique in the history of Argentina was the meticulously coordinated repression and goal to eradicate all political opposition. The military junta received public support as the dictatorship promised an end to the political chaos of the preceding years and set forth a plan that would stabilize and provide order to the nation.[14] This violent national makeover was termed by the junta leaders as the Process for National Reorganization. Historian Hugo Vezzetti notes that the tenets of the military regime pervaded all factions of Argentinean society, which aided in the regime's success; schools, offices, workplaces, and families acquiesced to the regime to varying degrees, a sign of the extent to which the ideology of the Proceso saturated various factions of Argentinean society.[15]

In order to achieve national order, the junta declared a war against subversion in which political opponents to the regime were considered enemies of the state. The junta crafted a narrative that positioned dissidents as part of a Marxist cancer that had to be extirpated from the national body. As a result, the three branches of the armed forces swiftly eradicated the armed Peronist wing, the Montoneros, and other armed leftist insurgent groups throughout the nation, and soon the regime targeted those who did not belong to armed organizations. As the governor of the district of Buenos Aires, General Ibérico Saint Jean, famously declared in May 1977, "first, we will kill all the subversives; afterward, their collaborators; then their sympathizers, and then those who are indifferent, and finally, those who are timid."[16] The years of the military regime were marked by extremely brutal state violence and included the following human rights violations: the disappearance of between ten thousand and thirty thousand individuals, the dumping of drugged prisoners from army planes into the Río de la Plata in the "death flights," sexual violence against prisoners, the theft of more than four hundred babies born to women in captivity, among other harrowing and cruel instances of organized, state-sponsored terrorism. Acts of state violence fomented a culture of fear, terror, and trauma in the national landscape, a cultural climate lasting until the dictatorship ended in 1983, though it has never been completely erased from national memory.

Gendered Dirty Wars: Women's Resistance to State Terror

Parallel tactics of state violence sanctioned by Mexico's liberal democratic PRI government and Argentina's military junta reflected the transnational reach of state terror during the Dirty Wars. They were, however, specifically *gendered* Dirty Wars that relied on what Jean Franco terms "extreme masculinity" to violently reinforce traditional gendered and sexual scripts that defined a national identity based on rigid masculine authoritarianism.[17] Latin American scholars have long discussed the gendered nature of Latin American state violence, particularly in the Southern Cone dictatorships and the racialized, genocidal state violence of the Central American civil wars. Argentina's history of state-sponsored terror has inspired a rich body of feminist literature on the gendered underpinnings of state violence. This genealogy of feminist anthropological, historical, and cultural scholarship on Argentina's dictatorship has often made transnational links to other historical epochs of state terrorism in Latin American nations such as Chile, Uruguay, and Brazil.[18] I build on their work by suggesting that we use this transnational frame to examine the normalization of gendered state violence in both nominally democratic states (Mexico) and military, fascist regimes (Argentina). This comparative approach not only makes important hemispheric links between the gendered nature of state violence instituted across the Americas during the Cold War era, but it also brings visibility to the unknown history of Mexico's Dirty War. Politically active women were perceived as a threat to the social ideologies and gendered nationalisms firmly entrenched in Mexico and Argentina. The politically active woman's body thus became a literal and figurative battlefield, as the authoritarian states attempted to wield their power and control over these dissenting bodies.

The global feminist, anti-imperialist, decolonization movements, and the Cuban Revolution of 1959 shaped the political consciousness of many women in Latin America, inspiring many of them to join socialist organizations in large numbers. The 1960s in Latin America was characterized by the *concientización* (political consciousness building) of many young people, including many young women. Social movements led many Latin Americans to protest social and economic issues afflicting their own countries, such as pervasive poverty, illiteracy, lack of health services and affordable housing, and extreme socioeconomic inequality. Across the Americas, many young women were participating in leftist social movements and entering the once-male dominated public sphere of politics to join demonstrations, marches, and other resistance efforts against their authoritarian governments. This political shift and women's resistance to political corruption during this time is best exemplified in the Spanish expression, "poner el cuerpo," which as Barbara Sutton explains, means "not just to talk, think, or desire but to be really present and involved; to put the whole (embodied) being into action, to be committed to a social cause, and to assume the bodily risks, work, and demands of such a commitment."[19] In effect, women were literally using their bodies as sites of resistance to their authoritarian, patriarchal, and capitalist nation-states.

In Mexico and Argentina, women were participating in embodied resistance efforts in both armed and unarmed organizations. Adela Cedillo posits that approximately 25 percent of urban guerrillas in Mexico were middle-class, university-educated women, and Deborah Cohen and Lessie Jo Frazier note that many more women joined brigades during the Mexican student movement and participated in public political events.[20] Leaders of leftist revolutionary movements recognized the importance of women's participation in the organizations and would stress the significance of gender equality and democratization in their movements. Lucío Cabañas, leader of Guerrero, Mexico's Party of the Poor, demanded of the guerrilleros that they "value the rights of women" and articulated that the guerrilleros must treat women participants as equals: "[the guerrilleras]— in addition to nursing the sick and serving as mail courier—are armed, and their gender does not make them more 'naturally' responsible to take care of the troops; the work we do here is done collectively."[21] Similarly, shifting cultural and social tides emboldened many Argentinean women to participate in leftist social resistance movements. Working-class and middle-class young women, many of them university students, joined armed socialist organizations; some women, such as the members of the armed group Montoneros, formed women's fronts of armed groups (such as the Agrupación Evita, formed in 1973), which organized women and their political interests at the local, neighborhood levels.[22]

By "poniendo el cuerpo," women were disrupting the ideal gendered subject-citizen, as either a docile, domestic mother and/or wife. Politically engaged women, especially those who took up arms, threatened patriarchal domestic norms and defied the social ideologies of the nation-state. In both Mexico and Argentina, and many other patriarchal Latin American nations of the time, the trope of woman as mother-nation was entrenched in nationalist narratives. Women's bodies literally and figuratively had to embrace and reflect motherhood, docility, and passive femininity. The "deviant, subversive" bodies of politically engaged women subverted the nation-state's definition of a proper feminine subjectivity, and the state, therefore, turned their bodies into a site of castigation and repression. As Anne McClintock notes, "all nationalisms are gendered; all are invented; and all are dangerous—... in the sense that they represent relations to political power and to the technologies of violence."[23] In this manner, the nation-state relied on "technologies of violence" in order to punish politically errant women who threatened Mexican and Argentinean gendered nationalisms.

There is a convergence between patriarchal social norms and gendered state violence, particularly as notions of proper femininity dictated the manner in which state officials treated women.[24] While women's involvement in political organizations transformed the cultural, sociopolitical landscape in Argentina and Mexico, women's bodies remained at the center of (often violent) political altercations between leftist resistance movements and the state. Although the state castigated the "deviant" bodies of both leftist men and women, it was the politically resistant bodies of women that provoked anxiety and fear among the capitalist-patriarchal heads of state. Diana Taylor reminds us that the "construction of [an Argentine] national identity" was essentially "predicated on female destruction" in both figurative and literal means; the systemic, organized repressive apparatus of the Argentinean regime depended on the violation, incarceration, and many times, disappearance or annihilation of subversive, gendered bodies.[25] Gendered violence, as Ximena Bunster-Burotto notes, is tied to a systemic, ordered gender regime. She claims: "these [state agents] are not simple males 'out of control with permission'; with a demonic irony, the sexual torture of women is named 'control' and is authorized state 'security.'"[26] In the 1970s, former head of Mexico's Federal Security Directorate's antiguerrilla task force, Miguel Nazar Haro, discussed the treatment of women activists they imprisoned: "in one way, we were somewhat concerned about the women we detained, but after we realized just how much more resistant and defiant they were than the men, we didn't care anymore about how we treated them."[27] This sentiment was echoed in Argentina; Adriana Calvo, a former detained-disappeared and survivor of the dictatorship, commented on a similar disdain for women political activists in her testimony: "The guards [of the concentration camps] would take sadistic delight in the torture of the women. They couldn't stand the idea that a woman could resist. To them, a woman who resisted was much worse than a man who resisted. The valor of the women drove them crazy."[28]

Gendered state violence, as evinced in the women's oral histories I examine throughout *Disruptive Archives*, was contradictory in many senses. The women were often verbally and physically denigrated for having strayed from proper national and cultural feminine codes of conduct, while at other times, women prisoners (especially pregnant women) were subject to paternalistic protection from officials. In both instances, women's abject, gendered bodies were controlled, scrutinized, and/or violated by masculine agents of the state. While politically active women's bodies were both the targets of state repression *and* embodied gendered resistance to this repression, the erasure of women from the dominant historical narratives reveals the struggles over historical memory in Argentina and Mexico.

Whose Historical Memory?
State-Controlled Narratives of the Dirty Wars

One enduring component of Dirty War state terror included the silencing and erasure of women from the histories of revolutionary struggle against the Mexican and Argentinean authoritarian states. While the states carefully managed the dominant narratives in order to portray activists as criminals, women were absent from this discourse, disavowing their active participation in these political organizations. In a similar vein, the historical memory narratives produced by leaders of the leftist revolutionary movements rarely incorporate a gender analytic when documenting their experiences of state terror. To this end, the dominant historical memory narratives of Argentina's and Mexico's Dirty Wars—whether controlled by the state, or by leaders of the revolutionary groups—tend toward a gender-neutral, or masculinist, account of this era of state brutality in order to produce cohesive and linear accounts of the past. And, although as Barbara importantly notes in *Surviving State Terror*, "the field of memory making is neither homogenous nor static within either side of the divide," it is critical to examine the dominant trends and sites of contention created by both the state and leftist political organizations and how women's memories were positioned, ignored, and/or managed to fit a particular narrative.[29] In this book I am concerned with the ways in which women survivors of state violence had to create alternative modes of collective storytelling that brushed against the dominant collective memories managed by the state as well as male-led revolutionary groups.

In an effort to contain the historical memory of the Dirty War period, and in an effort to legitimize their power, the Argentinean and Mexican authoritarian regimes created a narrative that positioned leftist activists as criminal, subversive individuals. The Mexican and Argentinean heads of state deployed vernacular that positioned leftist activists and guerrilleros as terrorists and sexually deviant criminals who attempted to violently overthrow the government.[30] The intent of the government was to strip away any political autonomy from these organizations and position them as criminal, terrorist entities. In Mexico, for example, PRI leaders depicted leftist activists as violent gangsters, influenced by foreign communist infiltrators who wanted to dismantle Mexico's democratic institution. This was evident in President Echeverría's public stance on the armed insurgencies in Mexico. With the assistance of the mainstream media, the government denied the existence of political armed organizations in Mexico, and only declared that criminal organizations existed. In May 1971, General Hermenegildo Cuenca Díaz, the minister of national defense, declared that "there are no guerrillas . . . in the state of Guerrero or in a party of the Republic. . . . [but only] bandits."[31]

This criminalization of political dissidents engendered a dominant narrative referred to as "la teoría de los dos demonios," or the "Two Devils theory." This refers to the notion that two opposing factions, from both the left and the right, were equally responsible for the violence that was institutionalized during the Dirty War era. It erroneously suggests that the states' systemic methods of violence and extermination (including the disappearance of thousands of individuals, torture, sexual violence, theft of babies, and death flights) were equivalent to acts of violence committed by armed insurgencies (including targeted kidnappings of high-ranking officials such as diplomats, and ransacking of army barracks). This false equivalency not only erases the difference in the magnitude of violence and repression generated by the repressive Argentinean and Mexican state apparatuses, but more importantly, it signals the extent of the state's control over the historical memory of this era, one that reveals the hetero-patriarchal power of the state.

The Two Devils discourse erased the political, social, and gendered underpinnings of the revolutionary movements that challenged the authoritarian measures of the capitalist patriarchal state, and further erased the power dynamics between the state and the political organizations. Both states positioned Díaz Ordaz, Echeverría, and Videla as all-knowing, austere patriarchal father figures of the nation who had to discipline their errant, misbehaving children (activists) for deviating from the proper political, gendered, and capitalist subject-citizen. In this vein, the state associated political dissidence (communist and socialist ideologies) with gender and sexual deviancy. The state portrayed political dissidents as sexually debased, effeminate "terrorists," as evidenced in Echeverría's 1974 presidential address to the nation, when he called young political activists lost youth "with a propensity for sexual promiscuity and high incidences of female and male homosexuality."[32] Similar concerns were expressed about politically active youth in Argentina, where the military junta violently reaffirmed proper gender, sexual, and political behavior as exemplified in the hetero-masculine, authoritarian father figures of the nation.

The states' management of the public discourse of political dissent profoundly shaped the historical memory of the Dirty War era and the theory of the Two Devils became firmly entrenched in the national consciousness. While the state-controlled narrative of the Two Devils theory is most commonly associated with the Argentinean dictatorship, the reach of this discourse was transnational, as it also became part of public discourses on the history of Mexico's political movements in the 1960s and 1970s. The Two Devils theory has now become Mexico and Argentina's dominant mode of conceptualizing the history of leftist social movements. In the transitional era, both states managed the historical memory through state-centered human rights commissions, which addressed the violence of the Dirty War era, yet they relied on this Two Devils theory. In Argentina, the management of historical memory appeared in the first publication of the official state-mandated human rights report on the dictatorship, *Nunca más*. In the original prologue by Ernesto Sábato, he refers to the Two Devils theory in order to explain the cause of the dictatorship's use of violence: "During the 1970s, Argentina was torn by terror from both the extreme right and the far left. This phenomenon was not unique to our country." Although this prologue was omitted from subsequent publications of the report, it evinces how the state's control over the historical memory of the Dirty War era was crucial to the legitimation of the contemporary, transitional government, and importantly eschews any connections between past and present. Many human rights activists, survivors, and academics have since contested this problematic discourse in an effort to regain control over the historical memory of this era, but it has remained a deeply ingrained narrative in the collective consciousness of Argentina and Mexico.[33]

The states' containment of the dominant narratives of the Dirty War shaped the contemporary governments' management of the historical memory of that era. This resulted in a disavowal of any connection to past violence and a subsequent elision of women's participation in these histories of struggle. The transitional governments could easily explain the extreme violence that occurred in the past and delinked any connection between the current political establishment and the past. The selective narration served to further reaffirm the capitalist, patriarchal state as purveyor and controller of the nation's history, and furthermore erased women from the historical memory of the Dirty War's political struggles, or portrayed them as hyperbolic, crazy women. The management of this historical memory is apparent to this day, as I encountered iterations of this discourse in my trips to Mexico and Argentina. During a trip to Argentina in 2009, a friend of an acquaintance asked the reason for my visit to Rosario, casually declaring that the women I were interviewing were "exaggerating" and that they *must* have done *something* to warrant their detention. Despite the international awareness of Argentina's human rights violations during the Proceso, his comment is not particularly surprising and it alludes to the success of the state in its control over the historical memory of the Dirty War, positioning activists as criminals or inventing accounts of past state violence. In Mexico, the state's management of the historical memory of the Dirty War had an even greater impact, as little public awareness of its secret Dirty War has resulted in greater silence and elision of a gendered history of resistance to the legacy of state terror.

Dominant Masculinist Narratives of Social Movements and Women's Struggle for the Historical Memory of the Dirty Wars

While the contemporary state regimes carefully managed the historical memory of the Dirty War era and denied any connections between the present and the past, survivors, activists, and members of leftist political organizations struggled to regain some agency by writing their own historical memories of resistance. Survivors of state violence and their advocates worked tirelessly with independent human rights groups to document their testimonies that challenged the states' official discourse on the Dirty Wars. However, as I explore more thoroughly in chapter 3, the male leaders of the revolutionary movements in Argentina and Mexico were often the spokespeople of the historical memory projects that sought to recuperate the buried history of the Dirty Wars. While these histories are critical in subverting the dominant state narrative that continues to criminalize survivors and relegate their histories to oblivion, I argue that some male leaders privilege a masculinist historical perspective of the Dirty Wars, often rendering women's voices silent in these stories of social resistance.

In the attempt to regain control over the historical memory of the Dirty War, and in an effort to decriminalize the history of socialist revolutionary struggle, the historical memory steered by male leaders of these organizations often relied on a cohesive, uncritical account of the movements themselves. The central objective was to construct an historical memory that not only honored the legacies of resistance to state violence and the memories of those who had been murdered by the state, but it also included subverting the discourse of criminality that positioned these activists as terrorists. In several of the oral histories of women participants of these organizations, they asserted that this central goal was critical in their memory work against the hegemony of state-controlled memory projects. As further developed in chapter 3, survivors of state violence prioritized challenging the state's disavowal of past violence and recuperating the historical memory of the Dirty War era, and therefore it was critical to maintain a linear, contained narrative of the past. Any critical perspectives of the organizations, such as the criticism of the gender inequality within the groups, were perceived as contradictory to the linear narratives created by masculinist historical memory groups.

When a gender analytic has been used to assess the history of the Dirty War, women have often been portrayed as passive victims of state violence and/or possibly traitorous collaborators who relied on their sexuality to survive. Such simplistic renderings of women's active political participation, as I argue in chapter 3, have stripped women of their agency and positioned them on the periphery of these historical memory projects. Here, I would like to consider the gendered dynamics of memory work and memory making and how women have intervened into these dominant historical memories of the Dirty War not merely in *what* women's experiences reveal, but *how* these experiences are articulated. The final two chapters of the book center on the critical memory work of women political activists; their memory projects challenge dominant framings of this epoch of violence and ultimately create alternative feminist epistemologies of the gendered history of the Mexican and Argentinean Dirty Wars.

Returning again to Alejandra's comment at the start of the introduction, women's memories of political activism have provoked anxiety among male-dominated state institutions and revolutionary groups. Alejandra's words evince the legacy of women's political activism in the Americas and the anxiety that gendered resistance produced—and continues to produce—especially among figures of power and institutional forces, as well as male-led historical memory projects. Historical memory work that centered on women's radical, revolutionary activism does not fit into the neat, linear narratives of both the state and leftist revolutionary groups. Cynthia Enloe notes that women are seen more as symbols than as "active participants" in nationalist movements, and this is evident in the historical memory and human rights organizing in the transitional moment.[34] In the human rights movements in both Mexico and Argentina, many women came to occupy significant roles in memory making, yet many of these roles, as Elizabeth Jelin notes, reflect the "public expression of pain and grief" that therefore "reinforce stereotypes and traditional roles."[35]

Centering on only their roles as grieving mothers, wives, grandmothers, and other maternal identities does not account for the agential, politicized parts of their subjectivities. This is not to say that women could not be both grieving mothers *and* political subjects, but it is the more traditional image of woman-as-passive, grief-stricken human rights victim that has gained social currency in Mexico and Argentina. Women survivors of state violence have noted the limitations of such roles, as their activism subverted traditional national narratives that reduced their bodies to their passive, reproductive, and maternal functions. During the Dirty Wars, women were "poniendo el cuerpo," putting their gendered bodies on the line in order to achieve political revolution, or as Sutton explains, "putting the material body in action to affect the course of society."[36] These women defied the state's attempt to destroy and eradicate errant gendered bodies, yet the dominant historical memory narratives of the Dirty Wars in Mexico and Argentina have not fully accounted for women's agented, active participation in resistance movements during this era.

In effect, this form of silencing among fellow leftist activists in human rights organizations *and* state-centered historical memory projects has led women to form historical memory groups that challenge the ongoing erasure of women from the historical archives. Women's histories of resistance challenge the contemporary state's narrative of progress and their attempt to shift away from past violence; women's memories pose inconvenient reminders of past state violence and disrupt the state's attempt in the post–Dirty War era to produce a linear historical narrative based on progress. As I show in chapter 1, the state in the transitional moment worked to construct a national image based on progress and attempted to shift away from its violent past, and therefore the national conversations on Dirty War–era violence veered away from making uncomfortable connections between past and contemporary forms of state violence. Women's memory projects also provide critical insight into the gender dynamics of leftist revolutionary groups and subvert the masculinist hold over the historical memory of the Dirty Wars. Many women have commented on their erasure from these dominant historical memory projects, such as Rodríguez Márquez of the 1968 Mexican student movement: "before, only the men narrated the histories until we women began to speak . . . women's participation in the political struggles was not visible."

This is not to say, however, that all women survivors of state repression insist on centering the gendered nature of state violence and the gender discrimination they often faced within their leftist organization. Chapter 4 explores how many women did not feel comfortable criticizing the men in their leftist organizations and many others preferred to use a gender-neutral analytic framework when discussing their experiences of repression and survival. Indeed, when I refer to women survivors of state violence, I consider the heterogeneity of the social category of "woman," as well as the diversity of women's experiences of activism and surviving state terror. While it is critical to focus on these heterogeneities involved in women's memory making, I consider how some women survivors called for an alternative collective memory that evinces the specific gendered nature of state terror and survival.

Many women survivors of state violence have created memory projects focusing specifically on the gendered histories of repression and the unique experiences women faced during this era. These memory projects articulate new, alternative modes of documenting the past and many women remain persistently vocal in the face of these systemic forms of silence. Their memory work furthermore alludes to the possibilities of transnational feminist historical memory projects that produce new knowledge of the gendered history of the Dirty Wars. For example, in 2002, many former guerrilleras, activists, and academics convened in Mexico City to form the first national reunion of former guerrilleras. During this conference, Rosa María Gonzales Carranza of the People's Union stated that "in the history of war, we women are not visible. For that reason, it is important to approach this history with a new perspective."[37]

It is precisely this "new perspective" that this book is preoccupied with, carefully attending to and centering the heterogeneous, and at times, contradictory historical memories of women survivors of state terror. A Latin American feminist epistemology emerges in these gendered memories of repression and survival and this book critically interrogates the new knowledge formation that these women's words articulate and theorize. To this end, *Disruptive Archives* interrogates and challenges long-standing, entrenched masculinist historical memory discourses on the Dirty Wars and invites us to consider more deeply what's at stake in the battle over historical memory of this epoch of violence; what's more, this book invites us to engage with the alternative Latin American feminist theories that the women's memories present as they challenge these dominant narratives of the Dirty War era while they also seek accountability for past human rights crimes.

Archives of Terror, Archives of Resistance

Disruptive Archives turns to the memory projects of women survivors of Latin America's Dirty Wars and their resistance efforts against the legacy of state trauma and violence. Women's historical memory projects represent what I term "disruptive archives," and they serve as archival sources that contest hegemonic forms of knowledge on the Dirty Wars. More recently, Latin American historians and archivists have questioned the role of knowledge building and the role of the state in the formation—and control—of that knowledge and have turned to what Mexican historian Laura Castellanos calls "independent archives" to best represent the history that has been elided by official documentation.[38] Similarly, *Disruptive Archives* relies on disruptive archival sources that challenge masculinist, official histories and hegemonic canons and forms of knowledge and archival research in order to address the gendered erasure of Dirty War historiography. In the process of constructing these disruptive archives, women are able to transform dehumanizing, violent memories of repression into politicized projects that seek comprehensive justice for crimes of the state.

At its core, *Disruptive Archives* centers on the power of storytelling found in the disruptive archives of women involved in revolutionary struggles in 1960s and 1970s Latin America. The book examines how women's storytelling vis-à-vis oral histories, testimonial literature, and other cultural mediums engender a collective solidarity that has been critical to the formation of women's political subjectivity. As transnational feminist scholar Chandra T. Mohanty notes, "feminist analysis has always recognized the centrality of rewriting and remembering history, a process that is significant not merely as a corrective to the gaps, erasures, and misunderstandings of hegemonic masculinist history but because the very practice of remembering and rewriting leads to the formation of politicized consciousness and self-identity."[39] As chapter 4 shows, the act of retelling and sharing histories of repression *and* resistance to state terror does not merely combat legacies of impunity, but they reflect the processes involved in women's collective solidarity based on this shared "politicized consciousness." Women's persistent efforts to speak out against gendered injustices of the past leads to the formation of a pluralized political consciousness based on collectivity that is feminist in nature. Their memory projects, disruptive archives, and pluralized political consciousness building all constitute an alternative feminist epistemology of Latin America's Dirty Wars, as they intervene in accepted masculinist, hegemonic historiographies of this epoch of violence.

The disruptive archives examined in this book present a range of perspectives on the Dirty War era. Disruptive archives invoke knowledge from firsthand accounts (oral histories, documentary film, and testimonial literature) and literary imaginings (fiction and narrative film), and these texts serve as critical disruptive archival sources to empirical findings on the Dirty Wars. However, *Disruptive Archives* is not solely preoccupied with "recovering" empirical data found in women's disruptive archives of the Dirty War, nor is it invested in merely filling the "gaps, erasures" of masculinist historiographies. While the oral histories and cultural texts examined in these pages provide critical historical content that had been systematically erased by hegemonic narratives, the unrecoverable nature of loss and how organized forms of gendered violence and trauma influence the manner in which the women articulate these histories are the primary focus. To this end, the book centers the transformative possibilities of trauma as many survivors refer to the crimes of the past in order to challenge the dominant (masculinist) narratives and knowledge of the Dirty War era.

By referencing histories of Dirty War trauma, these disruptive archives serve as a constant reminder of the legacy of state terrorism and create a feminist epistemological shift by producing new knowledge on the gendered history of the Dirty War. In essence, disruptive archives refer to embodied archives of terror and, importantly, embodied archives of resistance to this terror. The embodied knowledge on the gendered history of the Dirty Wars has been omitted by official state documents as well as from masculinist historiographies and are often downplayed or belittled as too personal, too biased, or not factual. *Disrupted Archives* focuses on what Diana Taylor terms the repertoire, or knowledge that has been omitted from more traditional forms of the archive. As Taylor explains, the repertoire differs from the archive, which centers the narrative or textual document as the locus of truth and knowledge, whereas the repertoire "requires presence: people participate in the production and reproduction of knowledge by 'being there,' being a part of the transmission."[40] In this manner, this book considers how these disruptive archives challenge more conventional forms of knowledge production, particularly in *how* this knowledge is produced, documented, and disseminated. Embodied archival sources, then, provide us with alternative ways of representing and documenting gendered histories of the Dirty War era.

This book carefully examines the embodied expressions of loss, trauma, and resistance found in these disruptive archives that are manifested in pauses, silences, gasps, sighs, and laughter. These embodied expressions involved in the production of the cultural texts directly shape the very form of these cultural products. *Disruptive Archives* considers how the *form* of these cultural texts stand in opposition to state-centered models of storytelling, as well as the linear masculinist narratives of leftist groups. Both the content *and* the form of the cultural texts on the Dirty War era differ from hegemonic, masculinist memory projects produced by the state and leftist groups, thereby creating alternative feminist epistemologies on the Dirty War.

This book adopts a Latin American feminist cultural studies analytic to explore how cultural producers represent tensions and gaps in this period of Latin American history. As Jean Franco states, "cruelty leaves long-lasting memory traces—hence the recurrent theme of buried books, faded photographs, fragmented testimonies, exhumed bodies, harvests of bones." This "harvest" appears in various literary forms, oral histories, embodied expressions, and visual cultural texts that exhume buried memories of gendered, state-sponsored violence. As Bolaño articulated in his acceptance speech for the Romulo Gallegos award in 1999, "all of Latin America is sown with the bones of [its] forgotten youth."[41] *Disruptive Archives* engages deeply with the "fragmented testimonies," "buried books," and other disruptive archival sources that yield a "harvest of bones," the bones of the "forgotten youth" of Latin America's gendered Dirty Wars.

One critical way women resisted the legacy of state terror was to audio-record their memories and narratives, and *Disruptive Archives* engages with the oral histories of women survivors of Mexico's and Argentina's Dirty Wars. The oral histories of women I interviewed in Mexico and Argentina form the architecture and narrative arc of the book. This book alludes to the radical possibility of oral history as a Latin American feminist methodological tool that can combat systems of power, legacies of oblivion, state-sanctioned impunity, and masculinist narratives.

Disruptive Archives relies on a feminist methodological framework, however, I am wary of relying on a Global North/Eurocentric notion of feminist activism and knowledge building when we examine histories of political repression in Latin America (and the Global South in general). As Pascha Bueno-Hansen and Sylvanna M. Falcón note, transnational feminists located in the Global North must be attentive to the "multidirectional and contextual complexity" of our relationship with the activists we are researching in the Global South, and we must be wary of reinforcing "unidirectional," top-down theories of feminism "from north to south."[42] For example, while many of the women I interviewed became more involved in the public, political sphere in Mexico and Argentina, many of them did not identify as feminist and viewed that label as a Western, Eurocentric concept. Survivor of the Argentinean repression, Margarita Cruz, explained to me, "I don't consider myself a feminist but I do have a special way of considering myself a woman . . . but not a feminist, a very special way of thinking . . . the question of gender was not in place because it was not necessary to consider it . . . an ideology of change, change in society, for equality for friends and of possibilities." The oral histories here can teach us about different perspectives of gender and feminism, and they call into question Western, Eurocentric notions of feminism. For that reason, I center on the emergence of a Latin American feminist theory of justice found in the work and oral histories of these activists.

As someone trained in cultural studies and feminist theory, my interdisciplinary methodology turns to oral histories as a critical medium that presents new knowledge of women's resistance movements in Latin America. The oral histories invite us to engage with multiple modes of storytelling as a form of radical resistance to hegemonic, masculinist forms of knowledge. I am particularly drawn to feminist scholar Maylei Blackwell's conceptualization of oral history as a critical methodological tool used in feminist knowledge production: "Instead of using oral history like any other archival source, my work more deeply engages with and is influenced by feminist ethnography and the theorizing of memory in oral history and cultural studies. This is an oral history project that produces a different way of knowing and telling history that requires a shift in epistemology rather than a mere methodological orientation."[43] It is precisely this epistemological shift that I would like to examine, as *Disruptive Archives* invites readers to consider how oral narratives, along with the other cultural forms I examine, create new knowledge and feminist theories on Latin American histories of resistance.

This book relies on oral histories from twelve women I interviewed between 2009 and 2013, all of whom were involved in armed and unarmed political organizations in Argentina and Mexico. With the assistance and support of historical memory groups, El Comité '68 and the Association of Ex-Detained Disappeared in Mexico City and Buenos Aires, as well as connections made through friends and colleagues, I met women willing to participate in interviews. At the time of the interviews, all twelve women belonged to historical memory groups in Argentina and Mexico that centered on recuperating the history of state repression during the Dirty Wars. Almost all the women remain politically active today, which is also indicative of why they were eager to participate in my project.

Each of the women I interviewed had a different survivor status; that is, some of the women I interviewed, such as Bertha Lilia Gutiérrez Campos in Mexico and Mirta Sgro in Argentina, were officially detained and processed as political prisoners. Other women I interviewed, such as Nilda Eloy and Margarita Cruz, were considered detained-disappeared, which meant that there was no trace of their existence because the Argentinean government did not officially document their detentions. Some women, such as Nilda Eloy, were first disappeared and then moved to a prison, where they were officially documented as political prisoners, whereupon the families and loved ones were alerted to their location. These distinctions are critical, for they shape the memory and oral history narrative arc of each of the testimonies and impact the identity formation of the women after their release from captivity. Only one woman I interviewed, Sylvia Yáñez, was never officially detained; however, her interview divulges the history of the repressive Argentinean state apparatus as she bore witness to the Monte Chingolo massacre.[44]

It is worth noting that not everyone was keen to open up to me before I divulged my own political inclinations and Latin American lineage. The moments of transference established before the interview set an important context for the duration of the interview and also established a theory of embodied research that has shaped this book. Alejandra, for example, joked several times throughout the interview that I might be working with the CIA since I was from the United States. However, she began to trust me more once I told her that my Cuban grandfather was an ardent supporter of the 1959 revolution and a member of the Los Angeles Communist Party. After I disclosed this information, she smiled more, teased me, and touched my hand and arm during our interview. These moments of transfer, banter, and points of personal contact evoke what Taylor mentions as the power of repertoire, knowledge that "requires presence" as "people participate in the production and reproduction of knowledge by ... being a part of the transmission."[45]

My methodological approach to each interview was based on an open interview format; I would prepare a list of general, open-ended questions centered on gender dynamics in their political organizations, but in general, the women guided the arc of their storyline. Some of the interviews were on the shorter side, around two hours long, while some spanned several days and lasted around eight hours. And while many of the women I interviewed knew one another and even belonged to the same political organizations and memory projects, each interview was distinct in style, length, form, and content. This methodology served two purposes: first, it allowed the women the flexibility to narrate their own memories of the resistance movements without my interjections or questions shaping the trajectory of their narrative; and second, it highlighted the importance of not only *what* the women said, but *how* they articulated their narratives.

This latter point centers the significance of embodied forms of knowledge and resistance to legacies of violence. Embodiment is an integral part of the interview process, and as Laura L. Ellingson contends, embodiment "manifests a dimension that is often missing from published accounts of research." In the oral histories, embodied expressions often complement the content of what the women were relaying, and also evince what *cannot* be articulated in language. The gestures, sighs, laughter, tears, silences, and personal contact contribute to new knowledge formation on Latin America's Dirty Wars. To ignore the significance of these embodied expressions is to privilege "the mind over the body"; this, as Ellingson argues, "is deeply engrained in Western cultures and hence within conventional research methodologies."[46] My interviewees' embodied responses evince the importance of the *form* of the oral histories. In some instances, the women's own articulations of the Dirty War histories were contradictory, producing tensions and inaccuracies in the content of their memory projects, yet their embodied expressions captured the manifestation of these silences, inaccuracies, and tensions. We must pay attention to *how* these embodied expressions form new feminist theory on Latin America's history of state violence. *Disruptive Archives* is preoccupied with the messy, incongruous, and haunted nature of these embodied memory projects and engages deeply with new feminist articulations found in these very gaps and inconsistencies, in the process of exhuming the bones of its "forgotten youth."

I have translated into English all of the original interviews mentioned in these pages. Unfortunately, much is inevitably lost in the process of going from the audio recording to transcription and to its final translation into English. Despite what is lost and what cannot be captured within the scope of this book, *Disruptive Archives* is inspired and driven by the women's oral histories of bravery and resistance. As Sylvanna M. Falcón asked in our International Studies Association "Transnational Change and Decolonial Interventions in the Americas" panel in 2017, "what can we learn from their bravery?" Even years after I conducted the interviews, and after listening to the interviews multiple times, these women's words of survival continue to inspire me. Their stories, along with the other cultural texts examined in this book, form the beautiful architecture of resilience, persistence, and resistance to state terror and oblivion.

Organization of the Book

Each chapter of *Disruptive Archives* centers the historical memories articulated by women participants of the Argentinean and Mexican revolutionary movements. The book commences by examining conventional, masculinist narratives of the Dirty War era and women's critical responses to these dominant framings. The first chapter examines how Mexico's and Argentina's transitional governments mobilized a human rights discourse to claim that they were redressing the violence of the past; however, the states did so in ways that maintained the heteropatriarchal basis for their authority and legitimacy. In a similar vein, chapter 2 focuses on the masculinist perspectives in literary and cinematic texts produced by men who participated in or sympathized with leftist revolutionary organizations. These cultural texts reveal problematic portrayals of women survivors of state violence as traitors and these representations evince gendered tropes of woman-as-traitor to the revolutionary cause. This chapter examines how the gendered, sexualized, and reviled incarcerated body reflects the anxieties of both the hypermasculine military states, as well as the masculinist revolutionary leftist organizations. Chapters 1 and 2 incorporate cultural texts and oral histories that problematize the state's and leftist masculinist representations of women's histories of repression and survival. Chapter 1 ends with an analysis of activist-produced texts that challenge the limits of state-produced human rights texts, while chapter 2 concludes with women's own perspectives of the gendered nature of betrayal and survival.

These first two chapters of *Disruptive Archives* center on the masculinist left accounts that have elided women's narratives of resistance, as well as human rights texts that have produced deliberate silences that legitimate contemporary regimes. In essence, these chapters provide the context that establish why women survivors of state violence make the narrative and discursive interventions through historical memory work, cultural texts, and activist projects. Chapter 3 closely examines the haunting of Latin America's revolutionary past in documentary film and testimonial literature, as well as the interviews I conducted with former Mexican and Argentinean guerrilleras. The cultural texts and oral histories examined in chapter 3 reveal a gendered haunting that results from the disavowal of women's participation in the armed insurgency and the eradication of women's histories of resistance from Mexico and Argentina's national consciousness. Chapter 4 centers exclusively on the narrative voices of survivors of violence and explores the intersection of gender, trauma, and state violence in interviews I conducted with women participants in leftist organizations in Argentina and Mexico between 2009 and 2014. The women's oral histories offer different interpretive frameworks with which to assess histories of resistance and create new feminist knowledge on the gendered history of the Latin America's Dirty Wars. The oral histories in chapter 4 invite us to engage more deeply with the multiple modes of oral history telling and the knowledge that can be excavated through what cannot be articulated. It is precisely the tensions, gaps, and contradictions of their narratives that point to the unrecoverable nature of loss, trauma, as well as the systemic erasure of their histories of resistance from official discourses. *Disruptive Archives* concludes by turning to recent instances of state violence in present-day Mexico and Argentina and how women survivors of the Dirty Wars combat the legacies of gendered state violence in the present. Through their very articulations of survival and resistance, alternative Latin American feminist theories of justice emerge. Their narratives serve as critical forms of feminist knowledge that can work to combat contemporary instances of gendered state violence in the Americas.

Together, the chapters reflect the urgency and timeliness of these women's narratives and their contribution to radical Latin American feminist epistemologies. The cultural texts I analyze in these pages—human rights reports, literary texts, film, and oral histories—offer those of us invested in Latin American feminisms with alternative ways of documenting women's narratives that do not belie the political histories of women survivors of state violence. Instead, it is critical that we turn to the discourse of resistance employed by local feminists, activists, writers, and cultural producers in Latin America as an essential organizing tool that can seek comprehensive justice and accountability for past crimes. The women's narratives of trauma, resistance, survival, and solidarity serve as critical feminist knowledge on contemporary Latin American history that have been omitted from the official story and the archive. As Lelia Ferrarese explained to me in Rosario, Argentina, in 2009, "sigue siendo presente esto" (this continues to be present), and as scholars and activists we must tend to the haunting yet inspiring words of these histories of gendered resistance.

CHAPTER ONE

Critical Latin American Feminist Perspectives and the Limits and Possibilities of Human Rights Reports

> The language and discourse of human rights proves more useful to women and marginalized communities as an organizing tool, in lieu of entrusting the state to abide by the human rights standards adopted by the international community.
> —Collins et al., "New Directions"

After the demise of the Argentinean dictatorship in 1983 and the 2000 end of the seventy-one-year reign of PRI (Partido Revolucionario Institucional) in Mexico, the presidents of both transitional governments mandated official investigations into the human rights abuses committed during the Dirty Wars. These transitional eras in Argentina and Mexico marked a significant moment in the history of Latin American human rights movements. Argentina was one of the first Latin American nations to establish a truth commission and to take important steps toward reconciling a divided nation. In 1983, President Raúl Alfonsín (1983–89) formed the National Commission on the Disappeared (CONADEP, Comisión Nacional sobre la Desaparición de Personas), which investigated disappearances and other human rights violations committed by the military junta. Mexico, on the other hand, never established a truth commission, continuing to deny state-sponsored human rights abuses until the 2000 election of President Vicente Fox Quesada of the National Action Party (PAN, Partido Acción Nacional). Although Mexico's National Commission on Human Rights recommended establishing a truth commission, President Fox's administration decided to create the now-defunct Office of the Special Prosecutor for Social and

Political Movements of the Past (FEMOSPP, Fiscalía Especial para Movimientos Sociales y Políticos del Pasado) in 2001 to investigate Dirty War crimes.[1] The efforts did not result in any convictions, and FEMOSPP was considered a failure by many human rights legal experts and activists. In 1984 Argentina's CONADEP published *Nunca Más*, a pathbreaking, best-selling state-sponsored human rights report on dictatorship-era crimes. Mexico's government, however, remained silent, continuing to cover up Dirty War–era violence until the highly anticipated—and controversial—release of FEMOSPP's report in 2006.

The Argentinean and Mexican transitional governments' responses to state crimes committed during the Dirty Wars reflect what Andreas Huyssen notes as the "problem and promise" of the rise of a "global, [human] rights regime" in the past several decades, particularly as it relates to the gender politics of transitional governments.[2] Since the 1990s, the vocabulary of universal human rights has become the international standard to assess a nation's ability to protect the fundamental rights of its citizens, and it has become the global community's manner by which to measure a nation's modern, democratic values. The mainstreaming of this human rights discourse shaped the manner in which the transitional governments of Argentina and Mexico responded to their violent pasts and this is evident in the publication of human rights reports by CONADEP and FEMOSPP.

The FEMOSPP report and *Nunca más* evince what Dana Collins and colleagues have called the "central challenge *and* opportunity for re-envisioning feminist human rights political projects."[3] The emergence of the reports created a critical avenue for women survivors of state violence as the texts documented their histories of political activism and resistance to gendered violence. The formation of a national and international human rights platform in the last few decades, in addition to the publication of these reports, allowed for women to archive their experiences and to expose the gendered horrors of both authoritarian regimes. What's more, the formation of CONADEP and FEMOSPP was influenced by local survivor groups, human rights organizations, and other activists who had pressured their governments for official investigations into human rights crimes. Human rights discourse became a powerful medium used to hold previous regimes accountable for their crimes, and CONADEP and FEMOSPP relied on this language to pressure leaders to participate in their investigations.

Inasmuch as these reports have been critical to survivors of human rights abuses in Mexico and Argentina and have brought international awareness to these historical traumas and gendered violence, the texts reflect the limits of state-controlled transitional projects. The transitional governments relied on human rights discourses to claim that they were acknowledging the violence of the past, yet they maintained a hetero-patriarchal context for their authority and legitimacy. Male heads of state in Mexico and Argentina—as well as the CONADEP and FEMOSPP entities themselves, which were predominately male—desired a swift transition to a democratic future; they incorporated universal rights discourse in an attempt to deal with their violent pasts and to establish themselves as modern, democratic governments. In order to effectively distance themselves from the violent, authoritative nature of previous regimes, the transitional governments embraced the language of universal human rights to position themselves as paternal benefactors who sought to rescue vulnerable victims of previous state regimes. The reports relied on a protectionist, paternalistic narrative that proclaimed that women—and children—were the most vulnerable victims of egregious, masculinist state violence. Activists and feminist scholars have criticized transitional governments and human rights courts focus on women as either chaste subjects or helpless victims of authoritarian violence. As feminist human rights scholar Pascha Bueno-Hansen claims, we must engage with a critique of gender violence that moves beyond "always implicating bodies, and usually women's bodies."[4] Instead of focusing on the sexed, violated feminine body as a mere victim of state violence, it is important to examine the gendered, social, legal, racial, class, and institutional inequalities that have engendered systemic violence against these bodies. The focus on protecting the vulnerable, defenseless, and sexed body of woman-as-victim is a trope that emerges in both state-sponsored human rights reports in Mexico and Argentina.

The rise of a universal human rights movement in Latin America has achieved certain legal milestones. However, when this discourse is managed by transitional governments, it can minimize the gendered, radical political subtexts of the histories of Dirty War repression. Furthermore, human rights law and juridical approaches to justice can reinforce state power and, as Rosa-Linda Fregoso and Cynthia Bejarano assert, "[disempower] everyday people." For these reasons, it important to "go beyond the state, as well as beyond instruments and accords such as the Universal Declaration of Human Rights."[5] The paternal, transitional state relied on a universal human rights discourse to claim they knew what was best for the nation and for the survivors of Dirty War–era violence. Keeping the critical terms of human rights in the hands of those in power prevented survivors from effecting significant changes in laws or state policy or from influencing the official, dominant narrative of the state's recent violent past.

As a response to the limits of the state-controlled narratives produced by the transitional governments, many writers, survivors, and activists in Argentina and Mexico produced their own versions of human rights documents. In 1971, investigative reporter and feminist writer Elena Poniatowska published *La noche de Tlatelolco* (*Massacre in Mexico*), the first report to document the Mexico City massacre of October 2, 1968. Poniatowska was one of a few Mexican journalists to denounce the government for its orchestration of the massacre, giving visibility to the trauma and horrors of the PRI-sanctioned human rights abuse. Although *La noche de Tlatelolco* was published before the mainstreaming of a human rights discourse, Poniatowska's text is a critical feminist human rights project that includes gendered and political contexts that are absent from the FEMOSPP report. In 1997, two books appeared—*Ni el flaco perdón de Dios* and *A Single, Numberless Death*—that tackle the subject of the Argentinean Dirty War from the perspective of survivors and those who never learn the fate of their loved ones. *La noche de Tlatelolco*, *A Single, Numberless Death*, and *Ni el flaco perdón de Dios* are activist-produced reports that evince the gendered and political contexts of Mexico and Argentina's Dirty Wars. In addition to providing a comprehensive rendering of *why* these violations occurred, the cultural texts reveal a theory of gender justice that is absent in the reports from both FEMOSPP and CONADEP, and accordingly, they expose the limits of masculinist state-controlled human rights projects. The activist-produced texts offer alternative feminist human rights vocabulary and theories of justice to convey the legacy of trauma and gendered political violence that is etched into the national, cultural, and political consciousness of both nations.

This chapter provides an intertextual reading of state-sanctioned human rights reports as well as activist-produced texts that attest to both the limits as well as the possibilities of using official universal human rights discourse to account for the gendered nature of Dirty War era violence. By tracing the evolution of a human rights discourse in a Latin American context in official state-mandated reports and activist-produced texts, this chapter addresses the pitfalls and possibilities that the language of universal rights poses when the state becomes the sole guarantor of human rights protection. The chapter epigraph sets the stage for my examination of how human rights rhetoric can be employed as "an organizing tool" for women survivors of gendered state violence, rather than "entrusting the state" to manage the terms of human rights.[6] The state did not account for the gendered context of human rights abuses committed during the Dirty Wars, further silencing and eschewing the histories of gendered resistance to state violence.

Thus, we must be attentive to the survivor and activist responses to the limitations of state-sponsored human rights investigations and reports, and examine how local activists and writers integrated the rhetoric of universal rights in order to reconceptualize a human rights narrative that is inclusive of and illuminates the gendered and political underpinnings of histories of human rights abuse. This chapter also engages with oral histories of women I interviewed and examines how their oral narratives provide us with alternative framings of human rights that capture the gendered histories of repression. Through an intertextual analysis of oral histories, state-sponsored human rights reports, and activist-produced texts, this chapter sheds light on the gender politics involved in the framing of human rights reports and the activist and survivor responses to the critical limits of state-centered human rights reports. My readings of these texts reveal how state-centered models of human rights have created a discourse that reduces women to passive roles, whereas activist reports captured the subjectivity of women who were protagonists of social change.

However, this chapter does not suggest a dichotomous reading of state-sponsored reports as only producing depoliticized survivors' testimonies, rendering women as victims, while activist-produced reports and oral histories retain the political subjectivities of survivors of state violence. Instead, I examine the nuances and power dynamics involved in archiving and representing women's political agency and the possibilities and limitations of both state and activist narratives. Although my intertextual analysis illuminates the limits of a masculinist, state-controlled human rights discourse, I argue that ultimately we should not abandon a human rights framework altogether in our analysis of women's histories of resistance to state violence. Instead, we must use a critical feminist human rights lens to examine women's narratives of survival; these narratives offer new knowledge and terminology that can contribute and provide a critical feminist perspective of human rights struggles and the legacies of feminist resistance in activist-produced cultural texts and oral histories. Activist reports, writers, and survivors can enact social change by challenging the discursive limits of state-controlled human rights to encompass a broader understanding of why and how human violations occurred in the first place. While hetero-patriarchal, transitional governments deploy universal human rights discourse in an attempt to move linearly through time and away from the horrors of the past, the intertextual focus of this chapter disrupts this linearity by invoking the oral histories and activist texts that bring the unresolved injustices and legacies of trauma from the past to the present. The activist reports and women's oral histories establish the tensions that emerge when examining activists produced texts—that recall the gendered nature of state violence—alongside the genderless or neutral frameworks of transitional governments and state-sponsored human rights projects. These cultural productions introduce new terms into the discourse of human rights that typically are controlled by the state, governmental policies, and the judiciary. In so doing, the works transform and reclaim the terms of human rights discourse in order to reorient it toward more comprehensive, gender-based justice projects and visions.

CONADEP and *Nunca más*: Human Rights and the Argentinean Paternal Post-Dictatorship State

Nunca más (1984) was one of the first state-mandated human rights report to emerge in the Western Hemisphere. Sponsored by then-president Raúl Alfonsín, the text marked a significant moment in the evolution of human rights in the twentieth century. By the time President Alfonsín established CONADEP in 1983, very few transitional governments had adopted nonjudicial measures to deal with their violent pasts, and as Priscilla B. Hayner writes, there existed little "recognition of other non-judicial strategies now commonly considered during post-authoritarian transition."[7] The information provided by survivors to CONADEP yielded critical data in subsequent criminal justice proceedings and the ultimate conviction of former officers in the 1985 Trial of the Juntas. To many in the global human rights community, the successful domestic conviction of former military leaders of the junta represented the promise and possibilities of transitional justice.

Nunca más was published just as the universal human rights movement was gaining momentum but prior to the movement in the 1990s of women's rights as human rights. In 1975, the UN's first International Woman's Year Conference took place in Mexico City, and this led to the UN-sponsored Decade of Women (1975–85). These critical moments occurred during the height of the Argentinean dictatorship and the era of transitional justice, yet these movements were still coming into mainstream focus. The lexicon of women's human rights was only beginning to go global, which explains why *Nunca más* does not include a gender lens in its documentation of human rights abuses.

While the international recognition of Argentina's egregious human rights violations during its Dirty War period was due in large part to the creation of CONADEP and publication of *Nunca más*, many local, Argentinean activist organizations helped shape this modern human rights movement. During a research trip to Argentina in 2009, I worked closely with the Buenos Aires–based civic organization, the Association of Ex-Detained Disappeared (AEDD).

This human rights group, founded by former disappeared and detained survivors of the dictatorship, has been essential in shaping cultural and legal human rights responses to Argentina's recent history of violence. On the demise of the dictatorship, AEDD members compiled survivor testimony that was used in the first Trial of the Juntas in 1985, and they served as key witnesses for the prosecution after the amnesty laws were repealed in 2003. In my 2009 interview with AEDD member Margarita Cruz, survivor of the Escuelita de Famaillá clandestine center in Tucumán, she declared: "When we began to give our testimony to CONADEP, it was the most painful thing, but it was the only way for us to say that in those places [concentration camps], our 30,000 disappeared compañeros had remained. Through our testimonies, this was the only way to prove that the concentration camps existed—there was no other proof." Survivors and family members of the disappeared were able to use the state entity of CONADEP to make visible the grave violations that had taken place across the nation for years. In my 2014 interview with Liliana Forchetti, former member of Argentina's Worker's Revolutionary Party (PRT, Partido Revolucionario de los Trabajadores) and former political prisoner of the Villa Urquiza prison in the Tucumán province, she discussed the importance of CONADEP's *Nunca más*. To Forchetti, the report was a critical platform for survivors and families who had been silenced during the dictatorship, and the magnitude of repression that characterized those years: "CONADEP's report blamed the armed forces for the disappearances. The report gave evidence of the magnitude of the repression, and treated the disappeared as subjects with rights, and also, it gave voice to the families and survivors through their testimonies." Human rights entities like CONADEP, NGOs such as Amnesty International, and other human rights enterprises were able to work collectively with local activist and human rights groups to denounce Dirty War–era violence and seek legal retribution for crimes against humanity. As Cruz noted, CONADEP and human rights tribunals would not have been able to prosecute former military leaders without the collective organizing of survivor groups and their testimonial accounts.

Judicial modes of attaining justice, however, did pose some limitations, particularly for women survivors of dictatorship violence. Legal recourses to attain justice for crimes of the state often reflect the paternalistic nature of transitional governments. Many feminist scholars and legal theorists have grappled with questions about how to most effectively utilize the judicial system in order to condemn, prosecute, and provide justice for those affected by gender-based crimes. In 2011, several Argentinean courts finally began to prosecute rape and sexual violence as separate crimes committed by the dictatorship; thus Forchetti and other survivors were able to provide testimony in trials against former officers of the regime. However, after years of impunity, amnesty, and silence during the transitional years surrounding the topic of gendered violence, the judicial system was reticent to proceed with gender violence cases. "There is great reluctance on the part of judicial system operators [to move cases forward]," notes sociologist Lorena Balardini of the Buenos Aires–based human rights institute Center for Legal and Social Studies, adding that "the majority see sex crimes as falling in the broader category of torture, but classifying them as such is just another way of concealing them." As Bueno-Hansen claims, "human rights law provides the most salient political discourse to gender-based violence, yet this discourse can never capture the full scope of harm."[8]

Furthermore, the discourse of human rights and nations' penal codes reflects the paternal state's moralistic, Christian, and hetero-patriarchal views on sexuality and gender. Argentina's transitional government evinced this patriarchal, paternalist discourse in the legal terminology used to prosecute sexually violent crimes. Initially, Argentinean human rights courts did not acknowledge sexual violence as a separate cause from torture in general and instead centered on the universal subject/victim of human rights. However, once the courts recognized rape as a separate crime committed by the dictatorship, they did so in a way that reaffirmed the state as the patriarchal guardian of women's sexuality and honor. Until 1999 in Argentina, rape was considered a "crime against purity/honesty" (*delitos contra la honestidad*), and then the law was changed to "crimes against sexual integrity" (*delitos contra la integridad*). In our interview, Forchetti described the effects this patriarchal law had on cultural notions of women's honor and sexual propriety, even within the human rights legal community. As Forchetti was preparing her testimony for the prosecution during a 2012 human rights trial, a judge's legal aide asked her if she was a virgin when military officers raped her during her detention at the Villa Urquiza clandestine center in Tucumán. Forchetti described her reaction to this question: "I wanted to kill that woman—you understand, here we were talking about the violation of basic human rights—it [rape] wasn't a question of honor . . . the penal code also hurt us . . . rape was a question of honor, it wasn't a question of basic human rights for a woman not to be raped." Forchetti's interaction with the judge's aide reveals the manner in which gendered and sexual biases emerged in legal human rights discourses. As Forchetti declared, the sexual crimes committed by the junta were violations of "basic human rights," yet the courts tied this form of gendered violence to patriarchal, cultural norms based on protecting women's purity and honor. If the courts portrayed Forchetti and other survivors of sexual violence as chaste, virginal subjects who were violated by sexually aggressive military officers, then they would be more sympathetic victims of violence, and the courts could then emphasize their vulnerability as helpless, innocent victims of sexual violence in need of protection. In essence, defending women's sexual honor and propriety was deemed integral in the human rights trials, rather than centering on the violation of basic human rights.

Although bringing awareness to the state's systematic sexual-based violence against women represented a critical step forward for many survivors, the focus on women's survival of violence also had the tendency to reduce women to helpless victims. Some survivors who participated in Argentina's human rights tribunals criticized the court's emphasis of their sexual torture and the ignoring of their political activism, which rendered women activists as passive, depoliticized victims of state violence. In a similar vein, Fiona Ross's research on the South African Truth and Reconciliation Commission maintains that female survivors of state violence were portrayed solely as victims of sexual violence. Ross quotes from the testimony of Thenjiwe Mtintso during a 1997 hearing: "This consistency of drawing you away from your own activism, from your own commitment as an actor, was perhaps worse than torture, was worse than physical assault."[9] The elision of political agency re-traumatizes women by erasing their histories of activism and represents a psychic assault on survivors of political violence.[10] In her work on transitional justice in Peru, Katherine M. Franke indicates that many women survivors of state violence have felt restricted by human rights tribunals as they rely on their victimization in order to be heard.[11]

Many of the Argentinean human rights trials relied on the protectionist, paternalistic language that is established in CONADEP's *Nunca más* and frames survivor testimony in a way that divorces them from their politicized contexts. Inasmuch as CONADEP and *Nunca más* are important to survivors of human rights abuses, the report and transitional governmental bodies avoid unpacking and uncovering the economic, political, and social ideologies and practices that engendered systemic political violence. While FEMOSPP does indeed include a more comprehensive account of the causality of the Dirty War–era violence in Mexico, *Nunca más* is detached from the historical-political context that impelled these human rights violations. *Nunca más* forms a collective national memory that looks away from histories of state violence and instead hearkens toward a "democratic" future. The reports from both CONADEP and FEMOSPP, however, rely on protectionist, gendered tropes to defend the "honor" of women victims of state violence.

The use of a human rights discourse in post-dictatorship Argentina centered on rescuing human rights victims, particularly female victims. In an attempt to reconcile a nation, and in order for many Argentineans to gain legibility as survivors of state violence, a specific rhetoric was used that depoliticized their narratives and instead focused on their victimized status. Women in particular were construed as passive victims of a dark epoch in Argentine history in order to maintain the patriarchal mechanisms of the state power as guardian of its most vulnerable civilians: women and children. Cynthia Enloe's work on feminism and international politics reveals how common this phenomenon is, and she contends that we must be cognizant of "which kinds of nationalist movements rely on the perpetuation of patriarchal ideas of masculinity for their international political campaigns and which kinds see redefining masculinity as integral to re-establishing national sovereignty."[12] Much like the transitional PAN government in Mexico, the transitional Argentinean state's role as benefactor to victimized women not only perpetuates "patriarchal ideas of masculinity," it also emphasizes the importance of "national sovereignty" and unity in the post-dictatorship era.

However, state-sponsored human rights reports became critical in the effort to document women's survivor testimony, resulting in a more nuanced representation of women's agency. Women survivors of state violence utilized the very avenue (the state) that had once attempted to eradicate their presence. *Nunca más* allowed for women to archive their narratives and officially recognize the atrocities and this sense of national and international recognition indelibly marked their collective political agency. State-sponsored human rights reports in these cases served to reaffirm and legitimize women's histories of political repression, albeit in a way that can elide their agented political subjectivities, as well as erase the deeper historical roots of such gendered violence. A more nuanced portrayal of women's agency is best reflected in how *Nunca más* framed Adriana Calvo de Laborde's testimony.

Calvo was a physicist working at the University of La Plata when she was abducted from her home on February 4, 1977, and detained at a Buenos Aires concentration camp. At the end of the dictatorship, Calvo contributed her testimony to *Nunca más* and other sources. As significant as *Nunca más* is in the official documentation of survivors' testimonies, we fail to gain a comprehensive understanding as to why Calvo and others were targeted by the repression; the text emphasizes reuniting a divided nation. According to Kimberly Theidon, "a central tenet of transitional justice is that it includes . . . the reestablishment of group unity" as well as making steps toward the "beginning of a new moral community."[13] National unity had gendered implications since it was essential to protect the most defenseless victims of the dictatorship: pregnant women and/or mothers of young children. The transitional state deemed this demographic as the most vulnerable category of state repression, and according to paternal normative codes, the mothers were in need of rescue and assistance. *Nunca más* illuminated victims' gendered vulnerabilities and simultaneously evaded the political causes that resulted in their detention. In so doing, the transitional government could focus on creating a new "moral community" that condemned the violence of the past and focused on a new, democratic government. By examining Calvo's testimony in the chapter "Victims," it is evident that *Nunca más* reinscribes political, leftist activists within a culture of victimhood.

Since Calvo was pregnant at the time of her detention, *Nunca más* placed Calvo's testimony within the "Children and Pregnant Women who Disappeared" subcategory. The section commences with a biblical allusion, condemning the state's violence against "the defenseless, the vulnerable and the innocent": pregnant women and children.[14] As I later examine, this section parallels the structuring of FEMOSPP's presentation of women victims of state violence, as both state reports categorize violence against women along with violence against children. The collation of disappeared children and pregnant women's histories in this chapter limits the women's narratives to their physical condition and infantilizes the pregnant women by equating their experiences to those of children. While it is critical to officially document the processes of dehumanization the prisoners faced, the commission's deliberate redaction of Calvo's testimony signifies the state's interest in the most fragile conditions of the detainees. This defense of society's most "vulnerable" and "innocent" citizens is representative of paradigms in universal human rights that eschew engagement with overt political condemnation of state violence. *Nunca más*, preoccupied as it is with delving into the most egregious instances of abuse, tethers Calvo's experience to the universal human rights model: the protection of society's most vulnerable subjects is prioritized above all. As Wendy Brown states, human rights discourse is predicated upon "a pure defense of the innocent and the powerless against power, a pure defense of the individual against immense and potentially cruel or despotic machineries."[15]

The infantilization of women's testimony is exemplified in Calvo's account of giving birth in captivity. The commission omits passages of Calvo's testimony in order to reconstruct the spectacle of childbirth under horrendous conditions of the camps, even though she alludes to entrenched power structures and the hypermasculine ideology touted by the regime. Calvo's narrative in *Nunca más* evokes the horrors of her abduction, her torture, and the birth of her daughter while she was detained. Her harrowing experiences appear in the "Births in Captivity" category. Calvo recounts that after she delivered her baby while restrained and blindfolded, she was tended to by one of the regime's doctors: "In the car the doctor cut the umbilical cord and they took me up one or two floors in another place, where they got rid of the placenta. They made me disrobe and in front of the guard they made me wash the bed, the floor, my dress and made me clean up the placenta and finally they let me wash my baby, all the while they were insulting and threatening me."[16] Forcing her to undress in order to humiliate Calvo after just giving birth, as well as having to clean up after her "mess," displays the power of the military officials for whom the maternity of leftist "subversives" is tantamount to something shameful and subhuman.[17] *Nunca más* documents Calvo's experiences of bodily degradation, which importantly allows her to position her narrative within a site of resistance. The human rights movement in post-dictatorship Argentina inflected Calvo's political agency, as she not only provided testimony to CONADEP but also presented her oral testimony at the human rights trials against former officers in 1985.[18] However, the text reduces Calvo's testimony to depictions of bodily harm without offering alternative modes of comprehending political forms of violence other than through the lens of victim/victimizer. Ultimately, the report served to legitimate post-dictatorship Argentina's nascent democracy and commitment to the defense of universal human rights. The commission omits passages of Calvo's testimony in order to reconstruct the spectacle of childbirth under horrendous conditions of the camps.

It is well-known in the international human rights community that, since the demise of the dictatorship, Argentina has been vocal in its denunciation of the regime. CONADEP and *Nunca más* opened a critical space for the recognition of state violence and worked with numerous human rights organizations and activist-based reports to shed light on the horrors of the dictatorship. Although the FEMOSPP report and *Nunca más* provided international and national acknowledgment of the state's perpetration of egregious violations of human rights and illuminated the gendered nature of state violence committed during the Dirty Wars, the state-mandated reports are ultimately an extension of state power and special interests. *Nunca más* does not articulate a theory of justice, nor does it seek accountability for the gender-based crimes committed by the state. It is, therefore, more critical than ever that feminist scholars who focus on issues of gender justice in the Global South remain cognizant of the pitfalls of replicating state-controlled discourse. Consequently, we must reenvision how to achieve justice and truth seeking outside the realm of the state. In what follows, I will center on contemporary Argentinean activist-produced texts that serve as critical narratives of resistance. These texts challenge the limits of state-centered models and discourses of human rights, and do so while incorporating a universal, woman's human rights framework and lexicon.

Feminist Readings of Argentinean Activist-Produced Cultural Texts

Many activists and survivors turned to cultural and artistic expression to document their experiences of state repression and to expose the limits of state-controlled human rights documents. The most critical form of resistance is the oral and written testimony of survivors who challenged state-produced documents that redacted their stories from the final version of their reports (as did *Nunca más*). Other survivors and artists turned to experimental, postmodern modes of documenting their histories of violence and resistance, and these dissonant, nonlinear discursive texts capture the disjointed, fragmented sense of self and national unity or nonunity that historical traumas created. Many survivors and artists have used cultural modes to better capture complex, nuanced, and layered experiences of survival, trauma, and gendered political repression.

In post-dictatorship Argentina, writers and survivors crafted texts that challenged the limits of the state-controlled narratives produced by the transitional government. In 1997, Juan Gelman and Mara La Madrid compiled the testimonies of survivors and of the children of the disappeared into *Ni el flaco perdón de Dios* (Not even God's feeble pardon). That same year, survivor Nora Strejilevich published *A Single, Numberless Death* (*Una sola muerte numerosa*), her experimental, fictional memoir that reconstructs the Argentine modality of repression and centers on gender-specific forms of torture and repression that underpinned the regime. These two texts incorporate the language of universal human rights and women's human rights to challenge the egregious history of Dirty War state violence, yet they do so in order to criticize the limits of state-centered transitional projects.

Despite their difference in form and genre, *A Single, Numberless Death* and *Ni el flaco perdón de Dios* are activist-produced reports that evince the gender, class, and political underpinnings of Argentina's dictatorship. Both Argentinean cultural texts articulate a theory of (gender) justice that is absent in the FEMOSPP report and *Nunca más*, and accordingly, they expose the limits of masculinist state-controlled human rights projects. These activist-produced texts create new human rights vocabulary and theories of justice to convey the legacy of trauma and gendered political violence that is etched into the national, cultural, and political consciousness of both nations.

Reclaiming the Testimony: *Ni el flaco perdón de Dios*

In 1997, seven years after former President Carlos Menem pardoned the convicted officers of the dictatorship, the human rights organization HIJOS and

Argentinean cultural critics and writers Juan Gelman and De la Madrid published *Ni el flaco perdón de Dios*, an activist-produced testimonial text that includes firsthand accounts of those affected by the dictatorship. This text is one of many activist-produced texts that appeared after the dictatorship ended in 1983; it is part of a critical genre of work that recuperated the historical memory of the Dirty War by centering the firsthand accounts of survivors and individuals affected by the military dictatorship.

As critical as it was for survivors to see their testimonies and experiences appear in *Nunca más*, many have criticized the limits of the report because their unedited, full testimonies were not included in the final version. *Ni el flaco perdón de Dios* makes clear what elements of survivor testimony were deemed too radical or extraneous to the masculinist state projects of the transitional governments. Here, I center on Adriana Calvo's testimony to illuminate the difference in gendered and political contexts between state-sponsored reports (*Nunca más*) and activist reports (*Ni el flaco perdón de Dios*). Calvo's testimony recounts the same processes of dehumanization institutionalized during the regime, yet the editors allow Calvo's narrative voice to guide the trajectory of her testimony. As the book's foreword asserts, "this book wants to show not demonstrate" (*mostrar no demostrar*). This indicates that the testimonies are published in their entirety, with minimal framing or structuring by the editors. *Nunca más* limits Calvo's testimony to the torture she endured as a pregnant woman, while *Ni el flaco perdón de Dios* presents her politicized identification as a union activist and does not divorce her political identity from her experiences as an incarcerated pregnant woman. Calvo's narration of giving birth in captivity is reconstructed as an act of subversion rather than as a source of shame and demonstration of fragility. Meanwhile, Calvo subverts the state's abuse of power and reclaims agency by reasserting two parts to her identity, mother and political prisoner, which are not mutually exclusive.

In her testimony, Calvo clearly states the reason she was detained: she was a member of her university's union. "Our union represented a history of struggle ... I think this is the main reason behind my abduction," Calvo explained, adding that, "they [the military regime] had to finish with these kinds of organizations, ... [and] they had a clear objective: to dissuade student activism and union activity in the department."[19] However, the history of union activism in Calvo's account is not printed in *Nunca más*. Calvo attests to the dictatorship's criminalization of political dissidents and the methodical eradication of "subversives." Her account problematizes the reliance of *Nunca más* on the human rights' culture of victimhood as she reasserts her collective subjectivity as an activist in her union, not merely relating her experience as a woman who gave birth in captivity. Since the dictatorship criminalized political dissent and created a narrative that justified its use of violence against "subversives," focusing on the political subjectivities of survivors could possibly serve as an erroneous explanation as to why women activists were targeted. This legacy of the dictatorship is evident in the inclusion of the Two Devils theory in the first edition of *Nunca más*, which places equal blame on the political dissenters and state agents who officiated the violence. Therefore, CONADEP erased the political contexts to emphasize the passive conditions of the victims of society's repression (pregnant women and children). CONADEP had to be strategic in what information to include in the final report, yet these editing choices ultimately shaped the national and cultural memory of the dictatorship by criminalizing political dissent.

Furthermore, *Nunca más* evades mention of the systems of repressive power—such as gender-based violence—that functioned during the military regime. In a passage recounting the gendered dynamics of torture and the military regime's display of hypermasculine, patriarchal ideals, Calvo states in *Ni el flaco perdón de Dios* that the prison guards would deride the women prisoners while physically assaulting them: "'Bitch, take care of your kids, go and wash the dishes,' they would tell us.... To them, a woman who resisted was much worse than a man who resisted. The valor of the women drove them crazy."[20] Calvo's experience as a political prisoner addresses the hetero-patriarchal order underlying gender violence in the clandestine centers. Calvo and other prisoners were perceived as subversive threats to normative gender ideals of woman as mother and/or housewife, which the regime violently reinforced. As a union organizer, Calvo was one of the many activist women who contested social categories of gender upheld by Argentinean junta, and as such the women were castigated by the regime. State authorities targeted female resistance as a means of reinforcing the patriarchal order.

Nunca más also omits a critical portion of Calvo's testimony that recounted the birth of her daughter Teresa. Calvo describes a moment when fellow inmates fought prison guards who attempted to take Teresa away: "They [my cellmates] made a human barricade, screaming and fighting like lionesses in such a situation of utter and complete inferiority.... [The guards] would have had to kill them to take Teresa away. And they didn't take her away." The women's daring display of valor is suggestive of the possibilities of reinventing traditional models of femininity and motherhood in order to resist masculinist state authority. Their actions proved successful: the guards did not remove the baby from Calvo, momentarily inverting the power dynamic where the guards were intimidated by this enraged, politically active, feminized "human barricade." This comes toward the conclusion of Calvo's testimony: "Teresa and a conviction were born together. If Teresa lived and I lived, I would fight my entire life for justice. That is how I recall that moment, as if I were taking a path of no return."[21] Calvo's narrative recaptures her commitment to social justice and historical memory, and her political activism is reinforced during her experiences as a young mother and political prisoner.

Calvo concludes her testimony by relying on the language of universal rights to declare her dedication to justice and to dismantling years of impunity. She thus interweaves her positionality as an activist-mother who swore a lifelong commitment to justice if she and her daughter survived the camps. Thus, she politicizes her experience as a pregnant woman in the camps and converts this experience of abjection and gendered degradation into a feminist theory of activism and social justice praxis.

The Production of Feminist, Human Rights Discourse in *A Single, Numberless Death*

Oral and written testimonies in post-dictatorship Argentina have been a critical mode of documenting and illuminating critical feminist theories of justice for years of impunity and state violence, while also serving as important texts that reveal the limits of state-sponsored testimonial projects. Testimony as a genre has been applied to various literary and artistic expressions, and many writers have experimented with the testimony as a literary form. *A Single, Numberless Death* is one of the many experimental testimonial texts to emerge in the post-dictatorship era. Twenty-five-year-old Nora Strejilevich was preparing for a trip to Israel in 1977 when several men wearing civilian clothing burst into her apartment one afternoon in Buenos Aires and subjected her to beatings and interrogation before forcibly taking her to the nearby clandestine concentration center, El Club Atlético. Strejilevich's text, however, does not adhere to the traditional structure of the first-person format that many testimonies assume. Rather, her testimony is experimental in form, situating her personal narratives alongside the experiences of others who were affected by the repression. The text's format and disjointed structure captures the enduring effects of this trauma; the format of *A Single, Numberless Death* incorporates poetry, prose, quotes from political figures of the time, splices of media headlines, and excerpts from other prisoners' testimonies, producing a nonlinear, fragmented narrative that evokes the traumatic effects of her experience as a survivor of the regime.

Strejilevich's memoir reflects the vestiges of the historical trauma of the Argentine dictatorship on the national consciousness. *A Single, Numberless Death* is a disjointed testimony that situates the narrative of the past repression in present-day Argentina and disturbs the national discourse of progress. Further, the book questions the politics of a gendered memory and justice as it illuminates the limits of state-controlled human rights projects. This is apparent in its experimental form, which creates an aesthetic quality that disrupts a temporally progressive, linear format. In effect, this creates a sense of unease and structural confusion as the interlocutor is incessantly transported back and forth across various spatiotemporal realms. This particular literary technique challenges the Argentinean transitional government's attempt to "work through" and move beyond the trauma and state-sanctioned violence of the past.

A Single, Numberless Death's disjointed, fragmented form contrasts with the ordered, linear format of many state-sponsored reports, such as *Nunca más*. Strejilevich discursively reconstructs the chaos of the dictatorship and the effect it has had on her personally as well as on the national collective. The disjointed structure brushes against state-controlled human rights projects that seek linear order and temporal progression. This tension is evoked at the outset of the text, the episode about Strejilevich's kidnapping. The repetition, incomplete sentences, and fragmented prose are effective rhetorical devices to depict the actual destructive, chaotic moment when military officials invade her apartment, as well as the fragments and destruction caused by the dictatorship. In *Cultural Residues*, Nelly Richard reminds us that testimonial dictatorship literature assumes "the heroic task of having to reinvent languages and syntaxes to survive the catastrophe of dictatorship that submerged bodies and experiences in the dismembering violence of multiple shocks and shatterings of identity."[22] The following passage exemplifies how Strejilevich "reinvent[s] languages": "Dizzy you whirl in a vortex of scraps of yesterdays and nows crushed by orders and decrees. You get lost amid chairs overturned, drawers emptied, suitcases torn open, colors blanched out, maps slashed, roads severed."[23] "Yesterdays and nows" cleverly plays with the concept of linear time and furthermore evinces the invention of new language to attempt to capture this traumatic memory.

Strejilevich's fragmented narrative reflects the initial stages of disembodiment as she is reduced to mere body parts. During a torture session where Strejilevich is abused with electrical prods, she notices "white light, scorched mouth, shivers. Tendons, muscles, blood all roar guttural words, consonants and vowels."[24] Here, the loss of language control is intermingled with the loss of bodily control; Strejilevich's prose is indicative both of her physical breakdown and of the breakdown of language and grammar. The sentence syntax is disorganized and each body part is separated by a comma. In addition, the elements that comprise a word—"consonants and vowels"—parallel Strejilevich's use of biological terminology—"tendons, muscles"—that constitute the fundamental elements of a human body. The disintegration of sentence structure in Strejilevich's prose evinces the military regime's control over language.

During her incarceration, Strejilevich and the other prisoners were constantly monitored and their interactions severely prohibited. As she notes, "the disappeared are forbidden to talk." This statement demonstrates the loss of language and communicative abilities among the prisoners who inhabit a communal space. The regime not only physically dominated the detainees but also limited their ability to communicate with others. Without language, a definitive element of communal interchange, the prisoners were stripped of their humanity. The temporary restriction of language separated prisoners from one another while simultaneously presenting the correlation between existence and language: "in the cells of not being, speaking is strictly forbidden."[25]

A Single, Numberless Death resists the state's attempt to elide the narratives of brutal violence institutionalized during the military regime. During a harrowing torture session, Strejilevich iterates the importance of memory and providing testimony: "Right then I seal a pact with Nora-to-Come: to remember."[26] Memory as a form of activism and resistance echoes Calvo's commitment to justice in *Ni el flaco perdón de Dios*. Despite the state's attempt to destroy and break Strejilevich and Calvo and their social bonds within the camps, future political activism and solidarity movements were essential to their very survival. According to human rights scholar Fiona Ross, "In extremity, political commitments were important in surviving violence and sustaining a sense of self. They enabled activists both to withstand extreme hardship and to return to protest or resistance activities on their release."[27] Maintaining a sense of self is predicated on the preservation of women's political agency even during extreme moments of degradation, and this is particularly relevant when Strejilevich, Calvo, and other women detainees are subjected to gender-based physical and psychological torments due to their political activism.

Similar to Calvo's testimony in *Ni el flaco perdón de Dios*, Strejilevich also refers to gendered abuse in order to deconstruct patriarchal forms of repression, which evinces the absence of a gendered analytic in state-controlled human rights projects. When Strejilevich refers to gender violence, she emphasizes the military regime's masculinist ideology and criticizes their use of sexual violence to torture the prisoners in the camps. By alluding to the personal and collective experiences of sexualized torture, *A Single, Numberless Death* critically exposes the hypermasculine forms of repression that were systematically enforced during the dictatorship. The military officials' depictions of the female prisoners as debased, licentious women encouraged their degradation of the prisoners through sexual abuse. In the section titled "Men Quick to Unzip," Strejilevich presents the topic of rape as constitutive of the repressive state apparatus in the concentration camps: "How do you live . . . among men who, without a qualm, earn their daily bread by asking how you like it—from the front or from the rear? Men quick to unzip who open and close their flies with masterful swiftness, the result of extensive training. A very masculine way of subduing the enemy."[28] Here, rape is not an impulsive act of sexual domination but rather "the result of extensive training" by the military regime. Rape is reflective of systemic hetero-patriarchal violence that underpinned the Argentinean dictatorship, where gender roles were violently codified inside and outside of the camps. The women raped in this passage were demoralized when asked whether they "like it . . . from the front or from the rear." In this instance, the officials are underscoring their power over the prisoners by morbidly offering a "choice" in their method of rape. This form of "extreme masculinity" indicates that military officials primarily used rape as a method of torture.[29]

In a later passage, Strejilevich invokes the fragmentation and sexualization of the women inmates when the guards taunt the women on their way to the shower: "The guards rate us as soon as we start to pull down our pants. . . . The ass of the third one, the legs of this one, the tits of the first one in line—one hundred points. Any other bids? . . . Better enjoy it [the shower], this might just be your last time under water."[30] The women are verbally degraded and sexually dehumanized as the guards objectify them, concentrating on their distinct body parts, yet they also reinforce their absolute power as agents of the state. This particular sexualized abjection is in dialogue with the hypermasculinize power structure of the military regime that sexualizes, dehumanizes, and abnegates the existences of these women. While the guards degrade them sexually, they also remind the women of their ability to exterminate them at any moment, so that in such instances, sexual torture and death are intimately linked in a sinister form of repression and power.

A Single, Numberless Death uses the language of human rights reports—such as *Nunca más* and other state-controlled documents—to provide the audience with a feminist reading of gender-based violence and its legacy in post-dictatorship Argentina. Strejilevich includes the following excerpt from *Nunca más*, which further illustrates gender domination over the prisoners:

"What did they do to you last night?" "They raped me, sir."
"Bitch, (*slaps*) no one did anything to you here, understand?"
"Yes, sir." "What happened to you last night?" "Nothing, sir."[31]

However, this excerpt is framed in her section on gender-based violence, a section that is absent from both *Nunca más* and the FEMOSPP report. Strejilevich uses the language of human rights that appears in *Nunca más* and the FEMOSPP report, yet she does so by creating feminist terms in order to criticize the history and legacy of state-sanctioned gendered political violence of the dictatorship. The processes of dehumanization and bodily and psychological fragmentation were gendered, and Strejilevich evinces the complexities and effects this has had on survivors. That the prisoners were treated as less than human demonstrates that they are now politically and socially irrelevant to Argentina during the dictatorship. However, this process does not merely reflect the dehumanization of the women, it alludes to the critical role sexual abjection plays in this process of degradation. In essence, the prisoners in the concentration camps were incarcerated and abused for their political affiliations and for being perceived as subversive threats to the junta. The passage therefore iterates the process of sexualization via rape and also underscores the dehumanization vis-à-vis the officials' denial of the sexual abuse.

Furthermore, *A Single, Numberless Death* invokes human rights terminology in order to contribute to and carve out a new feminist understanding of the history of Argentinean state violence. In a later passage, Strejilevich genders the term Dirty War in order to illuminate the sexual underpinnings of this term so often referred to in human rights discourse. While settling into her parents' home after her release from El Club Atlético, she remembers hearing about a young British woman named Diana, who was detained in another concentration camp. Both Strejilevich and Diana were subjected to torture and rape: "When they were ready, one [officer] said, 'Take off your clothes!' We took them off, Diana. And right then a new battle began. The Dirty War. . . . The hazing episode lasted three days and three nights. 'If you say a word, you're history,' she was told. We're history, Diana . . . Triumph, terror, booty, and ravaged land. Dirty War. Ten days later Diana was able to leave the country. We were able, Diana."[32] Strejilevich refers to the human rights term Dirty War as a figurative and literal act of violating thousands of prisoners sexually, physically, and mentally. The term was originally used by the government to depict the warring factions between the military state and the "subversives," but it was later appropriated by some human rights advocates to condemn this era of violence. In this context, Strejilevich reclaims the traditional definition of the term Dirty War and makes a clear connection between the systemic use of rape in the concentration camps and the military government's quest for a new sociopolitical order. Both Diana and Strejilevich not only metaphorically represent the "booty and ravaged land" of the war, but more importantly, they represent how this moment of torture irrevocably altered their lives. As she notes, "we were able, Diana." This ambiguous statement can be read as indicating that, while the two were able to survive the concentration camp experience, the military regime was able to dehumanize the prisoners. The past tense reveals that Strejilevich is no longer an able-bodied individual with subjectivity, but rather she is redefined by the military government as an abject being. These particular instances in Strejilevich's text expose the process of her own sexual abuse and dehumanization as well as the abuse of other women sexually brutalized in the camps. *A Single, Numberless Death* documents the silenced, gendered narratives and brushes against the military regime's systematic attempt of eliding the past. More importantly, the book's emphasis on gender violence brings visibility to the systemic form of sexual abuse instituted during the regime, and in so doing it exposes the limits of state-controlled human rights projects, vocabularies, and discourses that systemically erase or overlook critical histories of gendered state repression.

Strejilevich relies on a narrative style that alludes to the brutalities of sexualized torture, yet it is grounded in a political criticism of these hypermasculine modes of repression. In her depictions of the sexualized, gendered forms of torture, Strejilevich does not assume the narrative voice of a victimized, passive prisoner; instead, she criticizes the institutionalization of masculinist modes of domination that underpinned the military regime, and approach that is particularly evident in the re-ascription of the term Dirty War within a specific gendered context that criticizes dominant masculine epistemologies embedded within the terrorist Argentinean regime. In *A Single, Numberless Death*, Strejilevich counters state-controlled narratives' problematic infantilization of women detainees by subverting the dominant, masculinized paradigm that erases the narratives of survivors of sexual violence.

The Legacy of Impunity and Disavowal of Gendered Human Rights Abuse: Mexico's FEMOSPP

While the Argentinean transitional state swiftly and immediately addressed the crimes of the *junta militar*, the Mexican state did not acknowledge its culpability in Dirty War–era crimes for several decades. On November 27, 2001, at the General Archive of the Nation (AGN) in Mexico City, President Vicente Fox Quesada appeared before press, archive staff, human rights leaders, and politicians to announce the creation of a special prosecutor's office (FEMOSPP). Based on the recommendations of the National Commission on Human Rights (CNDH, Comisión Nacional de los Derechos Humanos), President Fox declared that the Special Prosecutor's Office would shed light on the past and "procure justice for crimes against people associated with past social and political movements."[33] Until 2001, the government's official response to the human rights concerns presented by activists, survivors, family members and local organizations was silence and denial. However, the defeat of the PRI in 2000 by the conservative PAN ushered in an era of transition and pivoted to a more open democracy in Mexico. The newly elected Fox sought to distance his administration from the authoritarian tone and legacy of the PRI, and he strategically embraced a universal human rights discourse in order to create a more positive image of Mexico in the international community. President Fox ran his presidential campaign on the promise of investigating human rights crimes of the Dirty War era, and his advocacy of human rights concerns served to reaffirm to the global community that Mexico "met standards for human rights, for environmental protection," and was able to partake in global economic treaties.[34] The creation of FEMOSPP signified a critical first step toward justice for survivors of Mexico's human rights abuses of the Dirty War era.

In December 2005, the authors of FEMOSPP presented an eight-hundred-plus-page report to Dr. Ignacio Carrillo Prieto, head of the FEMOSPP office. The Fox administration, however, hesitated to make the report accessible to the public. In November 2006, the Attorney General's office finally uploaded a redacted version of the report on its government website, which remained online only briefly.[35] Anticipating that those in power would edit the original report and make it difficult to access, the authors of the report leaked the original version to prominent Mexican writers, journalists, and activists. Kate Doyle of the nongovernmental, nonprofit National Security Archive in Washington, D.C., released the original report on their website in February 2006.[36] Although President Fox had promised in 2002 that he would promote "a Mexico where nothing is hidden and everything is done open to all citizens," the inability to access the report, along with major redaction, exposed the limits of state-centered transitional justice projects.[37]

As significant as this report was in unearthing the buried history of Mexico's Dirty War, many activists, scholars, and human rights experts have exposed the limitations and conflicts of interest that had doomed the FEMOSPP report from the start. Few activists and scholars, however, have remarked on the gender politics of Mexico's transitional project. Unlike *Nunca más*, Mexico's FEMOSPP report was written years after the rise of international human rights movement and nearly a decade after the 1993 UN World Conference on Human Rights, which declared that women's rights were human rights. By the time President Fox mandated the Special Prosecutor's Office in 2001, universal human rights and women's human rights had become integral to the vocabulary of many local and global rights–based organizations and governmental bodies. However, FEMOSPP does not specifically address women's human rights in its report, nor does it use a gender framework when documenting the human rights violations committed by the state. Transitional governments are typically male-headed entities, where many of the legal experts and policymakers are men, particularly men of significant power and influence. Indeed, the lead figures involved in FEMOSPP—Fox, the lead prosecutors, and other politicians—were mostly men involved in highly influential political circles, and some even had ties to the previous PRI regime.

Although the criticisms and analyses about the final redacted FEMOSPP report have not incorporated a gendered lens, they have illuminated its contributions and limitations. The report established an important precedent in Mexican history as the first official governmental response to the demands for justice made by many civic organizations, survivors, and family members of the disappeared. In twelve chapters, the FEMOSPP report details the investigation into the crimes against humanity committed by the armed forces during the Dirty War. The report links the history of the 1968 massacre to the extralegal killings of guerrilla activists in the 1970s and 1980s, also tying this era of state violence to the dictatorships of the Southern Cone. The report condemns PRI leaders for their role in 645 disappearances, 99 extrajudicial killings, and at least 2,000 cases of torture.[38] The report challenges the official discourse that had previously criminalized political dissidents in Mexico, and the authors use the language of universal human rights to legitimize their claims.

The report also provides some of the historical, economic, and political context of Dirty War–era repression. Chapters such as "Explanation of the Origins of the Dirty War" and "Genocide" explore the role the armed forces and intelligence agencies played in violently repressing political dissidence and guerrilla groups. The chapter, "Armed Groups: The Guerrilla Extends throughout the Entire Country," examines counterinsurgency groups, such as the Federal Security Directorate's White Brigade, that were explicitly created to monitor and "exterminate" the armed movements that had risen up throughout Mexico. The report details the excessive power used by the state in its efforts to "destroy this sector of society they considered their ideological enemy."[39] The FEMOSPP report importantly condemns the state for its excessive, extralegal use of violence against political dissidents, and the transitional government officially acknowledged that the state was directly involved in crimes against humanity.

President Fox's decision to create the FEMOSPP office was due in large part to the mainstreaming of the international human rights movement, as well as the pressure his administration faced from local Mexican human rights organizations. For many years during the Dirty War era, local activist groups, family rights organizations, and other civic organizations had been working collectively to document the violations committed against leftist political organizations and activists. Two activist organizations, Comité '68 and Eureka, have been instrumental in fomenting a human rights movement and in pressuring state and international agencies to investigate crimes committed by the government. In the early 1970s, these organizations worked alongside international organizations, such as the nascent Amnesty International, to seek accountability for violence sanctioned by the state. Ana Ignacia Rodríguez Márquez informed me in our 2010 interview that the German chapter of Amnesty International was instrumental in securing her early release from prison in 1971: "One of the things that helped me a lot was when Amnesty International sponsored political prisoners who had not committed acts of violence. I was incredibly lucky when they sponsored me . . . the [Amnesty International] Frankfurt group worked very hard on my case, they sent me letters, and they sent letters to Díaz Ordaz requesting my release from prison."

After her early release in 1971, Rodríguez Márquez joined forces with other former political prisoners and former members of the 1968 student movement to form what is now the Comité '68. As Elaine Carey and Jose Agustin Ramon Gaspar note, "Despite little recognition in governmental and international agencies' reports, the Comité is one of the motivating forces behind the modern human rights and democracy movement in Mexico."[40] Local activist groups such as the Comité '68 and international human rights entities like Amnesty collaborated to put pressure on Fox's transitional government.

These key events and the internationalization of the human rights movement pressured Fox's transitional government to respond to the demands of local coalitions such as the Comité '68. Indeed, Rodríguez Márquez and other Comité members were important social actors in the indictment of former president Luis Echeverría (1970–76) in 2004 for his role in orchestrating the Tlatelolco massacre. Although his indictment only led to house arrest and eventually to an overturned conviction, the FEMOSPP office and local activist groups such as Comité '68 were instrumental in taking this important step toward justice. Rodríguez Márquez emphasized to me the importance of local human rights groups in the transitional government's attempt to reckon with its past: "In Mexico, there had never been a former president who was condemned to house arrest. That is the achievement of the Comité '68." The activist work of these locally based civic organizations also influenced Fox's decision to offer reparations to those affected by PRI-era state violence. Reparations remain a controversial subject among various human rights and activist groups in Mexico, and survivor groups ultimately rejected Fox's reparations offer. However, some survivors viewed this as an important step in the state's attempt to reconcile with its violent past. In my 2013 interview with Maricela Balderas Silva, former guerrillera of the Sinaloa chapter of the 23rd of September Communist League, she expressed her belief that Fox's attempt to offer reparations was an important move by the government. "The point is that the government broke the law," Balderas Silva explained, "and this is a recognition by the government for the errors they committed, for the injustices they committed."

Despite the symbolic achievements made by the Fox administration, the Special Prosecutor's Office faced serious limitations that impeded its ability to successfully achieve transitional justice. The transitional government of the PAN sought to establish itself as a paternal guarantor of human rights for its citizens, and it attempted to situate itself as a nation-state that was decidedly different from the violent, paternal authoritarianism of the PRI government. However, as Sergio Aguayo and Javier Treviño Rangel note, the PAN did not eschew the political power and influence of the PRI.[41] The PRI still held many governorships and seats in congress, so if President Fox wanted to accomplish any significant political goals during his tenure, he would have to work with PRI politicians.

Another significant drawback of the FEMOSPP office was its inability to obtain a single criminal conviction during its five years of operation. Mexican human rights scholar Javier Treviño Rangel observes that the Fox administration's appropriation of a universal human rights discourse not only reinforced the power of the ruling political party, but it resulted in the creation of de facto impunity for perpetrators of state violence, which is evident in former president Echeverría's case. Treviño Rangel comments that the human rights legal terminology used in the cases against the perpetrators ultimately protected them from prosecution.[42] The Special Prosecutor's Office declared that it would only investigate "federal crimes perpetrated, directly or indirectly, by public officials," yet this stipulation occluded the prosecution of local agents, police, and paramilitary groups, such as those responsible for the October 2 massacre.[43]

These compelling and critical analyses of the FEMOSPP report, however, do not assess the gender politics involved in the framing of survivor testimony. The final report, as well as its many criticisms, use a gender-neutral, universal subject (victim and/or political activist) of human rights, which is inherently a masculinist subject. The report, like other state-sponsored human rights texts, uses a human rights discourse that exposes the tactics of state terrorism instituted by the PRI. This discourse, however, does not reveal the gender or cultural politics that engendered such forms of violence. When gender is referred to in the report, it merely refers to women as a separate category of human rights abuse, but does not evince the relationship between state power, patriarchy, and political resistance movements. Using a feminist lens here to assess the FEMOSPP report illuminates the ways in which Mexico's transitional government promoted itself as a *proper* authoritarian yet benevolent father figure of the nation with a vested interest in upholding hetero-patriarchal gender relations.

The FEMOSPP report documents various methods of state torture used by federal agents against political dissidents and guerrilleros; however, little context is provided for the gendered nature of these forms of state violence. For example, the "Genocide" chapter includes exhaustive information and testimonials on extrajudicial killings, disappearances, massacres, sexual violence, and other egregious violations of human rights instituted by the state against perceived threats to national security. However, the framing of survivor testimony violence in this dense, hundred-page chapter verges on the exploitative side, as the report does not provide sufficient context or basis for the state's reliance on sexual-based torture against political activists.

This is evident in section 8.5.4 "Methods of Torture, Part B. "Rotisserie Chicken and Sexual Torture." The authors include detailed testimonies by male survivors of sexual-based torture inflicted by federal agents, including castrations of suspected "subversives." However, there is no mention of causality or context as to why PRI agents deployed this form of violence against political dissidents. Instead of analysis or insight into the context of sexual torture against the men, the report delivers graphic and exploitative depictions of sexual violence. In Poniatowska's *La noche de Tlatelolco*, while sexual and gendered violence is included in the text, it is done so in a manner that links these forms of violence to the hetero-patriarchal power of the PRI's authoritarian government. The FEMOSPP report does not permit readers to develop a firm understanding of the state's use of excessive sexual and gendered violence, and the manner in which it is framed in the report is gratuitous and is delinked from its historical and social contexts.

Sexual-based violence was common in other Latin American states during the Dirty War era and was used to underscore the hetero-patriarchal power of the repressive state. Former president Echeverría's own public denunciations regarding political dissidents and guerrilleros during a presidential address to the nation on September 1, 1974, derided guerrilleros as individuals from broken homes who exhibited sociopathic tendencies, were sexually promiscuous, and expressed homosexual desires.[44] Echeverría's national address reaffirmed the authoritarian, hetero-patriarchal matrix of the PRI regime, and this provides context as to why sexual torture was used against dissidents who had deviated from prescribed gender and sexual norms set forth by the state. Echeverría and other PRI leaders linked the guerrilleros' sexual and gender depravity to political deviancy, which they viewed as a threat to the hetero-masculine and capitalist identity of the authoritarian nation-state. Thus, systemic use of sexual-based violence and torture of political dissidents upheld the authoritative power and control of the regime. This hetero-masculine identity was intimately tied to the PRI's political ideology, which was reflected in the violent castigating and policing of political dissidents. In this way, Echeverría and other PRI leaders publicly confirmed their role as paternal authoritarians, and clearly defined the ideal gender and sexual roles alongside an ideal capitalist political ideology.

While the FEMOSPP report mentions that many male detainees were castrated as a form of sexual torture, it fails to investigate the gendered, political contexts of these crimes. What's more, the report does not mention the castration of Martha Alicia Camacho's husband, José Manuel Alapisco Lizarraga, instead including Camacho's account of witnessing her husband being murdered while she was eight months pregnant. Her harrowing account is relayed in full detail in the 2007 collection of testimonies of former guerrilleras, *First National Assembly of Ex-Guerrilleras*. In this activist-produced text, Camacho gives testimony of her abduction and torture; she recalls army officers stating "he [your husband] thinks he's so ballsy, the asshole, well look here, now he doesn't have any more balls" before castrating and then murdering him in her presence.[45] The absence of this portion of her testimony in the FEMOSPP report divulges the important relationship between masculinity, political ideology, and state violence. The violent authoritarianism of the PRI deemed guerrilleros and other male political dissidents as exhibiting homosexual tendencies, as not proper men. Castration as a violent act of sexual torture thus reasserted the hypermasculinity of the state, while also ensuring that a political dissident was removed of his ability to procreate further "subversive" offspring. This correlates with the Argentinean military ideology that led to the theft of more than four hundred babies during the dictatorship; the officers of the dictatorship placed many of the babies stolen from the disappeared into military families and other families who sympathized with the regime, so that the children would be raised with what were deemed to be proper Christian, capitalist, and conservative political ideals set forth by the Argentinean dictatorship.

While the testimonies of male victims of sexual state violence are presented without context in the FEMOSPP report, women victims of sexual violence are grouped in another section of the same chapter. In the chapter, the authors rely on gendered tropes and protectionist terminology to illuminate the vulnerability of women, children, and elderly victims of the Dirty War. This paternal benevolence is best exhibited in section 8.7, "Harm against the Most Vulnerable and Defenseless Sectors of Society," which consists of four subsections: "Illegal detention, Forced Work and Disappearance of Children," "Torture of Children in Front of Family," "Mistreatment of Women Who Gave Birth in Captivity," and "Rape of Women and Minors." State-sponsored human rights texts adopt a discourse that positions women as feeble and vulnerable to the violent masculine agents of the state. The ostensible role of the transitional state is to assist them in reclaiming their positionality as honorable women. Curiously, however, this section on violence against women, children, and the elderly invokes the rhetoric of women's rights as human rights: "National and international legislation has come to adopt protective legal measures, particularly for women, children, the elderly . . . [and] under the law, women will be especially protected against any attack against their honor, and in particular, against rape, against forcible prostitution and against any attacks against their modesty; to not be subjected to humiliating and degrading treatment; to the protection of their privacy."[46] The report relies on an international human rights legal discourse that is intended to protect women from sexual-based violence, yet it does so in a manner that evokes the patriarchal state's perspective on women, gender, and sexuality. That is, the transitional government, embracing a women's rights as human rights framework, did so in order to protect women's "honor" and "modesty," which reflects Judeo-Christian values that link women's sexuality to their worth and integrity. Thus, any "attacks against their modesty" must be defended and protected by the paternal transitional state.

Furthermore, the final FEMOSPP report infantilizes women survivors of state violence by including their testimonies alongside histories of violence against children. This particular positioning of women's testimonies and narratives of surviving gendered, sexual state violence not only evinces the authoritative power of the PRI regime but also illustrates the paternal project of the PAN's transitional government. This is also showcased in Argentina's transitional justice project, which revealed women's vulnerability to the excessive, violent dictatorial state and the need to be protected by Raul Alfonsín's transitional government. Like the FEMOSPP report, *Nunca más* also situates the testimonies of pregnant women alongside those of children. In this manner, both reports highlight the spectacle of women's experiences of gender violence while overlooking women's histories of resistance and political activism during the Dirty War.

Elena Poniatowska's *La noche de Tlatelolco*: A Feminist Criticism of State-Sanctioned Violence and Precursor to Universal Human Rights Discourse

The egregious and harrowing acts of violence committed by the Argentinean and Mexican states during the Dirty Wars occurred prior to the mainstreaming of a universal human rights movement, as well as the "women's rights as human rights" movement of the 1990s. Prior to rise of these movements, Elena Poniatowska published *La noche de Tlatelolco* (*Massacre in Mexico*), the first report to document the massacre of October 2, 1968, when paramilitary forces opened fire on peaceful demonstrators in the Plaza de las Tres Culturas in the Tlatelolco area of Mexico City, killing hundreds of people. The Tlatelolco massacre has become one of the most public and internationally recognized instances of Dirty War–era human rights abuse committed by the Mexican state. However, at the time of *La noche de Tlatelolco*'s 1971 publication, the term *human rights* was not widely used in national or international lexicons.

In this final section, I turn to *La noche de Tlatelolco* in order to examine the ways in which activist-produced texts published before the rise of a global human rights movement can capture the gendered, social, and political underpinnings of Mexico's Dirty War–era violence. Poniatowska was one of only a few Mexican journalists at the time to denounce the government for its orchestration of the 1968 massacre, giving visibility to the trauma and loss that many Mexicans endured. Incorporating oral histories, poetry, photography, written accounts, and media headlines, *La noche de Tlatelolco* documents the events that transpired between July and December 1968 and exposes the mechanisms of repression implemented by the Mexican state. The text weaves together the narrative voices of the survivors to condemn the state's legacy of impunity and silence in their efforts to maintain secrecy in their role in the massacre. The state did not initiate an investigation of the 1968 massacre until early in President Fox's first term, in 2001. Years of impunity denied victims and families any recognition of human rights violations or the ability to seek justice. *La noche de Tlatelolco* not only recuperates an historical memory that has been elided by the dominant national narrative, but it brings awareness to a history of gendered activism that is absent in the FEMOSPP report. Read against and alongside state-sponsored human rights reports, I consider *La noche de Tlatelolco* as a model of a critical, feminist human rights cultural text that contravenes the state's obfuscation of histories of Dirty War violence—especially women's histories—from the official narrative.

Poniatowska's framing of the report captures the socialist rhetoric of the student movement and the growing participation of women in the resistance efforts of the time. *La noche de Tlatelolco* importantly positions the testimonies of young men and women as equal to one another, while also illuminating the gendered tensions that emerged within the movement. Poniatowska commences the textual portion of the report with testimonial excerpts from former student activists Raúl Álvarez Garín and Margarita Isabel. Positioned next to each other, these testimonies explain why Álvarez Garín and Isabel joined the movement, and they reflect a critical aspect of the movement's historical-political context. For Álvarez Garín, being involved in the movement was not arbitrary: "I didn't join the movement; it was already a part of my life for a while . . . it's a question of defending everything we believe in." According to Isabel, the escalation of police brutality on her campus prompted her to form an actors' brigade and join the movement.[47] Poniatowska is careful to highlight the political consciousness of both young Mexican men and women; by pairing the two testimonial accounts together at the commencement of *La noche de Tlatelolco*, women's political subjectivities are not overshadowed by the men's histories of activism. Historians Deborah Cohen and Lessie Jo Frazier explore this particular silencing of women's history of political activism during the Mexico student movement, claiming that "even though the idea that women could and should play a more visible political role was gaining currency, individual women were too often not considered legitimate political actors."[48]

Furthermore, it is important to acknowledge Poniatowska's privileged status and how it affected the legibility of the massacre nationally and internationally. A prominent figure in Mexican journalist and intellectual circles, she was able to utilize her upper-middle-class, European-Mexican background to be an arbiter of history and use a feminist lens to document this silenced history of violence. In *La noche de Tlatelolco*, the agency of young men, women, family members, and other activists is not merely represented; agency formation is dialogic in nature, as Poniatowska's and her interlocutors' political consciences are molded and shaped by interactions with survivors, witnesses, government officials, and other Mexican civilians. This is evident in the photographic essay in the beginning of the book. The photographs serve as a visual index, aesthetically presenting the political momentum of the movement months before the massacre, while the final photographs capture the violent repression of the demonstrators on October 2. There is a direct relationship between the photographic essay, the fragmented testimonies of the survivors and witnesses, Poniatowska as the journalist-activist, and the readers. In one photograph, we see the body of a young boy with a bullet wound visible in his chest and the following caption: "Who ordered this? Who could have ordered this? This is a crime."[49] This haunting image coupled with the denunciation of Mexican state violence is meant to provoke the reader into further critical interrogation and action.

Additionally, Poniatowska incorporates her own voice alongside the voices of those she interviewed, as the photographs' captions are taken from the interviews she conducted. Her own agency as a feminist, investigative journalist is informed by the narratives of the movement as well as the interactions with those she interviews. Furthermore, the visual index creates a visceral dimension to the text that is absent in state-sanctioned human rights reports. *La noche de Tlatelolco* includes images of people involved in the movement—such as the aforementioned boy—and utilizes this visual index to render legible the violence sanctioned by the state and to archive a history that the government was intent on erasing from its past.

While *La noche de Tlatelolco* captures the momentum of the student movement, it is also documents women's participation in the political sphere and their involvement in the student movement, whose aim included a social paradigm shift.[50] The movement was critical in Mexico's history of gendered activism as there was a surge in women's participation in the political sphere, marking a decided shift in Mexico's sociopolitical terrain. Poniatowska's report portrays women not as mere victims of state violence or as shadows of the male student leaders of the movement but rather as independent activists. Clearly, Poniatowska's work is important for considering the politics of gender that is not explored in the FEMOSPP report. It is important to be cognizant of the ways in which human rights discourses portray women, and how the varying, shifting language of activist and state-produced texts indelibly shape women's agency. Poniatowska's text offers a feminist human rights model to archive and document women's political histories of activism without relegating them to secondary roles. The reports from both FEMOSPP and CONADEP failed to incorporate narratives of women's political activism and archived their histories according to their experiences as mothers and/or wives.

In *La noche de Tlatelolco*, Poniatowska evokes the tensions and various social, political, and gendered realities in 1960s Mexico. Many women in the movement grew up in middle-class homes, signaling the politicization of this sector of Mexican society and the inclusion of women in public political demonstrations. As one young woman states, "my mother isn't a monster—she is a symbol of the majority of mothers of the middle class . . . with her head in the sand." Poniatowska contrasts this statement with testimonial excerpts of individuals who voice their concern for the sociopolitical and generational changes by centering on the bodies of female activists rather than their political consciousness: "why is your skirt so short?," "it [the violence and political climate] is the fault of the miniskirt."[51] State-sponsored patriarchal values are reflected in the Mexican nuclear family unit, and Poniatowska aptly captures the generational and gendered dissonance in these testimonies.

Furthermore, *La noche de Tlatelolco* illuminates the gendered power dynamics of the movement, particularly the double burden women of the movement faced: the violence of the authoritarian, paternal state directed toward women activists and the internal gendered hierarchies present within the movement. Poniatowska refers to the gender politics without deriding the movement as antifeminist. Many of the testimonies, in fact, indicate that women were integrated into Mexican politics in ways that were not typical before the 1960s. At various moments within the text, we are exposed to the complex gender dynamics and entrenched gender norms that were present in leftist Latin American movements. For example, male protagonists of the student movement, such as Eduardo Valle Espinoza, told the members during a group meeting that they shouldn't cry like women. The female activists challenged his statement, but they eventually ceded to Espinoza, as he claimed that he was using a harmless expression. The women apologized and later brought a cake to the men of the group.[52] This particular testimony evinces the masculinist subtext of the student movement and the manner in which gender norms and roles were perpetuated within socialist, leftist political movements.

Women activists also contended with the violence of gender policing by Mexican authorities. Poniatowska incorporates testimonies of women who allude to the state's normalization of sexual violence in a manner that is drastically different from the way state-sponsored human rights reports refer to it. Poniatowska's accounts of gender violence are not divorced from the political context of the massacre, whereas the FEMOSPP report and *Nunca más* sensationalize the violence enacted by hyper-violent male authorities without delving into the gender norms that incited such violence. In *La noche de Tlatelolco*, Poniatowska connects the gender violence enacted by the Mexican government to its hypermasculine, authoritarian character. In the text, Rodríguez Márquez mentions that while she was detained after the massacre, she was psychologically terrorized by prison guards threatening rape and physical assault.[53] Similarly, former political prisoner Roberta Avendaño Martínez recounted the prevalence of gender-specific torture in the prisons where many women protestors were detained after the massacre.[54]

While Martínez relates the types of gender violence committed by prison guards, Poniatowska frames her testimony in a way that does not focus solely on the sexual violence that incarcerated women experienced. Poniatowska's text, therefore, presents an untold facet of the history of the student movement: the use of corporal and psychological gender-based violence against women activists as a manner of policing gender, social, and political ideologies in Mexico. Martínez's testimony articulates the motivating cause for the murder and incarceration of hundreds of activists: "we are young people who fought for an ideal." This ideal, as she states, included a nation where political leaders "are not corrupt and do not abuse their authority; [we fought for] the ideal that the community have rights . . . [and for] true democracy and justice for all."[55] This echoes Calvo's testimony in *Ni el flaco perdón de Dios* as she clearly states why the Argentinean dictatorship detained her: she was a union member in her university. Thus, this ideology posed a severe threat to both the Mexican and Argentinean states, and they responded to these movements' demands for dialogue with violence, terrorism, and criminalization of activists.

This form of social control exerted by the authoritarian Mexican state also emerges in the oral histories of former activists of the Dirty War era. In interviews I conducted with former guerrilleras Alejandra and Bertha Lilia Gutiérrez Campos in Guadalajara, Mexico in 2012, they claimed that the government's surveillance and restricting of student organizing occurred across the country. As students at the University of Guadalajara in the early 1970s, Alejandra and Gutiérrez Campos witnessed the clashes between the University of Guadalajara's student-led Student Revolutionary Front (FER) and the right-wing student group, Federation of Students of Guadalajara (FEG). The FEG was a student group created, funded, and armed by the PRI government in order to maintain a conservative agenda on the university's campus and to intimidate leftist student organizations. As Gutiérrez Campos, a former member of FER, recounted, "we realized . . . that we were not only dealing with the FEG, but we were dealing with the national and state repressive apparatus." The increasing intimidation and targeting of FER members for their political ideology eventually led to violent confrontations between the groups, including the deaths of several of Gutiérrez Campos's compañeros and partners.

Alejandra also informed me during our interview that the lack of dialogue between the government and the student movement contravened basic human rights and reflected the violence of the state: "We wanted a dialogue with the government, we wanted to voice our opinion about what was happening in Mexico. It was the kind of violence where [the government] was essentially covering our mouths so we couldn't speak, for God's sake, it was terrible. And a basic human right is to engage in a public dialogue [with the government], right? And were not able to speak, to say what we were feeling, to say anything, we couldn't even hand out pamphlets or anything." While *La noche de Tlatelolco* documents the state's violent repression of the leftist student movement in Mexico City, Alejandra's and Gutiérrez Campos's quotations here reveal the national reach of the government's control of the social movements of the time. What's more, Alejandra invokes the term "human rights" to depict the violence committed by the authoritarian Mexican government; this demonstrates how the mainstreaming of a human rights lexicon in the contemporary moment shapes the way survivors articulate their memories of state-sponsored terror of the past. It took many years and the mainstreaming of a human rights vocabulary for many survivors of the Tlatelolco massacre—and other violent Dirty War episodes—to feel comfortable enough to share their experiences of trauma, repression, and survival. Poniatowska's *La noche de Tlatelolco* created a textual space where survivors and family members could archive their narratives of trauma and resistance to the authoritarian power of the Mexican state, particularly in their attempt to erase the gendered history of the 1968 student movement.

Despite the importance that Poniatowska's text represents for survivors, *La noche de Tlatelolco* does not have the same legitimacy as state-produced human rights reports such as *Nunca más*, nor did it have the backing of a global human rights movement to bring international visibility to the crimes committed by Mexican authorities. The lack of national and international attention given to the crimes of the state dissuaded many activists from politically organizing. As Rodríguez Márquez noted in our 2010 interview, women were less inclined to speak of the massacre than their male counterparts: "Many people have never spoken of it [the massacre] again. Many people were scared . . . there are many women who were protagonists of that history, that form part of that memory and who have not spoken of it." Many women in Mexico were terrorized into silence by the state during the Dirty War because they were repressed for transgressing their prescribed roles of apolitical mother and/or wife. In some ways, the authoritarian state succeeded in its violent castigation of politically active women since many of these women never returned to political activism after the massacre. Reading the activist-produced text of *La noche de Tlatelolco* with a feminist lens reveals the patriarchal, paternalistic, and, ultimately, violent authoritarianism of the PRI Mexican state. Poniatowska's work, a precursor to the human rights–centered texts of later years, offers us a glimpse of the critical gendered history of Mexico's Dirty War, a perspective that is decidedly absent from state-sponsored reports like those from FEMOSPP and CONADEP. Turning to the leftist and feminist framework of Poniatowska's *La noche de Tlatelolco* offers us critical feminist and human rights vocabulary that can help us shape new theories of comprehensive (gender) justice for human rights crimes.

Reading these activist-produced texts alongside the FEMOSPP report and *Nunca más* evince critical feminist human rights terms with which to assess histories of state violence and trauma. Activist-produced cultural productions reveal feminist theories of justice in their experimental literary and testimonial forms; as "amnesia-erasing" texts, they remind readers that this violent legacy "continues to be present" and they challenge the notion that state-sponsored human rights projects are the only avenue for attaining justice for state-sponsored crimes. Although the reports from both FEMOSPP and CONADEP are critical milestones in the evolution of human rights in Latin America, they are, after all, still projects of masculinist states. State-backed human rights projects essentially have managed the critical terms of human rights, and ultimately they had to appeal to audiences that were both victims of the regimes and those in favor of the regimes. As the next chapter demonstrates, cinematic and literary productions by former leftist survivors and activists can also perpetuate conventional, masculinist narratives of the Dirty War that effectively elides women's experiences in political movements. While these literary and filmic texts represent the horrors of the carceral state during the Dirty Wars, these cultural texts have relied on problematic gendered tropes that position women survivors as collaborationists and/or traitors to the revolutionary cause.

CHAPTER TWO

Sexual Necropolitics, Survival, and the Gender of Betrayal

> Betrayal looks like seduction. Like the image of a seduced woman.
> —Miguel Bonnasso, *Recuerdos de la muerte*

State-sponsored sexual violence committed by military officers during the Dirty War is a sensitive and polemical topic legally, culturally, and socially. As discussed in chapter 1, sexual violence was integral to the repressive apparatus of the state, yet it was only recently acknowledged in legal avenues and still remains a socially sensitive topic. While silence, shame, impunity, and apathy regarding sexual violence have been entrenched in the political, legal, and social worlds in Mexico and Argentina, cultural productions have validated survivors' experiences by portraying the horrors of the carceral state. At times, however, the representation of state violence in cultural texts can reflect dominant masculinist perspectives of leftist revolutionary groups and reinforce problematic gendered ideals. This chapter examines narrative film's and literary fiction's representation of sexual violence, survival, and gendered betrayal in Marco Bechis's Argentinean film *Garage Olimpo* and Mexican novelist José Revueltas's novella *El apando*.

Released in 1999, Bechis's *Garage Olimpo* is a fictional account of the disappearance and detention of twenty-year-old María Fabiani during the Argentinean military regime. María, a young political militant and literacy campaign teacher living in Buenos Aires, is taken to the clandestine torture center (in real life called El Olimpo), where one of the torturers is Félix, her former housemate, who has been fixated on María but whose affections she had previously spurned. In the carceral space where death is rampant, however, this dynamic shifts and

Félix becomes María's "protector" and her paternal savior who attempts, and ultimately fails, to save her life. *Garage Olimpo* cinematically captures the carceral logic of the military regime, where guards had absolute power over prisoners' bodies. The relationship between María and Félix in the carceral space of death illuminates the regime's fetishization and dehumanization of the captive female body. María's captive body serves as a site of desire and repulsion; she is castigated for her political transgressions and nonconformation to the state's desired feminine, neoliberal subjectivity. Although the film does not explicitly condemn María for engaging in sexual activity with Félix, the controversial nature of their relationship alludes to the concept of a hetero-masculine "revolutionary morality" that many leftist organizations espoused.

Revueltas's *El apando* (1969; *The Hole*) was published during his incarceration in Mexico City's infamous Lecumberri Prison (Palacio de Lecumberri), where hundreds of political prisoners were illegally detained during the height of leftist activism in the 1960s and 1970s. The novella, less than thirty pages in length, centers on three male prisoners who devise strategies to smuggle narcotics into their cell (the *apando*, the "hole"). Despite Revueltas's experience as a political prisoner, the text refrains from referring to the 1968 Tlatelolco Massacre or state violence during the Dirty War. The novella does, however, implicitly denounce the repressive carceral logics of the Mexican state. Despite *El apando*'s indirect condemnation of Mexico's carceral state and abjection of its prisoners, it is the women in the text who are subjected to physical and sexual degradation in the carceral space in order to assist with the male prisoners' addiction. Although the women in the novel are not incarcerated, they become subjected to the prison's control of their bodies while also being condemned by the male prisoners for using their sexuality to assist the prisoners.

Bechis's and Revueltas's fictional texts reveal the sexual necropolitics of the carceral state that structured the dynamic between the political prisoners, agents of the state, and the Argentinean and Mexican governments. *Garage Olimpo* and *El apando* illuminate the absolute power and systemic violence of the Mexican and Argentinean Dirty War states and show how power dynamics were strictly enforced within the carceral space, or space of death. In essence, the prison became a necro-carceral space where this authoritarian power and control over life and death was constantly wielded over the prisoner's captive body. In these cultural narratives, the carceral space is depicted as a place where death is imminent and where prisoners are constantly reminded of their impending deaths. In this chapter, *carceral spaces* refer not only to the film and novella's discursive representations of the confines of the literal prison, but also the way that carceral logics imbue and circulate through spaces *beyond* the prison. This, in turn, illuminates the logics of the Mexican and Argentinean carceral state in which prisoners and civilians were subjected to the necropower of the authoritarian regimes, inside and outside the carceral spaces of death.

Drawing on Mbembe's definition of necropolitics as "the subjugation of life to the power of death," this chapter establishes how the Mexican and Argentinean carceral states relied on a necropolitical logic that determined which lives were expendable and subject to constant threat of death.[1] The pervasiveness of death within carceral centers in Latin America was directly linked to the foundation of a neoliberal ethic and ideology. Latin American nations during the Cold War era served as testing grounds for neoliberal economic experimentation, and this hemispheric experiment relied on a necropolitical order that authorized the incarceration, torture, dehumanization, disappearance, and murder of thousands of political dissidents. The carceral space was a logical extension of the nascent Latin American neoliberal state—both in dictatorial and liberal democratic states—in exercising its necropower over people it deemed unworthy of their humanity. This chapter draws parallels between two authoritarian regimes in order to highlight the transnational scope of necropolitics that structured military states and liberal democracies. In both instances, the states exerted a "power of death" over incarcerated bodies.[2]

Although Mbembe's work on necropolitics has appeared in critical research on Latin American state violence, little scholarship addresses the gender dynamics of Latin American necropower. Biopolitics and necropolitics seemingly refer to a genderless being, yet it is essential to complicate this gender-neutral framework. The cultural texts I examine in this chapter reveal the gendering and sexualization involved in subjugating bodies to the power of death, processes that are integrative to the carceral logics of these states. While both male and female prisoners were subjected to the state's power of death in Latin America, the state sexualized and gendered incarcerated bodies according to entrenched social scripts. As Melissa W. Wright notes in her essay on the drug war and femicide in Mexico, Mbembe's and Foucault's theories on necropolitics and biopower are essential in comprehending the normalization of racialized violence in contemporary Mexico. But she goes further by arguing that contemporary forms of racialized and gender-based violence on the United States–Mexico border is "incomprehensible without a feminist analysis of the patriarchal state ideology that undergirds the violent status quo."[3] Similarly, Alexander Weheliye's *Habeas Viscus* provides a brilliant critique of Agamben's biopolitical discourse and turns to black feminist scholarship to address the absence of race and sexuality as critical categories that are constituted within bare life. As Agamben describes, bare life refers to "life [that] ceases to be politically relevant ... and can as such be eliminated without punishment."[4]

This chapter focuses on the patriarchal framework of Latin America's nascent neoliberal agenda and uses a feminist lens to examine the necropolitical and carceral setting of *Garage Olimpo* and *El apando*. In Mexico and Argentina, carceral spaces reflected the absolute power of the state over the dehumanized, abject—and sexualized—prisoner's body. The constant threat of death and the sexual abjection of prisoners occurred within the carceral space. Sexual torture was a normalized, integral practice of the repressive mechanisms of Argentina and Mexico during their authoritarian regimes.[5] With a feminist conceptualization of necropolitics and biopower in mind, I argue that sexuality plays a central role in necropolitics as the states reinforced absolute power over the death of captive bodies through sexual means, while captive bodies relied on sexuality to defy this necropolitical logic. It is critical to interrogate how the sexualization of abject, female captive bodies complicates a genderless necropolitical framework, as the masculinist state sanctions gendered violence and death.

Furthermore, this chapter examines the patriarchal, masculinist context of a leftist revolutionary ethos that emerges in both film and novella. In *Garage Olimpo* and *El apando*, women's bodies are manipulated, fetishized, and sexualized by agents of the state and by male prisoners within the prison. The sexual relationship between a prisoner and her captor in *Olimpo* yields a complex portrait of sexuality, subjectivity, survival, and death in the camps. As already noted, *Garage Olimpo* does not appear to judge María for her sexual relationship with her captor, yet the narrative of sexual betrayal in post-dictatorship Argentina has placed moral judgment on women who survived the carceral space of death. This raises the question of whether there is an appropriate way to culturally represent the concept of sexuality and survival in the Argentinean case, as these histories are considered as treasonous and debased in the cultural imaginary. In *El apando*, the prison exerts disciplinary power and control over its citizens, but the depiction of the prison is often feminized and gendered as female. The prison as woman/womb is an extension of a long-term hermeneutic paradigm in which the land-nation is feminized and where female betrayal is mythologized in transnational Latin America, evident in the figure of La Malinche.

Both texts reflect the eroticization of women's bodies as tied to state violence and they reinforce problematic masculinist renderings of women's sexuality by leftist organizations. They also center on female characters who utilize sexuality as a means of survival against state violence in the prisons, or the space of death. This, in effect, produces a tension between the dehumanization of the body and the sexualization of the female body as a site of castigation, revulsion, betrayal and desire, which discursively disempowers the women characters. The women's attempts to work with or resist the carceral state in both texts is portrayed as a form of betrayal as their bodies are privy to the masculinist power of the state. However, this reading of betrayal is gendered as female, and both the film and the novella explore the tension between abjection and fetishization of the women's bodies within the carceral space. While both *Garage Olimpo* and *El apando* document the harrowing conditions of the carceral space and the necropower of the Mexican and Argentinean states, they ultimately allude to a dominant narrative whereby leftist organizations maligned women survivors for betraying the revolutionary cause.

Women survivors of Latin American state violence often face gendered scrutiny that positions them as sexual traitors for acquiescing their bodies to agents of the carceral state and for submitting to the necropower of the state. As the Bonasso quotation indicates, betrayal is gendered as female, which alludes to the figure of La Malinche. Although originally a symbol of Mexican betrayal, Malinche-as-betrayer has now been codified in a transnational sense, as it has come to embody ultimate feminine betrayal in many Latin American cultural narratives.[6] In order to challenge this dominant narrative alluded to in *Garage Olimpo* and *El apando*, this chapter concludes by turning to the perspectives of women who survived state-sanctioned sexual violence. Here, politically militant women differently narrate the concept of gendered "betrayal" and thus express their own accounts of resistance against the sexual necropolitical structure of the prison and carceral state.

Gender and Necropolitics in *Garage Olimpo*

In September 1999, Chilean Italian director Marcho Bechis's second feature film, *Garage Olimpo*, was released in Buenos Aires, Argentina. Despite the marketing campaign involved in the film's highly anticipated release, *Garage Olimpo* did not perform well at the box office. Although upscale movie houses advertised the film, Amy Kaminsky notes that many cineplexes had misinformed moviegoers that the film had sold out. This led to low sales in the first week of its release, prompting theater owners to pull *Garage Olimpo* from movie houses. As she argues, the particular details surrounding the film's reception "[echo] the censorship period of the Argentine *Proceso*."[7] Film critic César Maranghello states that the box-office failure of *Garage Olimpo* "taught us a bitter lesson that, if an artistic work about the horrors of the *Proceso* is to be accepted, it must skirt the truth."[8] Even though many Argentinean films released during the post-dictatorship era have centered on exposing the horrors of the regime, there is still a cultural reticence to fully acknowledge the legacy of this past, particularly in relation to the topic of state-sponsored sexual crimes. The reception of the film evinces how post-dictatorship Argentina in the era of President Carlos Menem is defined by a politics of memory that is preoccupied with its forward-looking neoliberal present, eschewing any connection to the past horrors of the regime.

Despite the film's poor box office performance, Bechis's politically engaged film functions as a critical audiovisual source that documents elided narratives of state-sanctioned sexual trauma, as well as the legacy of the dictatorship that continues to shape contemporary Argentine society. It forces spectators to grapple with Argentina's relationship to its traumatic past and the continued effects of the period of the dictatorship. The film does not shy away from representations of the brutal violence of the dictatorship, and in so doing, *Garage Olimpo* bears audiovisual witness to an epoch of terror, degradation, fear, and death. It is critical to note that the filmmaker's positionality informed the thematic focus of the film. Bechis, an Italian national, is personally connected to the history of the dictatorship and spent ten days in El Club Atlético in Buenos Aires. Although Bechis casts himself in a cameo role as one of the many detainees in Olimpo, the film is not autobiographical. Instead, it centers on the degradation and dehumanization of a politically active young woman.

Garage Olimpo centers on the contradictory processes involved in the dehumanization and eroticization of María's abject body in the Argentinean concentration camp. The film introduces one of the central paradoxes of the narrative: the conversion of an agented subject into an abject entity, which is contingent on the vilification and sexualization of the subject within a space of death (the prison). This vilification and sexualization of women characters also emerges in Revueltas's *El apando* and this paradox forms a central driving force to both cultural works. At the start of *Garage Olimpo*, we are introduced to María Fabiani, a young, self-assured political activist and literacy teacher living with her mother in Buenos Aires. When we first see María, she is giving literacy classes to poor, indigenous Argentineans in the shantytowns of the capital city. The initial scenes of María at her job and as a political activist portray her as an independent and politically conscious young woman, as is evident in the film's representation of her body and gender expression.

María's confidence in her political convictions and gendered body is evident in an encounter with Félix, her housemate who becomes her captor in the camp. In one early scene, María returns home from her literacy job to find Félix lying on the couch, and commands that he remove his feet from the couch, telling him, "this is not your house." Sharing a beer on the couch, Félix attempts to flirt with María and asks her, "would you like to see a photo of my girlfriend?"

He pulls out a photo of María in his wallet and she, agitated, tries to retrieve it from him. Félix offers her a photo of himself. She takes the photo and quips, "you're better looking in your photo" before getting up and handing back his photo; she tells Félix to pay the rent and then leaves the room.[9]

The positioning of the characters in this scene is important, as the first shot reveals María standing up, towering over Félix, who reclines on the couch in her home. At this moment, María is self-assured, confident, and rebuffs Félix's flirtatious advances. It is clear that his feelings go unrequited. Félix, attempting to exert some control over the situation, shows María the photo of her he presumably stole from her belongings. The fact that he possesses María in this medium foreshadows his control over her physical, abject body in the concentration camp. María's teasing, slightly insulting, response to Félix's photo indicates that she is assuming a playful role, yet she is clearly disinterested in his amorous advances.

These opening scenes of the film set forth the carceral logics that extend beyond the prison walls; although María has the advantage in these scenes, audiovisual cues foreshadow her future abject status as bare life in the necropolitical space of the camp. Although the literacy class scene and the scene with Félix on the couch establish María's political agency and unbounded subjectivity, the film's somber soundtrack—a solo cello, and its arrhythmic, *staccato* notes—informs the audience of the ominous context. *Garage Olimpo*'s careful use of soundtrack heightens the tension between its presentation of one of the key dyads of the film: the spatial unboundedness of María living in the city versus the spatial cloistering of María as a (sexualized) prisoner. It further establishes one of the central paradoxes of the film: the river as both a symbol of life and a signifier of death. The film's opening scene provides us with an aerial shot of the murky brown waters of the Río de la Plata set to the cheerful song, "Brilla el sol" (The sun is shining) by the popular Argentine duo of the 1970s, Barbara and Dick. While this is ostensibly just an aerial view of the river, the film introduces the trope of death by alluding to the death flights during which thousands of prisoners were drugged and disappeared in the Río de la Plata and Atlantic Ocean from military planes.[10] The lighthearted lyrics and melody depicting the innocence of young love are contrasted against a representation of death and state terror; this paradox of life and death unsettles the spectator as we bear witness to the necropower of the state in its decision to condemn thousands of young lives to death.

The opening scenes of the symbol of death—the river—reflect the necropolitical, carceral audiovisual logic that structures the film. Here, the paradox of life and death are reflected in the film's representation of the river. Repeated aerial shots of the river and the city center—again evoking the death flights—punctuate the film's narrative and relay the authoritative necropower of the military regime. While rivers are typically associated with life and rebirth, in *Garage Olimpo* it serves as a trope of death. The muddy waters of the Río de la Plata serve as the film's final scene, when we learn that María becomes one of the many regime victims who is drowned, evincing her status as life unworthy of being lived.

The aerial scenes of the river furthermore evoke the trope of surveillance that parallels the military regime's policing of "subversive" sexed bodies, which ties to the carceral logics and sexual necropolitics of the film. The film's use of spatiality reflects the expansive necropower of the regime and its control over gendered bodies. Before María's abduction, we see that her body is her own, as she expresses control and command in her home and in her interactions with Félix. At this point in the film, María's body does not appear to be an object for the spectator of what Laura Mulvey calls scopophilic desire, especially since we are viewing the film from María's perspective. This shifts, however, in the moments prior to her abduction. The spectator begins to partake in the fetishistic gazing of her body as we view María in her living room wearing a long-sleeved shirt, shoes, and underwear. Unknown to María at this point in the film, plainclothes military officers have surrounded her home, monitoring her movements. María, half-naked, begins to lose her autonomy as soon as she rifles through a box of clothes Félix brought home. The clothing, we later discover, belonged to the abducted political prisoners Félix oversees in the Olimpo detention center.

As soon as María slips on a brown, long-sleeved dress from the box, she notices the armed men standing in her living room. Earlier in the film, María wore 1970s-style blue jeans and a turtleneck while going about her daily interactions. She discards a signifying element of her identity—her own clothing—and unknowingly dons the clothing of a detained-disappeared woman, thus commencing her transformation into the Agambian definition of bare life.

The scenes illustrating María's confidence in her body, her feminine expression, and political consciousness end abruptly when she is abducted. Steady camera work and long shots depicting María in her living room before her detention signify the last moments of control and agency she possesses. As soon as she realizes that officers have arrived to detain her, the scene erupts into chaos, with María's growing terror and panic accompanied by intense cello strings in minor tonal keys. In a futile attempt to defy the necropower of the state and to retain her agency, María tries to escape. Ultimately, she is captured in her backyard. As an officer drags her back to the house, a shaky, handheld camera follows as he commands her to kneel, then stand, then kneel again, contributing to the sense of chaos, fear, and growing terror of María's uncertain future. Furthermore, the officer's physical command over María's body portrays the absolute power the state has over her now-detained body, shown in a physically submissive position, kneeling before the officer. In the following scenes, María is transported to the dark, dingy underground of the clandestine center, Olimpo, where she is processed and stripped of her identity, clothing, and autonomy. Soon she is taken to the *quirófano*, or the torture chamber (lit. operating room) as she transforms into bare life.

The film's presentation of María's captive, sexualized body in the torture chamber highlights the link between sexual necropolitics and the carceral state. The ultimate power of the dictatorship's carceral state was dependent on the surveillance and regulation of subversive—and sexed—bodies inside and outside the camp and which bodies would be condemned to death. The film's portrayal of an incarcerated, sexualized detainee illuminates the absence of gender and sexuality in Agamben's concept of bare life and Mbembe's concept of necropolitics. If we are to consider Agamben's bare life as life that can be "eliminated without punishment," then I would like to question the role gender and sexuality play in the definition of the "sacred man," or *homo sacer*.[11] In *Garage Olimpo*, María's sexual degradation and dehumanization evinces the limitations found in Agamben's gender-neutral definition of bare life. In *Habeas Viscus*, Weheliye criticizes Agamben's assertion that the *homo sacer* transforms into an "absolute biological substance," anterior to gender, race, nationality, or other markings: "The flesh epitomizes a central modern assemblage of racialization that highlights how bare life is not only a *product* of previously established distinctions but also, and more significantly, aids in the *perpetuation* of hierarchical categorizations along the lines of nationality, gender, religion, race, culture, sexuality, and so on" (emphasis added).[12] Weheliye posits that racialized, gendered political violence that produces this bare life further perpetuates hierarchies based on power and difference. The sexualization of captive bodies in Argentina's camps evinces part of what black feminist scholar Hortense Spillers has termed pornotroping. Spillers describes pornotroping as a voyeuristic form of objectification that transforms the black, female captive body into mere flesh, a "thing" that "becomes a source of an irresistible, destructive sensuality."[13] To be sure, my analysis does not center on racialization and, therefore, it is important to make the distinction between María's white, sexualized captive body, and the black, sexualized bodies that Weheliye and Spillers analyze in their scholarship.[14] However, black feminist scholarship helps theoretically anchor my analysis of the eroticization and sexualization of bare life in *Garage Olimpo*.

Sexual torture with the threat of death was routinely used against politically active women who deviated from their appropriate gender roles as mother and/or wife. As Mexican feminist anthropologist Marcela Lagarde notes, the trope of the mother/wife, or *madresposa*, is codified in Latin American patriarchal cultures and their predestined femininity is directly linked to ideologies of nationalism. Hence, these "bad women" contravened their expected roles as *madresposa* and betrayed the masculinist, authoritative state.[15] María is therefore marked as a bad woman for not upholding the gendered tenets of nationalism and for eschewing the typical role set forth by the regime. Accordingly, the officers in Olimpo deride her political activism and her job in the literacy campaign, calling her "the famous little teacher." Having dared to educate the poor, subaltern, and indigenous population, she is subjected to electroshock torture, marking the conversion of her once-politically active body into bare life, a sexualized spectacle.

After a grueling torture session in which María is left unconscious and near death, the film depicts her nude upper body restrained on the torture table. While it is unclear at this point if María has endured sexual violence, the portrayal of her bare breasts in the carceral space presents the theme of sexual necropolitics and invokes Spillers's concept of pornotroping. On one hand, this shot exposes the degradation of incarcerated bodies that was normalized during the dictatorship and the conversion of bodies into mere flesh and bare life. On the other hand, the depiction of María's nude, tortured torso evinces the "destructive sexuality" of subjugated female flesh, alluding to Mulvey's critique of narrative film's scopophilic tendencies and its fetishization of the violated female body on screen.

Garage Olimpo's portrayal of María's tortured, eroticized body presents complex questions of the politics of representation and fetishized spectacles. María's captive body evinces what Weheliye has termed the "visual logic of pornotroping" as that which "cannot help but eroticize the brutality that the filmmaker seeks to denounce."[16] This presents a central problematic: is it possible for narrative cinema to represent the gendered atrocities committed by the masculinist authoritarian state without further exploiting the victimized body? In her essay on *Garage Olimpo*, Mia Mask criticizes the film for "plac[ing] the story's moral weight on the awkwardly titillating spectacle of the tortured female [. . .] body."[17] According to Amy Kaminsky, "narrative cinema cannot seem to escape the reinscription of the female body as fetish or those discourses of power that in the end seem to be about, or symbolized by, heterosexual, patriarchal gender arrangement."[18] In a similar vein, Diana Taylor argues that the eroticization of the female body makes it difficult to talk about gendered violence during the Dirty War without yet again making a spectacle of the body.

These scholars pose important critiques of filmic portrayals of sexualized state violence, and in many ways, *Garage Olimpo* represents the "visual logic of pornotroping" that replicates voyeuristic fetishism by exhibiting María's naked, captive body on screen. However, I would argue that the film ties this scopophilia to the surveilling necropower of the state, presenting to the viewer the critical intersection between sexual necropolitics and carceral logics that undergirded the Argentinean dictatorship. The film presents a critical paradox of the film in the relationship between María and Félix: she is at once an abject subject as well as Félix's property and embodiment of feminine passivity. By setting up this paradox, the film criticizes the fetishistic male gaze that represents the regime's hypermasculine, aggressive sexualization of the abject body *and* its investment in reinforcing "heterosexual, patriarchal gender arrangement[s]." *Garage Olimpo* importantly exposes the expansive reign of the regime's necropower and the fundamental role that gendered degradation plays in what Mbembe calls the "subjugation of life to the power of death."[19] Stripped of political agency, María is simultaneously dehumanized and sexualized and remains powerless to Félix and the state's control over her death. While the film portrays the spectacle of the eroticized, tortured female body, *Garage Olimpo* also focuses on women's resistance to patriarchal control and protection. One of the film's primary focal points, then, is to expose how sexual abjection was *constitutive* of the carceral state's necropolitical processes in exerting masculine power over subjugated bodies.

This is evident in the first scene of María's torture when the detention center's doctor examines her after she suffers cardiac arrest from electroshocking. The film does not depict the gruesome torture on screen, merely alluding to the violence. María's nude torso and breasts are in the foreground of the shot, and we cannot see the face of either the torturer or the doctor. Here, the doctor checks her pulse, uses defibrillator paddles to revive her, and reprimands the torturer for using excessive voltage on María. While the scene evinces what Mask terms the "titillating spectacle" of showing María's naked breasts, the film does not exploitatively portray the graphic details of her torture. The scene evokes images of death, evident in the flies buzzing around María's unconscious naked body, illuminating the necropower of male agents of the state. The men's faces are outside the frame, which reinforces their masculine omnipotence over her prostrate body as they "play god" in determining whether she will live or die. As Pilar Calveiro writes, "Death is administered randomly, displaying an intentional arbitrariness. It is these arbitrary acts where power is affirmed as absolute. . . . The suspension of life; the suspension of death; divine attributes exercised not from the heavens but from the basements of the concentration camps."[20] Furthermore, by exceeding the typical voltage in her electrocution, the torturer exposes his impatience with María's defiance to his authority for not "speaking a single word" during the interrogation.

This scene further relays the paradox of María-as-abject-subject and María-as-passive-feminine-object. María's abjection invokes her status as a gendered, sexualized bare life that becomes completely dependent on Félix, her captor. When Félix first sees María after the first torture scene, her abject body is lying on the torture table with sweat and other bodily fluids visible in the frame. Deborah Covino, referencing Kristeva's definition of abjection, notes that "the intolerable, or abject, body leaks wastes and fluids, in violation of the desire and hope for the 'clean and proper' body, thus making the boundaries and limitations of our selfhood ambiguous, and indicating our physical wasting and ultimate death."[21] The "clean and proper body" is evident when Félix first notices María in the torture chamber, as he rushes to her side. Lifting her off the table, Félix comforts her and provides her with a towel to cover her naked, tortured body. Covering her body displays Félix's paternalism and protectionism and furthermore evinces the paradox created between the abject, dehumanized bare life facing imminent death, and the gendered, sexualized body in need of protection and a reinforcement of feminine propriety.

The encounter between Félix and María highlights the dyad that emerges in the camp: the escape from this space of death is dependent on the proximity of bodies and sexual intimacy. María, cognizant of her status as an abject, bare life, turns to Félix and her sexuality as a means of survival within the death camp. Furthermore, the abjection of her bare life is contradicted by Félix's insistence on her propriety, reinscribing her desubjectivized flesh with markings of proper femininity and passivity touted by the Argentine regime.

In the detention center, María and Félix's relationship transforms the power dynamics established in the first few scenes. Félix exerts control over María's abject body by bribing his fellow officers in the camp in order to have sole access to María's cell. Despite his control over her captive body, Félix offers María false claims of agency by informing her that the information she provides will result in her release. This occurs in a scene that parallels the moment on the couch between María and Félix; in a later scene, Félix visits María in her cell, bringing a bottle of her favorite beer and telling her, "we have to celebrate that you are alive." As he attempts to come closer to María on her bed, and in perhaps a minor act of resistance, she tells him to stay away, stating that she is filthy. Upset that she does not want to be near him, he gets up and tells her before leaving, "I'm your only friend in here." María's body is seated, with Félix standing over her, indicating a role reversal from the first scene on the couch when they shared the same brand of beer. Within this space of death, Félix is in control, leveraging his power in order to "protect" and dominate María's body. In the earlier scene, we see María teasing Félix, exhibiting her gendered agency. In the later scene, however, María eschews his advances due to the condition of her abject body.

The dialogue in this scene also highlights the necropolitical context of the camp, as Félix ironically states that they must celebrate that María is alive, even though death, abjection, and dehumanization define her existence now. This sentiment is exacerbated when he looks around the dank, dingy gray walls and tells her he will bring her some photos and other items to decorate her cell. Despite her status as bare life, Félix reinscribes María with proper feminine markings, offering her naked body clothing and providing her with sanitary napkins. The details portray the paradox between María as a dehumanized, sexualized entity, and María as the object of Félix's desire: a passive, proper woman who is utterly dependent on him for survival. Although María is transformed into an abject, dehumanized being in the camp, she also becomes the typical figure of proper womanhood and femininity as she turns to Félix for protection.

Félix's role as masculine protector over María's abject, feminized body evinces the paradox that emerges in the film's sexual necropolitics. This is evident in his claim that he will protect her from death, even though he repeatedly reminds María of her status as a bare life, meaning that if she does not cooperate, she could die like many others have. His role as savior also extends to protecting María from sexual violence by other guards; however, María offers her sexualized, abject body to Félix, believing that by doing so she can escape from the camp. Although María seemingly exerts a certain amount of agency in her decision to have a sexual relationship with Félix, the very nature of the death camps prohibits exercising personal agency or domain over one's embodied existence.

Sexuality, Survival, and Betrayal in the Argentinean Death Camps

Despite relying on her sexuality to survive, at the end of the film María is one of many political prisoners disappeared into the Río de la Plata. María, in her attempt to escape from prison as a space of confinement, depends on sexual intimacy with her captor. It is precisely this intimate relationship with Félix that can be inferred as a betrayal, and thus, we need to think more complexly about how sexuality complicates our understanding of necropolitics. When sexuality appears in the necropolitical realm of the death camps, the notion of agency and choice needs to be interrogated. The previous section illuminates the paradox created between the space of death and the intimacy that inflects a sexual necropolitics, and here I center on sexual intimacy as an act of survival that evokes questions of agency and betrayal. The topic of sexual intimacy alludes to the trope of gendered betrayal that emerged in various revolutionary groups in 1970s Argentina; in many of these leftist groups, surrendering to the agents of the state—especially surrendering one's body—was considered to be worse than death. Furthermore, it is also worth exploring the film's paradoxical final message: on the one hand, the film illustrates the state's repressive necropower over María, and on the other hand, it depicts (in moralizing terms) her agential subjectivity as ultimately a failure.

Garage Olimpo does not deal directly with questions of gendered betrayal. Instead, the visual narrative focuses our attention on the question of culpability and the state's absolute power over sexualized, dehumanized captive bodies. This is evident in the film's multiple aerial shots of Buenos Aires, which are juxtaposed against scenes of the subterranean detention center. Omnipotence is evident in the name of the camp itself, Olimpo, as Calveiro notes that the guards referred to this detention center as "the place of the gods."[22] The film spatially demonstrates the carceral logics of the regime in its representation of the dictatorship's power, which extended from the depths of the camp functioning beneath the city center to the all-seeing and all-knowing omniscient presence from above, as represented by the aerial shots. The cinematic use of spatiality captures the dictatorship's use of extreme violence and reveals that this violence was not arbitrary or random, but rather organized, structured, and pervasive.

This necropolitical logic and visual narrative is evident in the film's portrayal of the regime's power inside and outside of the camps and evinces how the carceral logics extended beyond the physical structures of the real-life prison and camps. The space of death of Olimpo bleeds into "civil" society, implying that the regime's control over life and death was not confined to the camps, but that it formed part of the larger societal matrix. As Calveiro suggests, the constant presence of military power "exhibits itself as a perpetual threat, a constant reminder for the whole of society."[23] While the film portrays the Olimpo camp as a subterranean clandestine center located under the bustling metropolis, it comprised an entire city block and operated at street level. In 2003, the Argentinean government deemed the center an historic site, and human rights activists and survivors have since worked to educate the public on the history of state terrorism and human rights abuses that occurred in the center. In 2009, I visited the camp and local activists showed me the center; as we walked on the sidewalk of the exterior of the center, the guide pointed to a row of arched openings that were sealed with cement except at the top. Inside were the torture chambers, and the openings allowed for the prisoners' screams to be heard by passersby in order to instill fear and terror in the community. This architectural display of terror and violence evokes Agamben's concept of the "hidden matrix" of the detention center functioning as a "new juridico-political paradigm in which the norm becomes indistinguishable from the exception."[24] The film conflates spatial planes and attests to the way the regime functioned on a necropolitical, carceral logic: extreme violence and the necropower of the camp "becomes indistinguishable" from Argentine civil society and reinforces the absolute power of the carceral state.

The film's blending of spatial planes—of everyday life in Buenos Aires and of the horrors of the clandestine centers—links the gendered and political structures of "civil" society to the spaces of death in the camps. That is, the film does not separate the two spheres as distinct and disconnected, but rather, the seamless transition from scenes that depict the terror of the subterranean center to scenes that relay quotidian life in Buenos Aires suggest that the city functions as a figurative prison, as an extension of the carceral state. Bechis's presentation of the film's spatial conflation establishes the complex matrix of necropower and the carceral logics that defined the authoritative masculine Argentine state. In centering the narrative film on the dehumanization and subjugation of a politically active young woman, *Garage Olimpo* exposes the regime's reinforcement of gender and political normative scripts on abject, sexualized bodies, and questions the notion of agency within spaces of death.

Regarding the film's representation of agency, it is useful to turn again to Weheliye's *Habeas Viscus* to conceptualize the possibility of retaining one's subjecthood in dire situations. Weheliye questions whether agency or resistance or both are possible in a context where people are reduced to bare lives and are not fully agented subjects, as on slave plantations or in concentration camps. He notes that, "as modes of analyzing and imagining the practices of the oppressed in the face of extreme violence[,] . . . resistance and agency assume full, self-present and coherent subjects working against something or someone."[25] While I do not want to disavow María's sense of agency in the film, we must question whether indeed she could choose to engage in a sexual relationship with Félix, her captor, in the most abject of spaces, the concentration camp. Despite María's attempt to reassert her agency by sexually submitting to Félix for paternalistic protection, the authoritarian regime ultimately subjugates her to "the power of death." If we consider the term that Bonasso uses in the epigraph, "seduction," which implies a modicum of agency, I argue that such agency is absent in the necropolitical setting of Olimpo. Here I would like to examine the contradictory and masculinist undertones that frame María's sexual acts as betrayal. I would also like to consider how the necropolitical setting is ultimately one more instance of the masculinist state's sexualization and degradation of captive female bodies. In this sense, Bechis's message is contradictory and somewhat problematic: if his intent is to expose the systemic misogynistic necropower of the state, his ultimate portrayal of María's failed strategy in exerting her sexual agency evinces the notion of gendered betrayal that is entrenched in the revolutionary left's concept of sexual morality.

Although the sexual relationship essentially commences when María chooses to engage with Félix, *Garage Olimpo* constructs this narrative carefully while exposing the absence of choice and agency in such conditions. The first intimate encounter between María and Félix occurs when he visits María's cell to inform her of his new duties and brings her paintings and other decorations. Félix then tells her that he has been reassigned to street duty, thus limiting his ability to shield María from abuse by other officers in the camp. Realizing that his absence may result in more violence and degradation, María tells him she will worry for his safety if he is on the streets. Exasperated with María, Félix stands up and proclaims, "You know what? If we were on the outside, you would not be with me." Standing up to leave, María calls Félix's name and, grabbing him by the neck, proceeds to kiss him, asking him how she can leave Olimpo. "You have to behave yourself," Félix responds.

The scenes following their first kiss illuminate the lack of agency María possesses over her sexualized, incarcerated body. The next scene crosscuts to an aerial view of María's cell, where a reclining Félix is asleep on María's bed. Rousing from his slumber, María and Félix share a mug of coffee, and the camera transitions to a shot reverse shot of María and Félix looking at one another. The camera then returns to an aerial shot of the two characters, as María proceeds to sit next to Félix on the bed, running her hands through his hair while embracing him. With her face in the nape of his neck, she tells Félix, "Bring me real flowers next time. These plastic ones are very sad."

If we were to disengage from the context of this scene, it would appear that we were witnessing a tender moment between a young couple in their humble home. However, the extradiegetic sounds of the other officers playing Ping-Pong echo in María's cell, an unavoidable reminder of the close proximity of power and death over the prisoners. The close-up of María's face also conveys her desperation and powerlessness, as she looks away from Félix, as if scouring for an exit from her cell. Furthermore, the aerial shots in her prison cell parallel the aerial scenes of downtown Buenos Aires and the Río de la Plata, reinforcing the prison as a microcosm of the dictatorial state.

The relationship between María and Félix illuminates the critical role sexual degradation plays in the patriarchal state's repression of women's agency. By highlighting the harrowing context of their "relationship," the film alludes to the violence that can result when women do not adhere to the state's proper gender scripts. As Félix reminds María, in order to survive the camp, she must behave according to *his* standards. The repetition of Félix's authority and paternalism exposes the horrors of the repressive patriarchal state to which María must comply. These horrors are portrayed in the mundane, "romantic" details of María and Félix's interactions. Toward the end of the film, Félix complies with María's wishes and brings her fresh flowers for her cell. At this point in the film, María has attempted to flee Olimpo, and the futility of her circumstances leads her to a breaking point, when she screams and bangs on her cell door. When Félix discovers that she has attempted to escape Olimpo, he grabs and shakes her, yelling that he is the only one who can save her. Ultimately, Félix's threat rings true, as he is unable to stop her death.

María's dire situation and absence of agency is best exemplified during a "date" when Félix sneaks María out of the detention center. During this perverse date, Félix exhibits his masculine authority over María, while she portrays an ideal, passive—albeit abject—femininity deserving of protection and rescue. Throughout the scenes of their outing, María's body language evinces the powerlessness she possesses, a visual logic that is structured by sexual necropolitics. Here, the film's carceral logics and sexual necropolitics converge: the relationship between María and Félix is initiated in the space of death (the camp), thus sexual necropolitics undergirds all their interactions as she futilely tries to resist the state's power over her death. While walking through the city streets, Félix has his arm around María in a manner that restricts her movement; the scenes portray a passive, feminine surrender to his masculine protection, which she submits to in an attempt to survive. Throughout the date, María frantically glances around her, anxiously looking for an escape route, which she attempts to take in vain before returning to the camp. This sequence of scenes is accompanied by the melancholic strains of the cello heard earlier in the film, the minor key evoking the same sense of dread, despair, and anxiety that María experiences during the scene of her abduction.

While María engages in a "consensual" sexual encounter in a hotel room with Félix in this sequence, she is ultimately sexualized and possessed by Félix, an agent of the state. Although the sexual act takes place outside the camp, it is clear that María possesses no agency and is fully under Félix's control. The scene portrays the entire cityscape of Buenos Aires as a space of death, a logical extension of the carceral state. While the sex scene in the hotel could be interpreted as María attaining a sense of bodily autonomy, I would argue that such an interpretation merely erases the far reach of the power of the patriarchal Argentinean state, as they exercised their power over the abject bodies and subjugated them to death. Bechis's depiction of María's nude torso in the hotel room evokes the earlier scene of her sexualized subjugation in the camp after enduring her first torture session. What's more, before their "date," Félix lets María shower and gives her clothing that he acquires from other detainees so that she can blend in seamlessly with other people in the city. María selects a brown dress similar in color and style to the dress she wore when she was first abducted, and the symbolism of the brown dress shared among captive women in *Garage Olimpo* evinces how the city functions as a prison; the brown dresses she wears inside and outside the camp reflect how the carceral logics circulate through spaces beyond the prison and into the space of everyday life.

Ultimately, the film illuminates the limits of agency and resistance, and by that extension, questions the notion of betrayal when the logic of necropower governs the prisoners' actions. *Garage Olimpo* alludes to the complex and polemical topic of sexuality and betrayal that still affects the cultural landscape of post-dictatorship Argentina. The film's paradoxical and unsettling final message—that agential sexual subjectivity exercised by captive women is doomed to fail—illuminates the gendered scrutiny, moralizing, and judgment of women's sexual choices, even in a dire circumstance like the concentration camp. This topic is directly linked to nationalist ideas of morality, femininity, and gender scripts touted by both the leftist revolutionary groups and the regime itself. While *Garage Olimpo* implicitly denounces both the state condemnation of survivors who acquiesced to state power, the decision to portray María's death overlaps with revolutionary groups' judgment that women betrayed the cause if they attempted to use their bodies in order to survive. The film also exhibits not merely the gendering involved in the brutalization of transgressive bodies but also the gender dynamics of survival. If we turn again to Bonasso's statement that betrayal looks like "the image of a seduced woman," we must consider how María's sexual act with Félix could be interpreted as a sign of feminized weakness both by the leftist revolutionary groups as well as by the regime. This is evident when El Tigre, the director of the Olimpo camp, visits María in her cell and informs her, "I don't like those who talk," signifying that the prisoners who broke under torture and offered information were weak and feeble: the men were considered effeminate, and the women overly sexual and treasonous.

In the end, Félix sexualizes and possesses María's abject body, which converts her into an image of betrayal and treason to the revolutionary cause, a symbol of the violated, abject woman-as-betrayer. By surrendering her body to her captor and enemy, María seemingly defies the revolutionary cause, a sentiment reflected in many cultural works, such as Bonasso's *Recuerdo de la muerte*. As Ana Longoni asserts in her analysis of Bonasso's text, relationships between captors and prisoners provoke "repulsion" and such acts of "betrayal" are linked to the "female condition itself." As Longoni points out, even women prisoners who did not provide critical information about compañeros were still branded as having betrayed the cause because they surrendered their bodies sexually to their captors. Thus, as Longoni questions, "the militant woman, her sexuality and her feelings—are they considered her own or are they property of political organizations?"[26] While *Garage Olimpo* does not seem to condemn María's actions in the film, Bechis's decision to kill her off provokes questions of gendered betrayal that is etched in Latin American cultural history. The film portrays her death mere moments after she has a sexual encounter with Félix; thus, it could be argued here that the film inadvertently aligns with those judging women's strategies of survival (María's) as acts of "betrayal" and in the end "punishes" her (by death) for so doing. Furthermore, Longoni and other Latin American feminist theorists note that the criticism of women's betrayal in the detention centers mitigates the structural power of the masculinist state and its omnipotence, and *Garage Olimpo* centers on exposing the necropower of the state. In essence, my reading of the film differs from Weheliye's notion of *homo sacer* as agential, as María's attempt to use her body to circumvent the necropower of the state was doomed to fail.

Bechis constructs a narrative that reveals the impossibility of escaping the "hidden matrix" of the state's necropower in María's inability to escape the carceral logics of the dictatorship and its spaces of death, or the concentration camp. The narrative also reflects the gendered judgment of women who exercised sexual agency in this space of death, and the presence of sexual necropolitics that undergird the carceral state. In her brief moments of "freedom" in the city streets, María's bodily autonomy and movements are restricted and monitored by the agents of the state, and the cinematic use of spatiality (aerial shots and perspectives) reinforces the masculinist, dehumanizing gaze of the state. Thus, the film portrays the spatial characters—the city of Buenos Aires and the prison—as an extension of the masculinist repressive state apparatus that undergirds and governs the lives of all human beings living in the carceral state. The paradoxes between spatial and sexual politics of the repressive state apparatus is also evident in Jose Revueltas's 1969 *El apando*, yet in this novella we are presented with the feminization of the carceral space that functioned within a necropolitical context of 1960s Mexico City. The concept of gendered betrayal appears in the novella's feminization of the prison space as a maternal space that emasculates and dehumanizes its prisoners. In this manner, the novella portrays the repressive state apparatus as a feminine entity that, in turn, reflects the betrayal of Mexico-as-motherland.

El Apando: Abjection and the Commodification of Women's bodies in the Mexican Carceral Space

While Bechis's *Garage Olimpo* cinematically captures the necropolitical structuring of the Argentinean carceral state, Jose Revueltas's 1969 novella, *El apando*, offers a more subtle reading of the power dynamics of Mexico's carceral state and provides a complex picture of the politics of the sexualized body in the necropolitical space of the prison.[27] *Garage Olimpo* clearly identifies the victims of an expansive authoritative regime, reduced to their bare lives and subjugated to the state's power over their deaths. *El apando*, however, does not feature heroes or victims of state repression. The text's portrayal of decrepit, abject drug addicts confined in a prison cell parallels Revueltas's perspective on the demise of Mexico's revolutionary resistance movements. Revueltas discussed his choice of the prison for the novella's setting: "I choose the prison as an environment, that is, a symbolic environment. . . . The prison bars for me, the prison bars of the *apando*, they are the bars of the city, the bars of the country and the bars of the world. The prison is nothing more than a condensed reflection of society."[28] Yet despite *El apando*'s representation of the prison as an equalizer among the story's characters, it is the women in the text who are subjected to physical and sexual exploitation in order to assist with the male prisoners' addiction. *El apando* does not merely capture the necropower of the masculinist carceral state, but the prison converts into a maternal, feminized site that symbolizes the long-term hermeneutic paradigm of woman-as-nation and, ultimately, woman-as-betrayer to the nation. Similar to *Garage Olimpo*, the novella relies on a central paradox—womb and prison as life bearers and womb and prison as sites of death—to illuminate the critical intersection of sexual necropolitics and carceral logics that undergirded the Mexican authoritarian state.

The novella centers on drug addicts Polonio, Albino, and El Carajo and their futile attempt to bring drugs into the prison cell they share. Polonio's and Albino's girlfriends—La Chata and Meche—convince El Carajo's septuagenarian mother to smuggle drugs inside her body, as her advanced age and maternal appearance would not arouse the suspicions of the prison guards. Carajo's mother agrees and successfully passes the inspection process. However, the mother refuses to turn over the drugs until she sees her son Carajo, who is being held in the cell with Albino and Polonio. This prompts La Chata and Meche to demand that the men be released from confinement, and soon a riot ensues. Amid the chaos, Albino and Polonio corner two guards and attack them brutally. The novella ends with the guards violently quelling the uprising, and Carajo, upon being questioned about the riot, turns on his mother and reveals that she had smuggled narcotics in her body.

The nihilistic, pessimistic tone of the novella reflects Revueltas's complete disillusionment not only with Mexico's left political movement but also with the necropower of the Mexican carceral state. The context the novella was written in differs greatly from Bechis's *Garage Olimpo*, which was made sixteen years after the end of the Argentinean dictatorship. Revueltas wrote *El apando* during his incarceration in Mexico City's infamous Lecumberri Prison after having participated in the student movement that culminated in the harrowing events of October 2, 1968. Although not a member of the 1968 National Strike Council, Revueltas was accused of having led the student movement and was sentenced to sixteen years in prison. His involvement in radical politics and leftist movements led to his incarceration three times in his life (1932, 1934, and 1968), and by the time he was imprisoned in 1968, he expressed a disillusionment with the left in Mexico: "Generally, Marxists believe that the dialectic is progressive, that it goes from less to more, from regressive to progressive. That is false because the synthesis can be absolutely negative, as in the case of *El apando*. The dialectical synthesis that comes about with the combination of opposites does not give us something progressive, it gives us something somber and totally negative concerning humanity."[29] This disillusionment is evident in the absence of any political context in *El apando*. The protagonists are incarcerated not for their political activism but for drug addiction and other petty crimes. Lecumberri Prison at this time housed many political prisoners, Revueltas included; however, *El apando* makes no mention of the political backdrop of 1968 Mexico. The "something somber" of the political movement is affirmed in the portrayal of the abject existence of three drug addicts and their quest to smuggle drugs into their cell, relying on women's laboring bodies to sustain their addiction.

Many Latin Americanist literary scholars have offered insightful interpretations of the novella's absence of political context and relate this to the processes of modernization in Mexico. Elena Poniatowska claims that Revueltas's *El apando* "does not fit within any genre—it is a synthesis of all the elements Revueltas commands and it has significant political content without making any explicit political references."[30] *El apando* has often been read as a novella that illustrates the pitfalls of late capitalism and the degeneration of the ideals of the Mexican revolution, as well as the limitations posed by the rigidity of Marxist ideals. The novella relies on the trope of the prison to represent the confinement and necropower of the carceral state in Dirty War–era Mexico, but also in an important sense, the decrepit, maimed bodies of its inmates reflects the demise of the student movement. The setting of the prison also functions as a way to exhibit the carceral logics of the Mexican state and to underscore the central paradox of the novella: the prison is feminized as a womb, creator of life, but it is also a space of death. In this space of death/space of life, women's bodies are fetishized and manipulated by the characters in order to appease their vices, which ultimately highlights Revueltas's cynical view of the left and its future in Mexico's carceral state.

The violence and terror of Mexico's carceral state that Revueltas bore witness to on the night of October 2, 1968, makes no appearance in *El apando*, nor does the novella mention the infamous Lecumberri Prison or the clandestine prison Campo Militar No. 1. Also known as the Black Palace by many activists of the era for its fortress-like architecture, Lecumberri Prison housed many political prisoners, many of whom passed first through the Campo Militar No. 1, which was the site of many extralegal human rights violations, including rape, torture, and other repressive tactics that the government used to instill fear. Often touted as an architectural symbol of Mexico's modernization, Lecumberri worked in tandem with the Campo Militar No. 1 to reify the state's social ordering through the legal penalization of those it deemed a threat to national security. Like many other penal institutions in the West, Lecumberri adopted a panoptic architectural design, with a central watchtower providing maximum oversight of the prison without requiring many exterior guards.[31] The central watchtower is mentioned explicitly in *El apando*, and it alludes to the state's ability to monitor not only prisoners but also visitors and guards, and to subject them to its omnipotent and confining grasp.

El apando offers the reader a visual and textual representation of the prison space and the carceral logics of the authoritarian state, which parallels *Garage Olimpo*'s cinematic portrayal of Argentina's repressive carceral state. The panopticon used in Mexico's modern penal system is evident in the formal structure of the novella. Although they are not mentioned in *El apando*, Lecumberri's and Campo Militar's presence is evoked in the very prose and narrative structure. The thirty-page text consists of a single, long paragraph. Such a structural framework heightens the reader's anxiety as we are drawn into the narrative's starkly realistic portrayal of the carceral state. The discursive representation of the carceral spaces in the novella reflect the tight grip the carceral state had over its citizens, portrayed in the prose that does not incorporate breaks, indentations, or other pauses. The novella's opening sentence is eighteen lines long; while the reader expects to encounter a break or punctuation to terminate the sentence, the opening lines continue to build and narrate the subculture of the prison system. The first sentence textually establishes the increasing sense of dread and restriction of bodily movement, which parallels the literal confinement of the prisoners' bodies in *el apando*.

El apando denounces the necropower of the state in its portrayal of the city-as-prison, and exhibits how the prison functions as a microcosm of the state. The blending of Mexican civil society with the carceral realm is apparent in the first depiction of the prison. The prison guards "were made to be vigilant, to spy and to look around, so no one could escape from their control, nor from that city or those streets with prison bars, these prison bars everywhere."[32] *El apando* makes parallels between the "hidden matrix" of the state's biopower vis-à-vis the carceral system and its biopolitical control over its subjects. The novella discursively captures the necropower of the state's ability to decide who shall die and who must be subjected to punitive measures to ensure they conform to a proper capitalist subject within Mexico's carceral state.

However, *El apando* provides a complex perspective of state power in the carceral space. As agents of the state, the prison guards in the passage quoted just above seem to possess absolute power over the inmates, and thus the power dynamics place the guards in control of the inmates. Yet the opening lines of the novella clearly assign the prison guards to the same abject status as the prisoners: "They were imprisoned there the apes, no one but them, the [female] ape and [male] ape, the two of them, in their cage, not quite desperate, without despairing of anything, walking from one end to another, trapped but in movement, trapped by the zoological encasements as if someone, the others, humanity, cruelly did not want to bother with their situation, the situation of being apes . . . cruel and without memory, [female] ape against [male] ape within Paradise, identical, the same type and the same sex, but [male] ape and [female] ape, imprisoned, screwed."[33] In the novella's vision of the prison/nation, both inmates and guards are equally dehumanized and held captive by the repressive state apparatus. This opening sentence presents the text's omniscient narrator surveying the animalization and dehumanization of both inmates and guards from within the *apando*, a prison within the prison. The animalistic portrayal of guards and inmates flattens the power differential between both groups and describes them as ignorant, vile creatures oblivious to the powerful control of the state. Both guards and prisoners are dehumanized, degraded, and entrapped within the carceral state. Furthermore, the depiction criticizes Mexico's project of modernity, as inmates and guards are described as "apes . . . cruel and without memory." This reference to "apes" alludes to their pre-evolutionary state, regressing from their evolved state as Homo sapiens. It more importantly refers to the state's regression in its barbaric use of extreme violence and punitive measures in the prisons. Here, the novella reduces them to an animalistic existence, "screwed" and socially alienated within the confining cells of the Mexican state. However, in its denouncement of the state's absolute power, *El apando* does not feign to offer readers redemptive, heroic characters or even hapless victims of state control. Rather, it presents the readers with unsympathetic, decrepit, and abject beings who are imprisoned within the cell.

The most extreme example of the "screwed" abject being is the character of El Carajo, whose name literally translates as the "fucked one." He is depicted as a wholly degraded, dehumanized inmate whose body has become so abject that his fellow inmates named him Carajo because he "he didn't serve any purpose" (*no servía para un carajo*).[34] The moniker establishes him as the most decrepit character, with no redemptive qualities, in the prison. In many senses, El Carajo's character reveals Revueltas's vision of the trajectory of the left's movement in Mexico, and as scholar Javier Durán states, "Revueltas seems to send literally and verbatim all his struggles to 'hell,' and that is precisely what he does."[35] Revueltas's depiction of the maimed, degraded Carajo captures the crippling of the student movement, which was violently repressed on October 2, 1968. In their purest, animalistic state, the prisoners are equally violent, if not more so, than the prison guards, and Revueltas portrays the three inmates as unsympathetic, brutish men driven by their carnal desires to consume women's bodies and narcotics.

While *El apando*'s main characters allude to the degeneration of Mexican social ordering and Revueltas's disillusionment with both the rigidity of the left and the repressive apparatus of the state, the novella cannot escape a heterosexist and masculinist depiction of the female characters. Revueltas's *El apando* offers us a complex reading of gender dynamics within and outside of the carceral space, which evinces the intersection between the sexual necropolitical context of the prison and the carceral logics of the Mexican state. The three inmates depend on the women to maintain their drug addiction, and the women also fuel their erotic desires. The three female characters—La Chata, Meche, and Carajo's mother (who is never named)—crudely capture the dichotomy of the vestal virginal mother (alluding to the Virgin of Guadalupe, represented by Carajo's mother) and sexually wanton jezebels (La Chata and Meche). While all the characters are equally abject beings within the walls of the prison/carceral state, the novella relies on normative and hierarchical notions of gender and sexuality in its representation of the women characters. This paradoxical portrayal of women-as-abject and women-as-fetishized-or-sexualized-beings parallels the representation of María's character in *Garage Olimpo*. In *El apando*, this particular paradox appears in Polonio's observation of the guards and inmates as he thinks, "monkeys, apes, stupid, vile and innocent, with the innocence of a ten-year-old whore."[36] Polonio describes his masculine dominance over the other prisoners and guards, who are gendered and sexualized as young, childish prostitutes, both virginal and sexually wanton. This is a shift away from the first depiction of the guards and inmates as dehumanized, abject beings, equally "screwed" and "imprisoned." Revueltas relies on gendered tropes that reinscribe women within a heterosexist hierarchy, where masculine dominance is privileged over feminine weakness and ultimately, betrayal. In the novella, women's bodies are sexual objects to be consumed, or they are used as vehicles to deliver drugs. Using a feminist lens uncovers the heterosexist, masculinist portrayal of the female characters and also illuminates the feminization of the prison space.

The Feminization of the Carceral Space and Homoerotic Desire as Betrayal

Revueltas claims that the novella's depiction of the carceral space parallels "the prison bars of the city, and of the country." However, the "bars of the country" also refer to a heterosexist carceral state in which a dominant, hetero-masculine subject is the norm. In so doing, the novella portrays the women characters as erotic beings who exist for the sexual consumption of the prisoners and to reaffirm the inmates' virility and sexual prowess. Despite Revueltas's description of the abject, degraded status of the guards, visitors, and inmates, the novella primarily characterizes Meche and Chata as eroticized, sexually promiscuous women who illuminate the men's hetero-masculine desires and dominance within the carceral space.

This is evident in the first description of Polonio's girlfriend, La Chata, as she describes to Carajo's mother the process of smuggling drugs in their bodies past security. La Chata and Meche attempt to convince Carajo's mother to insert a few ounces of narcotics in her vagina, since the guards would not suspect her of smuggling drugs. La Chata claims that she and Meche cannot perform this task because they had been previously searched by the women prison guards: "Those apes have never attempted to search you, right? Because you are a respectable older woman, but us, in the registry, they always insert their fingers in us, those vile women." These statements arouse Polonio, and he recalls past sexual encounters with La Chata: "La Chata appeared before him, jovial, bestial . . . leaning her back against the balcony, her naked body visible under a light robe and her legs slightly open."[37] This invasive, clinical routine task performed by guards on the visitors is eroticized, stoking Polonio's hetero-masculine desires and memories, while relegating Chata to her purely carnal, "bestial" status.

The first detailed portrayal of La Chata is critical, as it establishes her function in the narrative and reduces women's bodies to sexual and other performative duties for the men's pleasures. While Revueltas also portrays the male inmates in disembodied terms, such as El Carajo's "neck, arms, thorax, testicles," they are not eroticized in the same way as Meche or La Chata. In the above passage, La Chata is reduced to various parts of her sexual anatomy, with her "legs slightly open," revealing her "pubic mound." In this sense, the inmates and the women are not equally dehumanized or depicted in disembodied terms, since the women appear in the text only in the context of sating the men's sexual desires. Polonio's recollections of La Chata's naked body reassert his virility, even though he is an abject being held captive by the carceral state.

Although the cavity search constitutes both a physical violation and a psychological violation of the women, Polonio projects his erotic fantasies onto this invasive act. His fantasy about the female prison guards and La Chata highlights Polonio's prostrate status as an imprisoned man, unable to sexually satisfy himself or his girlfriend: "The image [of his girlfriend] blinded Polonio with jealousy, but totally strange, not being able to be in that space . . . [creates] the sensation of jealousy in the throat and the solar plexus, with a strangely ticklish, loose and horrible involuntary sensation behind the penis."[38] Polonio is seemingly aroused yet upset by his own sexual fantasy of La Chata being searched by the guards, and this provokes a frustrated, impotent sexual response from Polonio as he imagines his girlfriend being searched vaginally by the prison guards. The penetrative act of digitally searching the women's vaginal canal for contraband emasculates Polonio, as he is unable to perform the penetrative duties he once did with La Chata. This erotic fantasy challenges Polonio's own impotent heterosexuality and highlights his status as a degraded, abject prisoner within the carceral space. The prison's carceral space of death is shaped and influenced by a hetero-masculine sexual politics, which evinces the sexual necropolitical context of the novella.

The realization of his dejected status and impotence within the carceral space is expressed in homophobic insults directed at the women guards. As La Chata describes the invasive search performed on their bodies, Polonio angrily thinks to himself, "Apes daugh-ters of their god-damn whore mo-ther, goddamn lesbians" (*Mo-nas hi-jas de to-da su chin-ga-da madre, cabronas lesbianas*).[39] Polonio ascribes a sexual context to the routine cavity search of the visitors, and his erotic same-sex fantasies between La Chata and the guard challenge Polonio's hetero-masculine virility. His anger toward the guards who, in his mind, derive pleasure from the cavity search, reflect a sexual politics that contests a rigid heterosexist framework upheld by both the masculinist Mexican leftist movement *and* the repressive state apparatus.[40] The deviation from a compulsory heterosexuality is thus perceived as the most abject, vile status, which incites Polonio's rage and disgust and characterization of the women guards as "goddamn lesbians" and dehumanized, animalized "apes."

In addition to this homophobic condemnation of the women, Polonio's remark refers to the abject status of all Mexicans, alluding to Octavio Paz's "Hijos de la Chingada." Although Revueltas depicts *El apando*'s characters as equally "fucked" as all "hijos de la Chingada," their abjection and dehumanization is gendered and historically connected to the vilification and sexualization of the original Mother of the Fucked Ones, La Malinche. The women in *El apando* are reduced to *malinchista* tropes of Mexican nationalist cultural discourse, either fulfilling their functions as sexual receptacles of men's hetero-masculine desires, or as virginal, maternal figures whose bodies provide sustenance and nurture (vis-à-vis narcotics).

Women's bodies serve as important vessels to placate the inmates' other central desire, their drug addiction. The women fulfill the men's carnal desires and reaffirm positions of male dominance and authority. Despite the women's apparent freedom, they are also subjected to the power of the Mexican carceral state and essentially, as Francisco Manzo-Robledo notes, "they convert, by extension, into victims of the system of discipline."[41] The women are subjugated to the disciplinary power of the carceral state and this disciplinary power involves a gendered process that illuminates the Madonna/Whore dichotomy.

However, Revueltas presents us with a nuanced representation of the Madonna/Whore binarism, as both tropes essentially reflect a gendered betrayal. While Meche and La Chata encapsulate the Whore side of the dichotomy and Carajo's mother reflects the Madonna descriptor, the women in the novella essentially fail in their gendered roles, which I argue is a form of betrayal. For instance, Revueltas's depiction of Albino's girlfriend, Meche, is portrayed in purely sexual terms, as an "honorable woman, a thief yes, but when she slept with other men she did not do it for money, she did it for pleasure, without Albino finding out, of course." In this passage, Meche illuminates the Whore trope as she is depicted as sexually wanton, enjoying the pleasures of the flesh. This, however, evolves into a form of betrayal against Albino, as the narrator describes Meche deriving sexual pleasure from the prison guard's search of her body.

As he did with La Chata, Revueltas introduces Meche vis-à-vis a routine cavity search by one of the female guards. In this passage, Meche has flashbacks of sexual encounters with Albino, while Revueltas describes the clinical details of the guard's inspection of her vaginal cavity: "with the middle finger, she began a suspicious interior exploration, delicate and kind." Yet the narrator notes that Meche experiences sexual pleasure during the search, as "it aroused her then, something that had not happened before, strange and with an indiscernible frame of mind." Meche's enjoyment of the cavity search stays with her even after she is admitted to the visitor's wing of the prison: "She still had fixed in her mind, those quiet, fixed, impenetrable and frightening eyes of the prison guard, black and with a deadly eloquence, as if she had been staring forever." To Meche, then, the desire she felt during the search reflects an "attitude of acquiescence" and Meche's body transforms into a "seditious" site.[42]

Similar to Polonio's eroticization of La Chata's search and homophobic reaction to his fantasies, Meche's lesbian desire for the prison guard is portrayed as a type of betrayal that challenges the hetero-masculinist authority of their men. The women are betraying a hetero-masculine logic of the left by "enjoying" their interaction with the prison guards, who are representatives of the carceral state. In Revueltas's portrayal of the power dynamic between the guard and visitor, the guard performs the dominant act of penetration on the passive feminized, sexualized body, and Revueltas describes her enjoyment of such an act as "seditious." Again, under the auspices of the panoptic layout of the prison's "surveillance tower," Meche's character is also eroticized and subjected to the disciplinary measures of the state during the cavity search. Yet this homoerotic passage importantly alludes to the dangers of deviating from proper heterosexual desires. Meche's character strays from the typical trope of the Whore in the dichotomy as she expresses same-sex desires. At the same time, she ultimately fails to sexually satisfy Albino or to provide narcotics for him.

Conversely, El Carajo's mother seems to encapsulate a proper passive femininity and nurturing maternal role, or the Madonna trope; however, her ultimate inability to provide her son narcotics positions her as a failed mother. The novella's depiction of the mother is critical, as this alludes to deeply entrenched notions of the gendered nation and the motherland. *El apando* offers a complex reading of Mother-as-Provider and mother of the nation, and she is framed as a metonym of the carceral state. The feminization of the carceral space in *El apando* reflects Revueltas's disillusionment with the Mexican state, the Motherland. The figure of Carajo's mother serves as a hermeneutic trope for the Motherland, and her inability to provide for her son is an allegorical representation of the Mexican state's failure to create a society based on progress, while also reflecting the nation's failure to fulfill the ideals of the Mexican Revolution.

In *El apando*, disciplinary power is not gendered as masculine, but rather, its feminine and maternal characteristics allude to the long-standing paradigm in which the land-nation is feminized. In this instance, the mother-as-nation and mother-as-prison not only infantilizes its inhabitants, it imprisons, degrades, and dehumanizes them. Like *Garage Olimpo*, *El apando*'s narrative is driven by a central paradox that discursively represents the carceral space as a feminized, womb-like entity that symbolizes life, as well as death and destruction.

As discussed earlier, Revueltas's disillusionment with both the left and the Mexican state is evident in his pessimistic view of human interaction in *El apando*. Trapped within the confines of the prison within the prison, the three inmates attempt to exert minimal control or agency over their abject, degraded status by arranging the smuggling of narcotics. At the start of the novella, the narrator depicts the *apando* as a "nondimensional, virginal space" that transforms into "a sovereign, inalienable territory."[43] In this passage, the prison-as-sovereign nation is gendered as virginal territory to be conquered and tamed by the three inmates. Revueltas makes a clear link between prison-as-virginal land and prison-as-sovereign-state, imbuing the nation with feminized markings. As many feminist scholars note, women have functioned as signifiers of the nation and, as Anne McClintock states, "women are subsumed symbolically into the national body politic as boundary and metaphoric limit."[44]

While the carceral space at first represents a passive, virginal, and feminized realm, it also functions as a maternal, womb-like enclosure that infantilizes and cloisters the men. While awaiting the visit of the three women, Albino attempts to look out of the small opening to the *apando* cell: "To introduce—or remove—the head from that rectangular iron, that guillotine, to move, to move the cranium with all its parts . . . to the space outside the cell . . . required careful, minute tenacity, the same tenacity used to extricate a fetus from its mother's insides, a tenacious and deliberate way of giving birth to oneself with forceps that pulled out chunks of hair and that scraped the skin."[45] This process of inserting or removing one's head from the opening of the cell is likened to a painful childbirth, where the infant is forcibly removed from the mother's womb, "that pulled out chunks of hair and that scraped the skin." What is important here is how the passage illuminates the necropolitical context of the novella through the rendering of the paradox between prison-as-womb/life-creator and prison-as-womb/site-of-death. Although Revueltas uses the image of childbirth to metaphorically capture the confinement of the men in the cell, he makes a direct link between the "rectangular iron" and a "guillotine," the apparatus used to carry out the disciplinary castigations of beheadings. Thus, the vaginal opening of the "rectangular iron" is not only depicted as a harsh, cold metal that restricts and confines the men, it symbolizes the necropower of the state in its ability to decide who will be subjugated to death.

The symbolic representation of the prison-as-maternal space highlights the gendered dynamic of Revueltas's disillusionment with the Mexican state, the Motherland. As Anne McClintock asserts, "nations are frequently figured through the iconography of familial and domestic space," and in *El apando* the gendered, domestic nation becomes a signifier for the carceral state.[46] In the novella, the maternal space of the prison is depicted as a restrictive, debilitating site that exhibits its necropower over its (male) subjects. Although the trope of the womb typically represents the creation of life, in *El apando* the womb-as-prison becomes intimately tied to the carceral logics of the Mexican state and the necropolitical structure of the prison, a site of death and degradation. In this case, Revueltas creates a paradox between the womb as bearer of life, and the womb/prison as the space of death and abjection, which parallels *Garage Olimpo*'s portrayal of the river as a site of death and life. Thus, the prison-womb comes to represent the metonym of the nation-state, and both nation-state and carceral-state are feminized.

This paradox of prison-as-womb-creator-of-life and prison-as-necropolitical-space is best reflected in Revueltas's characterization of El Carajo's mother. She is as abject and decrepit as her incarcerated son, with a large scar across her face, and with "an attitude heavy with resentment, reproaches and regrets." El Carajo's mother represents the prisoners' only hope to smuggle in drugs, and it is exactly her maternal visage and age that do not arouse suspicion from the prison guards. On the day she is supposed to smuggle the drugs, Revueltas describes her in the following way: "There were the udders, then; it was there, the vagina ... the milked cow passed as unsuspected as a virgin."[47] Similar to La Chata and Meche, the mother is reduced to corporeal, animalized fragments, "udders" of a "cow," and as innocent as a "virgin."

While the vaginal canal of El Carajo's mother serves as a critical vehicle to transport their drugs, her body also metaphorically represents the disciplinary, necropolitical site of the prison. El Carajo's dependency on his mother is described in vivid detail: "she still had not stopped giving birth to this son who grabbed on to her insides, looking at her with his criminal eye, without wanting to leave the maternal cloister, stuck inside the placenta sack, in the cell ... without being able to leave his mother's womb, confined inside his mother, in the cell." Instead of reproducing ideal subject-citizens for the Mexican state, El Carajo's mother has reproduced the most abject, degraded subject symbolized in the figure of El Carajo. As mentioned in the earlier passage of the *apando* as a guillotine/womb, El Carajo's mother figuratively is a site of death and decay, her "womb filled with worms."[48] Her womb becomes a site of death, with the image of worms representing decay and bodily disintegration. Her womb, instead of bearing life or "biological[ly] reproduc[ing] . . . members of national collectivities," becomes a space of confinement, imprisonment, and a necropolitical site that promotes the abjection of its Mexican subjects.[49]

The figure of El Carajo's mother as a metaphor for Mexico's mythical Motherland invokes gendered tropes tied to dominant, masculine notions of nationalism. Many postcolonial feminist scholars have noted that the female body has often discursively and symbolically represented the nation in the cultural imaginary. Deniz Kandiyoti notes that "women bear the burden of being 'mothers of the nation,'" although, as Anne McClintock observes, women "are denied any direct relation to national agency."[50] In *El apando*, the figure of El Carajo's mother most aptly conveys this trope of mother of the nation: "made of mud and stone from adobe, a broken and old idol."[51] In this description, the Motherland is mythical and of the Earth; however, she also represents the illusory and broken promises of an ideal nation promised set forth by the Mexican Revolution. Rather than signifying the idealism and glorification of the Mexican Motherland, the Motherland here is imagined as the aged, decrepit, and decaying female body of El Carajo's mother, an allegorical representation of the disillusionment Revueltas and other activists had of Mexico, and the carceral logics that undergirded the Dirty War–era Mexican state.

Malinchismo, Seduction, and Agency in Cultural Narratives

The two texts provide critical cultural renderings of the Mexican and Argentinean carceral state, but they do so from a decidedly leftist, masculinist perspective. In novella and film, we are presented with the concept of *malinchismo*, the notion that women have an inherent predilection toward betrayal. The word *malinchismo* derives from La Malinche, the Nahua woman often maligned as a traitor to the Aztec empire for being the interpreter, advisor, and lover of Spanish conquistador Hernán Cortez during the colonization of the Americas. The myth of La Malinche has become embedded in the Latin American imaginary, with La Malinche herself exemplifying the ultimate traitor. In Revueltas's *El apando*, *malinchismo* is evident in the representation of the feminized carceral space and the portrayal of the female characters. Mexico's carceral state, depicted as a feminized entity, subjugates the men to the power of death while it also emasculates and dehumanizes masculine beings. This prison/womb serves as a metonym for the Mexican state and Revueltas's clear disillusionment with the state captures the betrayal of the Mexican nation to provide for its (masculine) subjects. Revueltas genders this betrayal and disillusionment as female, which reflects the entrenched paradigm of woman-as-betrayer and woman-as-nation. The figure of Motherland and "madresposa," and other gendered tropes in Latin American social and cultural discourses allude to *la conquista's* history of gendered racialization and gendered betrayal. In "The Sons of La Malinche," Paz writes of Mexico's history of racialization and Eurocentrism that was borne from the maligned figure of La Malinche, to whom he refers as "la chingada" (or the raped/violated one).[52] As "Madre de los chingados," Malinche is the ultimate traitor who has come to symbolize the Mexican nation state and is a critical part of the formation of the Mexican national imaginary.

The trope of the Malinche as mother Mexico and traitor is evident in Revueltas's female characters in *El apando*. The figure of the El Carajo's mother signifies the betrayal of the Motherland and Malinche-as-mother, as she is ultimately unable to provide for or protect the men vis-à-vis supplying them with drugs. While El Carajo's mother passes through security, she fails to provide the drugs to her son and the other inmates, signifying a betrayal. Furthermore, instead of proffering a space of nurturing comfort, her womb highlights decay, death, and the men's ultimate inability to resist the necropower of the Mexican state. Similarly, La Chata and Meche reflect the sexual politics of betrayal in the lesbian pleasure they derive from the vaginal inspection from the female guards. The younger women are also reduced to gendered tropes and reflect the sexualized betrayal of Malinche in her sexual relations with the Spanish, the enemy (as Meche had "sexual relations" with the guard, an enemy of the inmates). Ultimately, the novella reinforces gendered tropes (woman as betrayer, woman as motherland) and eroticizes its female characters as it simultaneously condemns the authoritative power of the Mexican state.

Malinchismo takes a different shape in Bechis's *Garage Olimpo*. While Malinche is an historical figure from Mexico, the history of Malinche's submission to the Spaniards remains a powerful narrative of gendered betrayal etched in Latin America's cultural imaginary. Paz's depiction of Malinche's passivity links to the abjection of María's captive body in *Garage Olimpo*. Of Malinche, Paz states: "Her passivity is abject: she does not resist violence, but is an inert heap of bones, blood and dust ... she loses her name; she *is* no one; she disappears into nothingness; she is Nothingness. And yet she is the cruel incarnation of the feminine condition."[53] *Garage Olimpo* presents the abjection of the violated woman—albeit in the most extreme context of the concentration camp—that is rooted in the history of the European conquest of the Americas. Paz's depiction of Malinche's abjection parallels the degradation María experiences within the camp, and the state's enactment of gendered violence against sexualized, abject bodies is directly linked to this history of racialized, gendered violence in the Americas.

The most obvious representation of *malinchismo* is in the film's portrayal of the sexual relationship between María and Félix. María's decision to have an intimate relationship with her captor Félix alludes to the stringent, hetero-patriarchal standards of female sexuality that were upheld by many leaders of Latin American leftist revolutionary groups. While the film does not refer explicitly to what Isabel Cosse calls the "revolutionary morality" that governed gender interactions in leftist groups, it does refer to the politics of survival that is directly linked to gender and sexuality. As Cosse notes, many leftist activists and guerrillas were suspicious of those who survived the camps and prisons, particularly women, who were assumed to have survived by being "guilty of sexual involvement with the enemy."[54] A hetero-patriarchal sexuality framed the interactions of many women in leftist guerrilla groups. Sexual acts between prisoners and captors—even if committed under the guise of survival—defied the strict sexual and moral codes of armed revolutionary groups such as the Montoneros. Thus, this heightened scrutiny and condemnation of survival tactics is gendered in nature, as more women were suspected of relying on their sexuality to survive. María's sexual relationship with Félix betrays the left's notion of proper revolutionary femininity, and her actions would be considered treasonous to their ideas of a masculine, revolutionary ethos.[55]

Malinichismo and revolutionary morality are referenced in other Latin American cultural texts. Liliana Heker's 1996 novel, *El fin de la historia*, mentions a minor character, a Montonera guerrillera who refused to succumb to her captor, stating that she would choose death over sexual relations with the enemy. Chilean writer and former political prisoner, Hernán Valdés, describes interactions between female prisoners and prison guards in his testimonial novel based on his life, *Tejas Verdes*: "They [the women] were obviously drinking with them [the guards] . . . we couldn't figure the women's behaviour out. . . . We were all of us outraged. Someone recalled how in the National Stadium the women prisoners had preferred to be shot rather than let the soldiers lay a finger on them. We couldn't explain this kind of collusion."[56] Women's sexuality was policed in many leftist Latin American revolutionary groups, where militant women were to ascribe to the proper role of a revolutionary woman, even if adhering to such ideals resulted in death. Although I note again that *Garage Olimpo* does not explicitly condemn María for her actions within the camp, it is difficult to extricate the film from its cultural context and the revolutionary politics which placed moral judgment on the decisions many prisoners made while under the power of the carceral state.

"De eso, no se habla . . ." ("It's a topic that one doesn't speak about . . .")—Women's Perspectives on Survival, Sexual Violence, and the Carceral State

The cultural narratives of *El apando* and *Garage Olimpo* depict the violence of the hetero-patriarchal Dirty War era states as well as the political and social mores of masculinist revolutionary groups. However, we fail to garner the perspective of women who survived the carceral spaces of death. In this final section I reflect on the voices of the survivors and cultural critics who offered their views on survival, betrayal, sexuality, and the carceral logics that structured the Dirty War–era states.

Surviving the carceral space of death—the concentration camps and detention centers—and reintegrating into civil society was a fraught, difficult process (see chapter 4). In 2009, Margarita Cruz told me that no one wanted to hear about what the desaparecidos experienced. She explained that there existed "a paradox between disappearance and reappearance," noting that both actions placed the blame on the victim and survivor. When Cruz and others began to reappear from different centers, she told me, "family members of those who remained disappeared told us, 'If you reappeared, it is for some reason.'" Fellow former detained-disappeared Adriana Calvo recounted a similar experience when she was released from captivity: "People began to be suspicious of us. 'How come you were able to leave?' It was the same expression of 'for some reason you were detained,' but the other way around . . . there was an implicit assumption that we had collaborated with the regime to attain our freedom."[57] Surviving the necropower of the state and the space of death is often met with suspicion and as Cruz and Calvo allude to in their testimonies, it implies a sense of complicity and betrayal.

Survival and betrayal, as this chapter argues, is linked to the legacy of *malinchismo* that is a critical part of the Latin American cultural landscape. In Andrés Di Tella's 1994 documentary, *Montoneros: Una historia*, former guerrillera Ana Testa recounts that her husband, Juan Silva, refused to see her once he discovered she had been released from the Navy School of Mechanics (ESMA, Escuela de Mecánica de la Armada) detention center, one of Argentina's largest concentration camps. Testa was released from the ESMA in March 1980, months before Silva was disappeared and while he was still living clandestinely. According to their mutual friends, Silva assumed that Testa had cooperated with the regime to secure her release. In the documentary, Testa recounts the moment she discovered from other compañeros that Silva did not want to meet up with her. Testa says, with eyes downcast, "well, Juan dies thinking that I was a traitor."[58] Her fellow compañeros told Testa that Silva had said, "I could have seen Ana, but I don't want to see Ana because Ana is a traitor. Ana was able to get out of that place [ESMA] alive? What else could Ana be." This wrenching moment of the documentary reflects the gendered, heterosexist moral social codes that were a part of many of the leftist Latin American guerrilla organizations at the time.

This concept of revolutionary morality is best evinced in the case of Mercedes "Lucy" Carazo. Carazo, a high-ranking Montonera guerrillera, was kidnapped in 1976 and detained at the ESMA for two years. After enduring brutal torture, Carazo eventually complied with military officers, which resulted in her release from ESMA in 1978. Carazo was in a sexual relationship with Antonio Pernías, her former torturer who also led the mission that resulted in the execution of Carazo's husband and Montonero guerrillero Marcelo Kurlat. Carazo eventually denounced Pernías and provided testimony against him in the ESMA Mega Trial, which took place between 2012 and 2017. Despite her denunciation in court, it is the salacious and shocking nature of her sexual relationship with Pernías in the concentration camp that captivated the cultural imaginary of many Argentineans. Carazo's case has aroused disgust, ire, and condemnation in many cultural texts, including Miguel Bonasso's *Recuerdo de la muerte* and Liliana Heker's 1996 novel, *El fin de la historia*. Heker's novel is based loosely on Carazo's life and recounts the detention and torture of guerrillera Leonora Ordaz. Leonora cooperates with military officials and begins a relationship with the officer who assassinated her husband. Protagonist Diana Glass attempts to write a novel of Leonora's involvement in the Montoneros but is unable to complete the novel when she discovers that Leonora fell in love with her captor and torturer. In the novel, Leonora is not perceived as a victim of the dictatorship but rather is viewed as a sexually debased traitor who abandoned her revolutionary principles. Leonora, like María in *Garage Olimpo*, is depicted as a traitorous *malinchista* who is the object of repulsion, desire, and shame to both the leftist resistance movements and the authoritarian Argentinean state.

Heker's novel alludes to the trope of betrayal presented by the women's collaboration with the regime and defection from the revolutionary cause; it incorporates a revolutionary moralistic lens in her judgment of the women's actions. Heker's novel is controversial to many former guerrilleros and survivors of the dictatorship; some noted that it centralizes a history that was not common during the dictatorship, while others criticized the novel's unfair judgment of Leonora having cooperated with the regime for survival in the death camps, where free choice is absent. In Di Tella's documentary, Ana Testa and Graciela Daleo, who were both detained with Carazo at the ESMA, evade judging Carazo's actions. "Well, it [ESMA] was a very particular place to be," Daleo explains, "and you had to negotiate how you were going to survive, and well, she [Carazo] negotiated [her survival]." Regarding Heker's representation of Carazo's story in *El fin de la historia,* Daleo stated that the novel assumes that Leonora was freed from captivity because she "seduced" her torturer. In reality, "those of us who are alive," she contended, "it is because the military officers decided so. Was it benevolence, was it a prize, or was it out of pity? No. It is a far-fetched, perverse assumption that 'if they are alive, it must be for some reason.'"[59] Daleo and other survivors argue that applying a moralistic lens when assessing stories like the one relayed in *El fin de la historia* eschews the power dynamics and mitigates the necropower of the carceral state. Ana Longoni contends that placing moral judgment on the actions of Carazo and others ignores the "complexity of the actions and feelings of a human being in those conditions of extreme adversity."[60]

Miriam Lewin, survivor of the ESMA and former guerrillera, further elaborates on the gendered and sexual politics of survival and how the question of "choice" and agency did not apply in those dire conditions. In 2004 she was invited to participate in the Argentinean daytime TV show, *Almorzando con Mirtha Legrand,* Host Legrand asked Lewin, "is it true that you went out with Tigre Acosta?," referring to the infamous ex-officer of the ESMA concentration camp." The question stunned Lewin; it simultaneously fetishized and made a spectacle of women survivors of extreme sexual, gendered state violence, while also implying that she had a choice in "going out with" her captor. Of her experience, Lewin writes: "We women survivors suffered a double stigma. The general conclusion was that if we were alive, it was because we were informants and what's more, prostitutes. The only way that we survivors were able to leave the concentration camp was because we gave up information under torture, and what's more, because we engaged in a transaction that was considered despicable because it involved our bodies."[61] To this end, women's betrayal refers directly to the acquiescence of their bodily integrity and femininity, which was abhorrent to the revolutionary moral projects of the left, as well as the heteropatriarchal notions of womanhood set forth by the authoritarian state. In the 2012 documentary, *Campo de batalla, cuerpo de mujer* (Battleground, women's bodies), Lewin discusses this relationship between seduction, betrayal, and the masculinist state: "Winning the bodies of the widows of famous combatants ... well, that was like winning the war, in a sort of *malinchista* move, against the Montoneras women, the guerrilleras. And thus, they [the officers] would win a battle over their men, another battle, postmortem."[62] The captive female body not only becomes abject and dehumanized by the state, but it becomes a sexualized, degraded pawn used to reinforce the masculine power of the state and to erode the hetero-masculinity of the members of the revolutionary left.

Heker's novel, Legrand's question, and the social, cultural scrutiny and judgment of women survivors of gendered state violence ignore the power imbalances that existed in the masculinist, necropolitical carceral state. According to Longoni, the fixation on this narrative of women "seducing" their captors mitigates the brutalities of sexual violence in the detention centers and instead, centers on the "salacious act of seduction that places the blame on the women prisoners." Yielding their bodies to their captors, Longoni notes, is framed in terms of "betrayal, seduction, stigma," which is tied to "the inherent nature of their gender."[63] Lewin proclaims that this narrative dangerously assumes that "we women had the power to resist sexual violence and the advances of the torturers" and that the women should have resisted more in order to "preserve 'the altar' of [their] pristine bodies."[64] Similarly, Alejandra Cárdenas of Mexico's guerrilla Party of the Poor (Partido de los Pobres) relates that women survivors of violence in Mexico faced similar judgment: "the punishment for us women still has a sexual connotation that is very difficult," alluding to the sexual politics of survival and betrayal. In reality, for Cárdenas and other survivors of sexual state violence, the egregious sexual torture she endured irrevocably changed her life: "it left a mark on me and I want to let everyone know that even though I have gone to therapy and things like that, whenever I receive news [of this topic], I have nightmares, where I wake up screaming."[65] Women survivors of gendered state violence escaped the death grip of the Mexican and Argentinean carceral state only to be met with judgment, scrutiny, and skepticism. Such reactions have also prompted many women survivors to remain silent on the topic of surviving sexual-based violence. Margarita Cruz in our interview noted that, for many years, survivors would not discuss their experiences of enduring sexual violence in the camps, and that "it's a topic that one doesn't speak about."

These controversial, polemical cultural narratives outline the gender politics of the carceral state and display the necropolitical logic of the regimes. Instead of centering on the motivation of the prisoners to engage in sexual encounters, I argue that these relationships and the controversies they elicit are reflective of gendered social codes that existed within leftist organizations, and gendered moral absolutes that the authoritarian states upheld. These women were defying the heroic martyrdom of their leftist organizations, while also exhibiting sexual behavior unbecoming of a proper, apolitical, Christian woman. This condemnation ignores the critical role the carceral space played in the development of these relationships. Not only does such a criticism of women's use of sexuality for survival ignore what Cosse terms the "radical asymmetry of vulnerability and domination between tortured and subjugated prisoners and their captors," it furthermore illuminates the transnational scope of gendered and sexual propriety in Latin America.[66]

While the term *survival* has become a double standard for many women survivors of gendered state violence, it has importantly aided in the reconstruction their subjectivity and political agency after surviving the carceral spaces of death. Cárdenas asserts, "I am a survivor like I have mentioned here, and I like this term a lot because it clearly expresses that we are survivors of a terrible war against humanity."[67] As I explore in the following chapter, surviving gendered state violence is a process that invariably invokes a kind of haunting. The cultural legacy of the women involved in armed revolutionary movements remains an absent-present whose narratives remain silenced and unearthed within the Mexican and Argentinean national imaginaries.

CHAPTER THREE

"Ghosts of Another Era"
Gendered Haunting and the Legacy of Women's Armed Resistance

> The official history does not acknowledge us, they view us as ghosts of another era. And we are here to relate our histories, to show that this discourse that excludes us cannot aspire to be a universal discourse. And in this context, the history that we are recuperating, reconstructing in this space, is another history entirely.
>
> —Alejandra Cárdenas, the Party of the Poor, Guerrero, Mexico

After my interview in July 2012 with Bertha Lilia Gutiérrez Campos, former member of the FER and the Liga, she shared with me documents from her personal archive. Rifling through the papers, she pulled out a pamphlet made for a 2006 photographic exhibit in Guadalajara. Titled "To Forget Is to Forget Ourselves," the exhibit featured photographs housed in Mexico's General National Archive that captured the visual history of a past the nation had systematically kept from public record. Gutiérrez Campos explained that this exhibit had been organized by local civic organizations working on recuperating the historical memory of the Dirty War. Gutiérrez Campos handed me the pamphlet and recited Mexican poet Enrique Macías Loza stanzas reprinted in the flyer:

> It is not the streets
> that cause pain
> it is the dead
> our dead
> who do not let me

sleep
or live
and sometimes won't let me die.[1]

Afterward she added, "It says more—it says, it is not the streets that cause us pain, rather, what we left on the streets." She then offered to show me the area of Guadalajara that used to be the Penal de Oblatos, the prison where she and other guerrilleros were detained for several years.

As we approached the site, she informed me that the prison was demolished in 1982 and an elementary school erected in its place. As we circled around the block, she pointed to the playground and told me that this was where the guerrilleras were detained. With classes out for the summer, the empty playground created a sense of haunting and loss. Driving away from the site of the former prison, Gutiérrez Campos and I were silent for a few moments until she said, "spaces conserve a certain energy of the past, don't they?" We drove off in silence and away from the site of Gutiérrez Campos's trauma and experiences of political persecution, where she was just one of the many women protagonists of Mexico's little-known history of armed struggle.

This anecdote opens this chapter because it captures the theory of haunting and spectrality that has emerged in my research on the legacy of women's participation in Latin America's armed struggle during the Dirty Wars. Read alongside Cárdenas's epigraph, former guerrillas' accounts of the past reveal that a significant element is absent from contemporary Latin American historiography: women's participation in the armed socialist movements of the 1960s and 1970s. The history of armed movements in Mexico and Argentina hold a marginal place in contemporary Mexican and Argentinean history, yet there is even less information on the history of women's participation in these movements. Gutiérrez Campos and Cárdenas allude to the haunting of Mexico's and Argentina's revolutionary past and the unsettling of several dominant narratives of the armed struggle: the state's criminalization of armed organizations in contemporary cultural discourses, the infantilization of the armed insurgencies as utopic and idealist movements doomed to fail, *and* the masculinization and romanticization of the armed struggle narrated primarily by its male protagonists. I argue that these dominant narratives on the armed insurgencies evince a gendered haunting of Mexico's and Argentina's revolutionary past into the present, where the specters of the armed struggle unsettle and rescript the discourses that have failed to acknowledge the legacy of women's resistance.

While the history of the guerrilleras is rendered invisible in contemporary Mexico and Argentina, visual culture and testimonies have played a critical role in documenting women's histories of revolutionary struggle and capturing the gendered haunting of this past. This is evident in Luisa Riley's 2012 documentary film, *Flor en Otomí* (Flower in Otomí) and Marta Diana's 1997 collection of testimonies, *Mujeres guerrilleras* (Women guerrillas). *Flor en Otomí* centers on the life and death of Dení Prieto Stock, a nineteen-year-old member of the Mexican urban guerrilla group, the National Liberation Forces (FLN).[2] *Mujeres guerrilleras* is a compilation of testimonies of former Argentinean guerrillas and also includes Diana's own reflections on her personal connection to the women. By centering my analysis on *Flor en Otomí* and *Mujeres guerrilleras*, as well as the interviews I conducted with former guerrilleras in Mexico and Argentina in 2012 and 2014, I investigate how these cultural productions center silenced narratives and how the history of the guerrilleras is rendered illegible and irrelevant in contemporary neoliberal Argentina and Mexico. The works examined in this chapter document how Argentina's and Mexico's unresolved history of violence and the guerrilleras' erasure from state and masculinist discourses have resulted in a generation of specters whose histories of revolutionary struggle continue to haunt contemporary Mexico and Argentina.[3] The film and testimonies disrupt the neoliberal present as it documents both countries' violent histories and evokes the gendered memories of the ghosts who resisted the free-market economic policies of the 1970s.

This chapter uses the image of haunting as a heuristic tool to examine the systemic erasure of women's political subjectivity from the history of Latin America's armed struggles of the 1960s and 1970s. In *Ghostly Matters*, sociologist Avery Gordon defines haunting as "an animated state in which a repressed or unresolved social violence is making itself known, sometimes very directly, sometimes more obliquely." For Gordon, this "animated state" represents that which cannot be documented empirically beyond that which is not seen, but felt. In other words, haunting reflects a "structure of feeling that is something akin to what it feels like to be the object of a social totality vexed by the phantoms of modernity's violence." Gordon's evocative theories of haunting are an important methodological tool in making sense of the lingering presence of "abusive systems of power" that "make themselves known . . . in everyday life" in Latin America.[4] It is precisely this "structure of feeling" that theorizes the unsettled moment of silence I shared with Gutiérrez Campos as we drove away from the former prison site in Guadalajara; the "energy" she described feeling near the former prison site most aptly reflects the "seething presence" and ghosts of Mexico's Dirty War, "making themselves known" to us. In this chapter, haunting is an important conceptual tool that makes sense of the "structure of feeling" and social violences that are not seen but felt in the present. Furthermore, haunting moves us beyond empirical data and captures the loss and the lingering effects of the ghosts of Latin America's Dirty Wars.

What, then, is the effect of the haunting of the social violences of the past that are felt in the present? And what do these ghosts want? The reason for this kind of haunting vis-à-vis the "structure of feeling" is not to "chase away the ghosts," as Derrida asserts, but to "grant them the right . . . [to a] hospitable memory . . . out of a concern for justice."[5] This chapter investigates the ghostly presences of Latin America's armed movements in cultural texts, and I unpack the complexities their ghostly presences render in contemporary cultural representations. I am invested in exploring the ways in which haunting is present in the repressed cultural memory of Latin America's armed insurgencies and how it has made "itself known" in the public imaginary in contemporary Mexico and Argentina. I argue that "unresolved" histories of violence, and their subsequent erasure from dominant discourses, have resulted in a generation of specters whose histories of revolutionary struggle continue to haunt contemporary Mexico and Argentina. Ghosts and specters can emerge when artists, filmmakers, historians, writers, and cultural critics attempt to contend with unresolved past violences.

It is precisely out of this concern for justice that I base my readings of cultural productions that evoke the legacy of this gendered haunting of Latin America's revolutionary past on the present. These cultural texts not only address the official history's silencing, demonization, and infantilization of guerrilla organizations, but they also reflect the complex gender dynamics that existed within the guerrillas, challenging the masculinist historiography of Latin America's guerrillas. In *Flor en Otomí* and *Mujeres guerrilleras*, the structure of feeling evinces the gendered nature of haunting in precisely what cannot be audiovisually or textually captured in relation to the violence of Latin America's revolutionary past.

Cultural studies and literature allow us to contend with such ghostly presences, whereas more traditional disciplinary modes of conducting research may be limiting. It is important, however, that these narratives of gendered haunting are not read as "authentic" or true historical accounts of women's elided experiences in the armed struggle. Although this chapter relies on the methodological framework of gendered haunting, I am not primarily concerned with accurately capturing authentic accounts of women's marginalization; instead, I explore the impact the legacy of women's histories of repression has had on cultural productions and oral histories.

The recuperation of the historical memory of the armed struggle has recently been of interest to many activists and Latin Americanist scholars. Their work importantly challenges the legacy of the dominant narrative, which has led some former guerrilleros and sympathizers, such as former guerrilleros Mario Firmenich and Alberto Ulloa Bornemann, as well as public intellectuals Beatriz Sarlo, Hugo Vezzetti, and María de los Angeles Magdelano Cárdenas, to disavow the armed struggle.[6] However, recent critical scholarship by Alexander Aviña, John Beverley, Laura Castellanos, Fernando Calderón, and Adela Cedillo has challenged the official history that has criminalized and silenced the historical memory of the armed insurgencies. This is evident in the case of Mexico's armed struggle, about which there is even less literature available than there is on Argentina. These authors importantly contest the trope of what John Beverley calls the "guerrillero arrepentido" (the repentant guerrillero), and they question the dominant narrative that portrays the armed insurgency as a naive, utopic, and idealistic movement doomed to fail.[7]

If—as Beverley, Castellanos, and others have asserted—representations of the history are "dominated by a paradigm of disillusion" and youthful naïveté, then it is critical to examine to what degree this youthful, political idealism is gendered as masculine and erased by the official state discourse of the armed struggle or overlooked by male protagonists of the guerrillas. Dominant representations center on a masculine subject of "the new man," or what Ileana Rodríguez terms the "romantic revolutionary hero," who has been idealized and canonized in leftist revolutionary narratives.[8] As Jean Franco argues, the armed socialist movements in Latin America evoke a "masculine ethos," evident in "the photograph of the dead Che taken in Bolivia in 1969 [which] is still the ghost that haunts the social imaginary."[9] This haunting, however, is masculine, as Che Guevara has become the face of Latin America's revolutionary past. This masculine ghost has become the dominant referent point in the historiography of Latin American armed socialist movements.

It is critical to position the conversations on gender and Latin America's armed struggle within contemporary discussions on the political climate particularly as recent neoliberal, neoconservative shifts in the Americas have conjured the ghosts of the armed struggle.[10] The cultural texts I examine in this chapter disrupt the linear temporality of the neoliberal present in Latin America; that is, these texts evoke the gendered hauntings of the past crimes of the state by playing with temporality calling forth the ghosts of the past. Turning to Cárdenas's statement from the epigraph, I consider her depiction of the guerrilleras as gendered "ghosts" of a bygone era in Mexican and Argentinean history and explore how they emerge in recent cultural representations of the armed insurgencies. My interviews with former guerrilleras alongside my analysis of *Flor en Otomí* and *Mujeres guerrilleras* document the "muted presences" of these histories and evoke a haunting of Latin America's armed insurgencies as I situate the history of the guerrillas of the 1970s in contemporary discourses on Latin American culture and politics. This chapter considers how women are making discursive interventions in historical memory projects that unsettle and challenge the dominant narratives of the armed insurgencies.

Ultimately, I argue that *Flor en Otomí*, *Mujeres guerrilleras*, and the interviews I conducted with former guerrilleras are critical cultural texts that conjure the ghosts of the guerrilleras "out of a concern for justice." The cultural texts and oral histories center the narratives and hermeneutics provided by the women who were involved in the armed insurgencies. Furthermore, it is within the cultural texts' spaces of un-representability, gaps, and silences where the ghosts are conjured and given a chance for a "hospitable memory" that they have been denied for decades. The testimonies and film do not purport to offer the real history of the armed struggle in Argentina and Mexico, nor do they provide us with the guerrilleras' authentic experiences, but the texts' limits of representation creates a political space that allows "ghosts of another era" to teach us about histories of resistance and help us envision alternative forms of justice for human rights crimes.

"Fantasmas, fragmentos y huecos" (Ghosts, fragments, and gaps): Searching for the Ghosts of the Argentinean and Mexican Armed Struggles

As artists and writers intimately tied to their subject matter, Luisa Riley's film *Flor en Otomí* and Marta Diana's testimonial narrative, *Mujeres guerrilleras*, are immersed in the history of the armed struggle in Mexico and Argentina, respectively. In 2012, Mexican filmmaker Luisa Riley released *Flor en Otomí*, a documentary on the life of her childhood friend, Dení Prieto Stock, a nineteen-year-old member of the Mexican urban guerrilla group, the FLN.[11] In 1997, Marta Diana published *Mujeres guerrilleras*, a compilation of interviews with former guerrilleras who were active in various armed organizations in Argentina during the 1970s. The text also includes Diana's personal narratives and reflective essays on the historical memory of the guerrillas, as well as her own musings on her relationship with Adriana Lesgart, her childhood friend. In these texts, we learn that Prieto Stock and Lesgart are murdered by their respective states as a result of their participation in Mexican and Argentinean guerrilla organizations.

Despite the difference in medium and genre, both the documentary film and testimonial narrative grapple with the difficulty of audiovisually and discursively documenting the traumatic loss of young guerrilleras. In *Flor en Otomí*, Riley follows the brief life of friend Prieto Stock, born in Mexico City in 1955 to a Jewish American mother, Evelyn Stock, and a Mexican playwright father, Carlos Prieto Argüelles. Raised in a middle-class, politically left family, Prieto Stock's personal and familial worlds were immersed in politics, and this shaped her political consciousness and involvement in various movements. However, increasing state repression in late-1960s Mexico impelled her to pursue a more radical decision to go underground and join the FLN. On February 14, 1974, Prieto Stock and several other members of the FLN were killed when the Mexican army raided their safe house in Nepantla de Sor Juana Inés de la Cruz, southeast of Mexico City.

Diana's *Mujeres guerrilleras* similarly reveals the personal relationship she had with guerrillera sisters Adriana and Susana Lesgart, who were killed by the Argentinean state in the 1970s. The Lesgart family was from Córdoba, Argentina: father Rogelio Lesgart, a member of the Socialist Party, was a union organizer; and all the Lesgart siblings were politically active. In 1971, Susana Lesgart was arrested for her participation in Montoneros and was ultimately murdered by the state one year later at the age of twenty-two. Her younger sister, Adriana, one of the founders of the women-led subset of Montoneros, Agrupación Evita, was disappeared by the state in 1979, also at age twenty-two. Siblings Rogelio and María Lesgart were also disappeared and murdered by the state, which left Liliana as the only surviving sibling. The traumatic and haunting loss of the Lesgart family pervades Diana's text as she contends with the gaps and fissures their traumatic absence imposes on the formal structure of her text. While *Mujeres guerrilleras* consists primarily of testimonies of various former Argentinean *guerrilleras*, Diana's work cannot escape the legacy of trauma and haunting in her prose, as she interweaves personal narratives and reflections throughout the testimonial text.

Released decades after the deaths of Prieto Stock and the Lesgart siblings, both *Flor en Otomí* and *Mujeres guerrilleras* emerged during a time when human rights organizations and cultural producers are recuperating the historical memory of the armed struggle. The texts evince the importance of women's historical memory projects that illuminate the central role women played in the Mexican and Argentinean armed insurgencies. Both *Flor en Otomí* and *Mujeres guerrilleras* importantly document the unrecognized legacy of the guerrilleras and underscore the governments' role in committing human rights abuses. However, we are confronted with a central limitation apparent in the narratives: as many cultural theorists have noted, cultural productions are limited in their ability to accurately represent reality, especially when focusing on trauma and violence. In this section, I argue that the works are haunted by their own subject matter and by this difficulty—and urgency—of representing the violent loss of the (gendered) specters of Latin America's Dirty War. These specters cannot be audiovisually or textually contained or represented in *Flor en Otomí* and *Mujeres guerrilleras*, thus escaping the narrative logic of the cultural texts. However, neither text is preoccupied with documenting an "authentic reality" of the guerrilleras' experiences. Rather, both *Flor en Otomí* and *Mujeres guerrilleras* evince a "structure of feeling" that is central to haunting, and I would add, evoke a gendered haunting in the way both texts represent the gendered losses of the guerrillas, and also the "something-to-be-done" response to the lack of justice achieved for state crimes. The texts are eluded by the very subject they seek to investigate, encountering "fantasmas, fragmentos y huecos." Yet it is the ghosts of the guerrillas who represent the driving force of both works as they encourage us to find a "hospitable memory" out of a concern for justice.

We turn first to Riley's *Flor en Otomí*, where the haunting subject matter is revealed in the discordances presented in the film's narrative arc and limitations in portraying the "real" history of the FLN and Prieto Stock's life. In Latin America, many documentary films produced in the 1960s and 1970s captured political unrest of the time and provided counter sociopolitical narratives. Many of the films were released during a time of political turmoil—such as Patricio Guzmán's 1975 epic three-part *The Battle of Chile*—and the films reflect the political urgency of disseminating information to an international audience. Similar to Latin American social documentary films of the 1970s, *Flor en Otomí* documents a history of political repression and significantly contributes to the small body of films that explore this unknown history of Mexico's Dirty War. In the summer of 2012 I met with Luisa Riley to discuss her film and what she hoped it would accomplish. She stated that the film "is a little grain of sand; without a doubt it contributes to the recuperation of the historical memory [of the Dirty War]. It's about Dení, but Dení for me also represents the spirit of the youths of that era."

Flor en Otomí evokes the history of state-sponsored violence that took place thirty years before Riley began work on her film; this temporal remove not only indicates a haunting that is evident in contemporary Mexico's inability to reckon with its traumatic past, it importantly reflects a deviation from the emphasis on representing truth that many social documentary films purport to do. Rather than offer us a chronological, complete account of Prieto Stock's life and activism, the film is more invested in exploring the cultural legacy of these ghosts and what they can teach us about the audiovisual archiving of historical narratives.

In the attempt to track down Prieto Stock's ghost, *Flor en Otomí* includes various archival materials such as photographs, testimonials, personal letters, and news sources. The archival sources constitute an integral part of the film's narrative, and they relay the indexical quality of the film in the validation of the elided history of violence. As Roland Barthes notes in *Camera Lucida*, photography and other visual texts invoke a conflation of past and present, as the photo preserves an image of the past; this, he continues, "is a certificate of presence," which in relation to Riley's incorporation of multiple images of Prieto Stock in the film, serves as a kind of "certificate" of Prieto Stock's existence.[12] The historical sources used in the film contravene Mexico's mainstream discourse on the Dirty War and create an audiovisual space of validation for repressed histories, while reinscribing Prieto Stock's political subjectivity. While *Flor en Otomí* attributes this generation of activists with the legitimacy and subjectivity that was stripped from them by the state, the film appears cognizant of its own limitations in its ability to represent Prieto Stock's narrative and alludes to the lacuna inherent in documentary film's portrayal of the past.

The film's deviation from a specific type of documentary film and its preoccupation with truth telling is evident in Riley's personal involvement in the creation of the documentary, and further alludes to the materiality and indexicality of visual culture. Riley's presence in *Flor en Otomí* illustrates her role as documentarian and family friend, yet also refers to the impossibility filmmakers face documenting "the way things truly [were]" when tracking down the specters of the Dirty War.[13] Despite her absence throughout most of the film, Riley's positionality is clearly noted throughout the documentary as she retraces the political subjectivity and life of Prieto Stock. Riley has intimate access to material sources in the creation of her film, including Prieto Stock family videos, photographs of Prieto Stock, and—most critical in the film's narrative reconstruction of Prieto Stock's subjectivity—personal letters sent to her cousin Laura Stock.

Riley's personal involvement with the subject matter is depicted in the first few minutes of *Flor en Otomí*. The opening scene reveals headlines from the *Excelsior* and *El Universal* newspapers dated Thursday, February 15, 1974, praising the Mexican government for capturing "subversives" of a "red conspiracy whose objective it was to implement through violent means a socialist government." The camera then focuses on the text of the article, which claims that five "extremists" were killed in a "shoot-out" against the army and federal police.[14] These images are accompanied by the discordant, unnerving simple minor keys of a piano, which

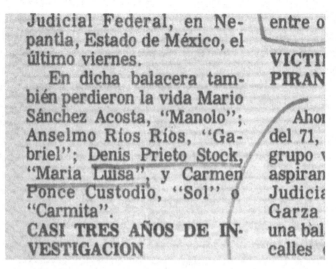

Figure 3.1. A close-up of the *Excelsior* newspaper article on the capture of "subversives," with director Luisa Riley's underlining. *Flor en Otomí*, with permission of Luisa Riley.

eventually give way to the brash sound of trumpets as the text of the article lists Prieto Stock as one of the deceased. The abrupt, forte notes of the piano in the first few minutes of the film are unsettling and represent the traumatic effect of the extralegal violence sanctioned by the Mexican state. The camera pans over the newspaper article documenting the ambush at the Nepantla safe house, revealing green underlining and handwritten marginal notes.

Riley's inclusion of headlines from Mexican newspapers challenges the official discourse of the armed insurgency and relays the immediacy of the filmmaker's relationship to Prieto Stock. The handwritten notes reveal the shock that Riley described to me when she read the 1974 *Excelsior* article while visiting the General Archive of the Nation (Archivo General de la Nación) in 2007. As she noted, she was left "paralyzed" the first time she read the newspaper in 1974, and, "when I saw it again [in the archives in 2007], I yelled. You get the impression that it is true [Dení's death]. It really happened."[15] The lack of resolution to the question "why this trauma occurred" is depicted in the film and reflected in Riley's personal trauma when she learns about the death of her childhood friend. Riley's absent-presence emerges in the commencement of the film while the loud, green ink underlining the name—Dení Prieto Stock—evokes the shock of re-encountering the reality of her friend's death in 2007.

Riley's inclusion of archival newspapers with her comments furthermore alludes to the relationship between materiality, indexicality, and haunting that is present in many visual cultural texts. Indexicality here refers to the relationship between the object and the subject of visual culture, which in this case can refer to Riley as director and the film, as well as spectator and the film. To this end, indexicality alludes to the imprint the visual images make on the spectator and the director, as well as to the perceived fixed moment of time that these images produce. Although the images of Dení, her letters, and so on are ostensibly from the 1970s, the indexicality of the images produce a sense of haunting that arises as we view the film in the present. According to Laura Mulvey in *Death 24x a Second*, film's and photography's preservation of fixed time arouses indistinguishable feelings of uncertainty—what I infer to be a haunting—that emerge between "the boundary between life and death" and "the mechanical animation of the inanimate, particularly the human, figure." This boundary is evident in the film, as the material sources that depict Prieto Stock's death are reflected in the present moment, contributing to the uncertainty in film's ability to portray "a real image of reality across time."[16] This sentiment of haunting is exacerbated as the film centers on the lack of justice for Dení and other victims of the Dirty War.

This haunting and uncertainty in *Flor en Otomí*'s portrayal of past traumas is evident in its narrative structure and the use of archival materials. Riley does not offer a historically chronological narrative, but rather, a film compressing temporal distance by moving between three narrative arcs and incorporating distinct sources. The first narrative line offers a biographical sketch of Prieto Stock's life leading up to her involvement with the FLN. In this part, Riley relies on testimonials, photographs, and letters to reveal the critical moments that shaped Prieto Stock's political consciousness. The second storyline centers on Prieto Stock's time in the guerrilla as "María Luisa" (nom de guerre), relying predominately on former FLN compañera Elisa Benavides Guevara's testimony to relate their experiences living clandestinely in the safe house. The third narrative takes place in the present day, as the film journeys to the safe house in Nepantla, where Benavides recounts the events that took place on the day of the ambush.[17] While *Flor en Otomí* shifts from one narrative frame to another, it is constantly pulled toward the third narrative, the site of the violent ambush.

A salient example of this temporal compression and the film's indexing occurs halfway through the film as Prieto Stock's cousin, Laura, reads from a letter that Dení had sent her in 1970, three years before she went to live clandestinely with the FLN: "I've had a sort of hazy feeling as though I'm really sick inside. It's like a deep disappointment, but like I'm too lazy to do anything about it. It's so hard to explain. Let me try and to put my thoughts in order. First I started thinking, why the hell I'm studying if in the end I'll probably leave everything and go to the mountains and fight guerrillas and probably get killed in the process."

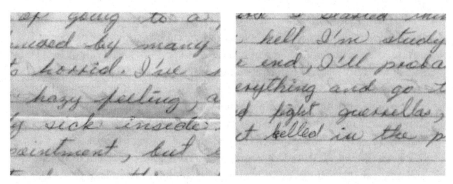

Figure 3.2 and 3.3. The camera lingers on several close-ups of Prieto Stock's handwritten letter to her cousin, Laura, emphasizing vital phrases. *Flor en Otomí*, with permission of Luisa Riley.

As Laura reads aloud from the letter in the present day, the camera pans over Prieto Stock's original handwritten text, where the phrases "hazy feeling" and "sick inside" are foregrounded. As Laura continues to read the letter, the camera switches to a black-and-white photograph of a young Dení, then returns to the text of the letter, as the camera draws in on the words "guerrilla" and "killed." As Laura Stock finishes reading the letter, the next scene crosscuts to the yard of the Nepantla safe house, as the camera pans skyward, with the final frame lingering on the Popocatépetl volcano.

Figure 3.4. An extreme close-up shot of a young Dení Prieto Stock. *Flor en Otomí*, with permission of Luisa Riley.

"Ghosts of Another Era" • 111

By repeatedly crosscutting to the scene of the ambush in present-day Nepantla, the film invokes the "seething presence" of the unrepresentable: the violent repression of the armed insurgencies in 1970s Mexico and the traumatic legacy of Prieto Stock's death. Her death is the seething presence that the film evokes by showing us that it *cannot* be represented. Yet the film is able to conjure the spectral qualities that her trauma—and the trauma of this historical epoch—represent. This is clear in the evidentiary editing as Riley blends images of the photograph, the letter, and the yard of the safe house (the site of Prieto Stock's death). The quiet and peaceful scenes of the Nepantla house is contrasted against the final words of Prieto Stock's letter, eerily foreshadowing her own death, as well as close-up images of the home's exterior showing the bullet holes from the day of the attack. The scene of the raid is always portrayed in the film as tranquil, evoking a sense of haunting as archival photos of the violent massacre of the FLN members in 1974 are positioned against the quiet scenes of the Nepantla house in 2012.

This sequence repeatedly centers on Prieto Stock's photograph, each frame providing a closer image of her face. In her discussion of Barthes and André Bazin on photography, Mulvey articulates the sense of uncertainty that results from the medium's allusion to death, or what Mulvey terms, the "embalmed index;" for Barthes, photographs reveal a simultaneous absence and presence in the "'return of the dead.'"[18] About photography's contribution to the film's sense of haunting, Mulvey states that "the photograph's suspension of time, its

Figure 3.5. Bullet holes are still visible from the exterior of the Nepantla safe house. *Flor en Otomí*, with permission of Luisa Riley.

conflation of life and death, the animate and the inanimate, raises ... a sense of disquiet that is aggravated rather than calmed by the photograph's mechanical, chemical and indifferent nature."[19] Thus, the combination of material sources used in this sequence reflects an absent presence in the "conflation of life and death," as the spectators view images of Prieto Stock's face, the Nepantla house and the text from her original letters. The haunting effect is heightened as Laura Stock provides the voice for the deceased sender of the letter, which in one sense imbues the film with life and animation yet simultaneously underscores the reality of Prieto Stock's absence and traumatic death.

The convergence of the three narrative arcs is disquieting, as the confluence of temporalities and archival sources reminds the spectators of Prieto Stock's death. The film evokes the "sort of hazy feeling" Prieto Stock wrote about, as it attempts to audiovisually track down the specters of the guerrilla movements, aware of its limitations in its ability to capture this unrepresentable subject matter and Prieto Stock's absent presence. What's more, the compression of temporalities in *Flor en Otomí* alludes to the belated impact of trauma in cultural representations of violence. The centrality of absence in the film emphasizes the elision of this narrative from the annals of Mexican history and reflects the traumatic and unrecognized legacies of this era. By playing with the temporal narrative lines, *Flor en Otomí* brings the violence of the Dirty War era directly into present-day Mexico and challenges neoliberalism's fixation on a notion of teleological progress. While contemporary neoliberal Mexico desires a shift away from the violence of the past, the multiplicity of temporalities in *Flor en Otomí* disrupts this attempt to look forward toward a modern, neoliberal Mexican state. In this regard, the film alludes to the Dirty War legacies in present-day neoliberal Mexico, where the vestiges of the violent past bear directly onto the present, as there has been no justice or resolution for the human rights crimes committed in the past.

In a similar vein, Diana's *Mujeres guerrilleras* is haunted by the gaps and silences surrounding the information regarding her childhood friends' deaths and disappearances. The personal impact of trauma on Diana's narrative is evident at the start of her text. One evening in 1972, Diana was in her Buenos Aires home watching the evening news as her young son, Esteban, played with his toys. As she was tending to laundry, she suddenly saw a headline flash across the screen, "Prison break attempt ... repression" accompanied by a photograph of Susana Lesgart, the older sister of her childhood friend, Adriana. She recalled: "Listed there were the names and the photographs of the dead. My shock did not allow me to register anything with clarity, except for the death of Susana, but it was not only her death. My shock was discovering that Susana led a life that I had completely ignored and, obviously, this involved Adriana."[20] Diana was referring to Susana's involvement in armed organizations in 1970s Argentina, prior to the dictatorship of 1976.

The news that stunned Diana in 1972 refers to the massacre of Trelew, where sixteen political prisoners—many associated with the People's Revolutionary Army (ERP, Ejército Revolucionario del Pueblo) and Montoneros guerrilla organizations—were executed by prison guards, allegedly for attempting to escape. At the time, officials of then-president Alejandro Agustín Lanusse's government (1971–73) stated that these prisoners were attempting a second prison escape after having been caught and reincarcerated after the first failed attempt. However, survivors of the massacre and human rights officials have since debunked this narrative, stating that it was instead a premeditated execution of prisoners.[21] The massacre and Susana's death shocked Diana, as she attempted to reconcile the memory she held of her childhood friends—studious, sweet, and musically gifted adolescents—and the realization that they were guerrilleras: "I could not (and I still cannot) reconcile both images," she said.

The irreconcilability of two subjectivities—Susana as her musically gifted childhood friend, and Susana as a militant in an armed revolutionary group—disturbs the linearity of *Mujeres guerrilleras*, and in so doing, establishes a sense of unease and unsettling that is echoed in Riley's *Flor en Otomi*. While Diana eventually becomes preoccupied with uncovering what led to the disappearance of her friend Adriana Lesgart in 1979, it is the initial shock and trauma of learning of Susana's violent death during the evening news that impels her to research the political activism of the Lesgart siblings.

This memory establishes an important parallel with Riley's *Flor en Otomí*, as both Riley and Diana learn of their friends' violent deaths—and involvement in armed struggle—through mainstream media outlets. The dominant media narrative—and indeed, the official narratives in both nations—has scripted the history of the armed struggles as treasonous subversion led by terrorists whose deaths were justified through the use of language such as "fugitive attempt," "subversives," and "conspiracy." The mainstream media also contributed to the dominant narrative that positioned the guerrillas as doomed to fail in their utopic quest for a socialist revolution. These official discourses in both Mexico and Argentina have shaped the public imaginary on the history of the armed struggle of the 1970s, eliding the voices of the protagonists of this era that seek to challenge the discourse.

Diana, like Riley, uses her text to unsettle the dominant narrative on Argentina's guerrillas and creates a discursive space to investigate the experiences of women militants. *Mujeres guerrilleras* importantly contributes to the historical memory work of women in Latin America's armed insurgencies and clearly centers the narratives, visions, thoughts, and experiences of the guerrilleras. Her project additionally portrays the ghosts of Argentina's revolutionary past as the gendered specters of the armed struggle, which have been effectively denied—and continue to be denied—an opportunity to seek justice. Diana is unsettled by the scope of her own project and the attempt to discern why her childhood friends would join the armed struggle. Traumatized by their violent deaths, Diana begins her investigation guided by the following question: "'What was the occurrence that had pushed Susana and perhaps Adriana... to the guerrilla groups?'"[22] The Lesgart sisters, as well as Prieto Stock, were academically ambitious students from middle-class families. Riley and Diana, both from similar backgrounds, attempt to ascertain what motivated these young women to leave their comfortable, middle-class homes to join armed militant groups where the risk of death was imminent.

Although Riley is an absent presence in her documentary film, Diana's presence is pronounced throughout the laborious process of reconstructing the subjectivity of her friend Adriana and other guerrilleras in her text. Much like Riley's film, Diana's work reveals the challenges and limitations of her project: many of the women protagonists of the Argentinean armed struggle have been killed or were disappeared, making it impossible for anyone to piece together an accurate portrait of their experiences. As she claims toward the end of *Mujeres guerrilleras*, "I was looking for people, but many times I encountered ghosts because the majority of these women (as they had informed me), *"are no longer here"* (original emphasis). Despite their absences, *Mujeres guerrilleras* evokes the "muted presence" of "ghosts of another era," and in essence, it is a text that rescripts the dominant narrative on Argentina's armed struggle. Indeed, it is Adriana's ghost that haunts Diana throughout her investigations, and while her specter serves as the organizing thread of the text, it simultaneously unsettles and dismantles the structural form. Diana notes that during her interviews with other guerrilleras, Adriana's figure "refloated" in her memory, as she tried to "look for some kind of trace, some kind of explanation, with the (vain?) attempt to reach some conclusions." As Diana immerses herself in her research on Argentina's armed struggle, she is confronted with "ghosts," "fragments," and "gaps" as she attempts to piece together a cohesive, complete account of women involved in the guerrillas.[23]

The presence of these "ghosts" and "gaps" is conjured by the temporally disjointed form of *Mujeres guerrilleras*. This is evident in the introductory section of her text; Diana commences the text with her earliest memory of meeting Adriana in 1963. Then the narrative shifts to 1992, when she first learns of Adriana's involvement in Montoneros. Diana then recounts her discovery of Susana's death on the news in 1972, and her introduction concludes in the 1990s, when she first began her research project. As Idelbar Avelar notes, "mournful literature will search for those fragments and ruins . . . that can trigger the untimely eruption of the past."[24] Although Avelar centers specifically on the function of mourning in post-dictatorial Latin American fiction, Avelar's notion of the "untimely eruption of the past" in the present correlates to Diana's narrative structure. *Mujeres guerrilleras* does not provide a linear, diachronic account of her involvement in the project or of Adriana's participation in Montoneros. As readers, we are unsettled by abrupt temporal shifts from past to present and back again. *Mujeres guerrilleras* clearly establishes that there is no sense of teleological progress to the history of women guerrillas of the 1970s, or indeed of the history of the Argentine armed struggle. Rather, these histories—subsumed by a neoliberal present that is forward-looking—upset, irrupt, and unsettle the present.

A clear example of this temporal shift is evident in Diana's memory of learning of Susana's death in 1972 while sorting through her laundry. She states, "I stayed for a long time, sitting on the bed, holding the clothes against my body. I suppose that faced with the shock of this news, those clothes connected me to earth, a reminder of the reality that only a few minutes prior had been my own real world."[25] Although Diana is writing about the trauma of learning about Susana's violent death, she is writing in the (then) present, in 1996, which signifies that more than twenty years had passed since her initial discovery in 1972. This parallels Riley's account of discovering the death of Prieto Stock in 1974, and again in Mexico's General Archive in 2007. The temporal compression of past and present is evinced in both Diana and Riley's cultural productions, as the violence and trauma associated with these young women's deaths at the hands of the authoritarian state haunts them both in the present. The vacillation from past to present and back to the past in *Mujeres guerrilleras* alludes to the irreconcilability of Argentina's violent past with the present, and furthermore, it reveals the unresolved placement of the armed struggle's history in present-day national discourse.

The irreconcilability of the armed struggle in the present is further evident in Diana's inability to create a cohesive narrative of the Lesgart sisters' involvement in the Montoneros. It is Adriana's disappearance that haunts Diana as she pieces together fragments of her activism from testimonies given by friends, survivors, and family members. Adriana's ghost simultaneously structures and disrupts the narrative arc of *Mujeres guerrilleras*, as we are constantly pulled back into the unknown void of the past. The first apparition of Adriana's ghost appears at the start of the text, as Diana recounts the first time she met her in grade school in 1963. As a new student, Diana felt nervous and apprehensive, yet such feelings of anxiety dissipated when she saw a piece of paper being pushed toward her. Then "came a hand, which reached toward me," she remembered.[26] The hand belonged to Adriana, who had given her a piece of paper with instructions on what books to buy for class. In one respect, this memory refers to the instant bond established between the young Diana and Adriana; however, it more importantly reveals a haunting that unsettles the narrative linearity of the text. Diana—writing her first memory of Adriana in the 1990s—first recalls her hand, a fragment of her corporeal whole, which alludes to the spectral element that undergirds this project. Indeed, this evokes Avery Gordon's account of the desaparecidos: "a disappearance is real only when it is apparitional because the ghost or the apparition is the principal form by which something lost or invisible or seemingly not there makes itself known or apparent to us."[27] Granted, Adriana was still alive in Diana's 1963 memory; however, Diana was attempting to document and conjure the first recollections of her now-disappeared friend. Diana's first memory of meeting Adriana establishes the text's tonal element of haunting as we encounter her hand, a fragment of Adriana's whole subjectivity.

Adriana's spectral apparitions continue to emerge throughout *Mujeres guerrilleras*, as Diana travels to their hometown of Córdoba to interview four former guerrilleras and Adriana's only surviving sibling, Liliana. As Diana approaches Adriana's childhood home, she notes: "The light from the corner was the same as I remembered. The night, like so many others. Was it then or now? For a few seconds I sank into a timeless vertigo in such an intense way that I had to hold the wall with one hand and ring the bell with the other while my heart was pounding."[28] Here, the past bears overwhelmingly on the present and creates "anguish" in Diana as she contends with the sense of "timeless vertigo" in her project. This passage denotes what Elizabeth Jelin terms the "multiplicity of temporalities at play" and the challenges of scripting a linear narrative of the history of Argentine women involved in the armed struggle.[29] The trauma and haunting resulting from the violent loss and disappearance of Adriana, Susana, and thousands of other political activists indicate that completing an accurate, comprehensive narrative of this epoch of Argentina's history is—and always will be—an impossible feat.

The difficulty is further evident in Diana's meeting with Liliana, who informs Diana that after the deaths and disappearance of Susana and Adriana, their parents did not touch their rooms or remove their personal items: "It seemed that they had gone out for a while and would return any minute. But it had been years. So one day I picked up everything. There had to be an end to the story."[30]

This passage establishes an important parallel with *Flor en Otomí*; Prieto Stock's announcement, "I'll be back later," before her death anticipates the haunting that was to emerge after her violent death by the Mexican state. The Lesgart parents similarly anticipate this "apparition of [specters]" of their dead and disappeared daughters, leaving their rooms untouched. It seemed that at any moment "they would return."[31] Although Liliana attempts to put an "end to the story" by putting away her sisters' personal items, *Mujeres guerrilleras* rejects the notion of teleological progress to this history of the armed struggle. Liliana's desire to end the story of this violent history exacerbates the haunting and unnerves us; until we are able to create a "hospitable memory out of a concern for justice," these ghosts of the armed struggle will continue to haunt Argentina's imaginary.

The historical context within which this text emerges is essential in understanding the apparition of ghosts and specters in Diana's work. *Mujeres guerrilleras* was released during the second presidential term of Carlos Menem, who under the pretense of "national reconciliation" pardoned about 280 former officers convicted of human rights abuse during the dictatorship.[32] Diana does not mention the pardons nor the rise of *menemismo* during this decade; *menemismo* was a neoliberal model that resulted in the privatization of national industries and social welfare programs, as well as increased rates of poverty and unemployment. But the absence of such details in *Mujeres guerrilleras* illuminates the tensions and gaps created by situating the ghosts of the armed struggle in the (then) neoliberal present. The fact that Diana avoids mention of Menem or the historical moment of 1995—and most significantly, the pardons—conjures the ghosts of Argentina's armed insurgent past, as the specters irrupt the present and disrupt Menem's and post-dictatorship Argentina's narrative of progress and reconciliation.

It is important to examine the notion of teleological progress that is often associated with neoliberalism and its relationship to the dominant narratives of Latin America's armed struggles. The dominant narrative that positions Latin America's socialist armed struggles as "failures"—as Argentine scholars Beatriz Sarlo, Hugo Vezzetti, and some former guerrilleros have asserted—has been interpreted as inevitable in order for the reign of neoliberalism to take hold in the Americas. The past of the armed struggle is also portrayed as a "paradigm of disillusion," where youthful and essentially political immature movements had to fail in order to give way to a mature, advanced political and economic system of neoliberalism. Beverley explains this further: "The illusion of the revolutionary transformation of society that was the inspiration for the armed struggle was our Romantic adolescence. It was generous and brave adolescence, but also one prone to excess, error, irresponsibility, and moral anarchy. By contrast, our biological and biographical maturity, represented by our role and responsibilities as parents and professionals, corresponds to the hegemony of neoliberalism in the eighties and nineties."[33] As I detail in the following section, many former guerrilleras I interviewed—and many of the guerrilleras' testimonies in *Mujeres guerrilleras*—directly challenge this dominant narrative that portrays these movements as guided by youthful idealism and destined to fail. Furthermore, the guerrilleras' testimonies evoke incompleteness, or what Diana calls "fragments," as the dominant history of the armed struggle has not fully acknowledged women's participation in the movements.

Gender and the Cultural Imaginary of Mexico's Armed Struggle

Although *Flor en Otomí* and *Mujeres guerrilleras* do not feign to offer "authentic" accounts of the armed insurgencies, the texts are also cognizant of the importance of survivor testimony in archiving women's experiences of this history and in the contribution to women's historical memory work. As Wendy S. Hesford and Wendy Kozol articulate, "cultural representations of the 'real' negotiate competing interests in the interstices of power, authority, and resistance." This is most evident in some cultural narratives' privileging of guerrilleros' accounts.[34] Kozol and Hesford argue that the privileging of subjugated people's narratives as the locus of truth and authenticity is problematic, but they also contend that it is important to contest historical inaccuracies and omissions of the experiences of these subjugated groups. The interviews I conducted with the guerrilleras do not purport to offer "real," "authentic" or all-encompassing versions of women's experiences in armed insurgencies in Mexico and Argentina. Instead, I am invested in the manner in which the gaps and fragments that are evoked in the narratives challenge the dominant masculinist discourse on the armed struggle and provide a place where the gendered ghosts of the armed insurgencies can seek justice.

Although both *Flor en Otomí* and *Mujeres guerrilleras* illuminate women's active participation in the elided histories of the armed struggle, both cultural texts relay what I believe are contradictory portrayals of femininity and motherhood. Turning first to Riley's *Flor en Otomí*, the film evokes a complex gender reading in the reconstruction of the guerrilleras' political agency. While much of the first half of the documentary centers on the development of Prieto Stock's political awareness during her adolescence, Riley also dedicates a significant portion of the film to addressing Prieto Stock's romantic relationships.[35] This can be interpreted as a contradiction in the film's intent, as it portrays Prieto Stock as an independent, politically conscious young woman who gave her life for a political cause. A critical limitation and tension emerges in the representation of Prieto Stock as, on the one hand, a politically radical young woman who made her own decisions, and on the other hand, a delicate, pretty teenager preoccupied with romance and dating.

The tension is exhibited in the film's first incorporation of Prieto Stock's personal letters addressed to her cousin, Laura Stock. Laura reads aloud a letter sent to her in 1969, wherein Prieto Stock recounts a new romantic interest, Juan. The next excerpt that Laura reads focuses on the political climate in Mexico as Prieto Stock mentions a political prisoner hunger strike that occurred in Mexico City. Afterward, Laura shares memories of Prieto Stock, where she notes that "hanging out with her boyfriends [and] going to parties" were just as important to Prieto Stock as her political activism.

After Laura Stock reads aloud the first letter, the film introduces a former childhood love interest and companion, Ramón, who discusses the first time he meets Prieto Stock. Accompanied by a sexy trumpet and guitar soundtrack, the camera then shifts to several photographs of Prieto Stock in alluring positions, including one photo of her lying in bed, smiling at the camera. Laura then reads passages of Prieto Stock's letter describing her attraction to Ramón, adding that "Dení was very flirtatious, really enjoyed having attention from all these boys ... she was very small, very pretty, very delicate." The comments are contrasted against Laura's follow-up observation that Prieto Stock "was her own thinker ... she wanted to read and understand things."

These key moments of the film reflect how Prieto Stock's political agency is mitigated by Riley's portrayal of a gender normative subjectivity. The film's first evocation of Prieto Stock's voice vis-à-vis the personal letters is centered on a romantic interest rather than a political memory. Riley's interview with Ramón represents Prieto Stock's gender in a way that emphasizes a teenage frivolity and a gendered sexuality rooted in normative assumptions. We must be critical of this particular representation, as Prieto Stock's political commitment is decentered in the film's repeated references to her diminutive, attractive physical form and multiple romantic interests, which reaffirm existing gendered notions of the guerrilleras.

Although *Flor en Otomí* does not explicitly claim that Prieto Stock joined the FLN and other political organizations due to her interest in young men, the assumption that women became politically engaged because of their male companions is a common narrative in the history of Latin America's Dirty War era. While some women were indeed exposed to political issues through their romantic partners, fathers, and so forth, it is important to examine the framing of such narratives. In my interview with Gutiérrez Campos, she informed me that her high school boyfriend, Arnulfo Prado Rosas, discussed politics extensively with her in 1960s Guadalajara, Mexico, and this connection exposed her to the political climate of the time. Prado Rosas was a dynamic leader of the student-led FER in Guadalajara, a group that challenged the presence of the government-backed right-wing student group, the FEG, at the University of Guadalajara. However, the brutal—and very public—murder of Prado Rosas by the FEG in downtown Guadalajara in 1970 ultimately radicalized Gutiérrez Campos and impelled her to join the *Liga*. "I found a meaning in my life, and that was to immerse myself completely in militant activism," she relayed to me, adding, "your commitment to service when you enter the guerrilla is a desire to serve humanity."

For Gutiérrez Campos, her political militancy is inextricably linked to the memory of her deceased partner at the hands of state officials. Yet, during our interview, she clearly asserted that her political agency was her own and that she made her own decision to join the armed struggle after his death. Hence, it is critical that we not represent romantic and sexual relationships among guerrilleros and political militants in ways that might mitigate the women's sense of agency. It is also important to remember that "typical" teenage girl interests—such as socializing and dating—should not be perceived as mutually exclusive from a politicized consciousness. That is, "typical" adolescent interests of the guerrilleras should not be perceived as interests that do not align with their commitment to radical politics; their multiple interests should be considered as different parts of the guerrilleras' multifaceted subjectivities, not as mutually exclusive interests.

While Gutiérrez Campos and other former guerrilleras are able to speak for their own histories, *Flor en Otomí* must rely on survivor testimonies to reconstruct Prieto Stocks's subjectivity. This contributes to the film's haunting, as Riley utilizes the voice of the living recipient of the letter to give voice to the deceased, while the camera simultaneously centers on images written in the deceased's hand. While Prieto Stock's personal letters are vital narrative resources in the portrayal of her life, we must carefully consider which excerpts are included in the representation of her subjectivity, since the letter excerpts reflect the pitfalls that appear in representations of former Mexican guerrilleras and contribute to the gendered haunting of the Dirty War era. Such limitations are not unique to documentary filmmaking. Narratives of loss, trauma, and death in oral histories must also contend with gaps, contradictions, and many specters. In my interviews with the former guerrillas, I was cognizant of the various limitations to which I allude in chapter 4 on feminist ethnographies and histories of political resistance in Latin America.

Despite the film's limitations, *Flor en Otomí* provides us with critical information that highlights the central roles women held in various guerrillas in 1970s Mexico. The film reflects the moments that shaped Prieto Stock's political trajectory and the conscious decision she made to join the FLN, which destabilize the masculinist historiography of the armed insurgency. Prieto Stock's political consciousness is presented in the film and many of the testimonies and excerpts of Prieto Stock's letters reflect her condemnation of the repressive political climate in 1970s Mexico. This is apparent in one sequence that commences with Laura Stock stating that "she [Dení] was responsible for her own education and opinions." The next scene includes an intertitle quoting from Prieto Stock's personal diary: "People are hungry, cold and all that. They ask me what it is to be a communist. My answer is: truly want everybody to have food, shelter, books, etc., and be willing to die for it. I'm simple, I know." Despite the self-proclaimed "simple" ideological beliefs that Prieto Stock espoused, this sequence shows that her political convictions were her own, as her cousin indicates. This appears in a letter Prieto Stock sends to her family explaining her decision to join the FLN: "You know that this is not a hasty decision but one made over years. Don't think I'm taking this as a romantic adventure." In her own words, she debunks the notion that women activists were overly romantic and spontaneous with their actions.

This portion of the film also challenges the dominant narrative of guerrilleros as idealistic, naïve, and impetuous; rather, it illuminates how the decision to join armed struggles is one that required forethought and careful decision-making. Maricela Balderas Silva of the Sinaloa chapter of the Liga echoes this sentiment. Reflecting on her decision to join the Liga, she stated that, while she did not fully consider all the risks involved, she ultimately joined the armed struggle because of her disillusionment with the one-party rule of the PRI in Mexico: "Yes, I want to change this country, I want to belong to that group, I think that that there should be liberty in this country, I don't think it should be one political party that controls everything in this country, where people cannot have their own opinion . . . to me it was very logical, very obvious that I would make that decision because I was not happy with the situation of my country." While Prieto Stock and Balderas Silva likely were unaware of the extent of the repressive mechanisms that the state would institute to annihilate their armed organizations, both women clearly articulated that theirs was not an impulsive or "hasty decision" to join the armed struggle, but rather one based on logic and political conviction.

Furthermore, the narratives question the tradition of documenting guerrilla activism as a male-centered revolutionary movement. *Flor en Otomí* also relays Prieto Stock's criticism of the gender politics that existed in many male-dominated guerrilla groups. The frame following an intertitle revealing her decision to join the FLN is a close-up of Benavides, discussing the chauvinism that surfaced at times in the Nepantla safe house. She recounts a moment when the compañeros asked the women to wear discreet clothing so they would not appear attractive to them: "María Luisa thought that was ridiculous. It made her laugh, and get upset . . . there came a point where she couldn't take it anymore. She would make fun of them, but sometimes she said: 'Look, stop calling me babe, stop calling us babes or else I'm going to start calling you . . . whatever.'" This sequence attests to Prieto Stock's exasperation with masculinist traditions that were embedded in many guerrillas and exposes her willingness to contest gender norms.

While *Flor en Otomí* alludes to the gender inequalities within the FLN, the concept of gender discrimination within the armed organizations is sometimes a contentious and contradictory topic for some former guerrilleras I interviewed in both Mexico and Argentina. The day before my interview with Gutiérrez Campos in Guadalajara in July 2012, I had the opportunity to interview her friend and former compañera in the Liga, Alejandra. When I asked Alejandra about the gender dynamics of the Liga and the People's Union (Union del Pueblo), she replied:

> Listen, those jerks of La Liga criticized me for being insubordinate, and because I didn't agree with some things . . . and then the others, members of the FRAP [People's Revolutionary Armed Forces, Fuerzas Revolucionarias Armadas del Pueblo], they also thought highly of me, but they were *machistas*, and for example they criticized Tita [Bertha Lilia Gutiérrez Campos], and criticized another compañera, and that bothered me, and with the People's Union . . . I reached a position of leadership, and they appreciated me a lot, they told me . . . at least those men in that moment who were in charge of the People's Union, because the most misogynist, the most radical was in prison . . . the People's Union called him a Guerrilla Hero but not me, not for me . . . because he was authoritative and misogynist . . . feminism is implicit in my political views, so that was what bothered them.

While Alejandra recalled Gutiérrez Campos being subjected to gender discrimination, Gutiérrez Campos stated that she did not experience this: "I never felt discriminated against, I always felt like I mattered, now I know that the men were in charge . . . and I never felt disrespected, rather the dynamic was one of brotherhood and respect. . . . My compañeros felt and we believed that we were creating the 'new man,' and the 'new woman,' and we wanted to be that, and so nobody ever had the intention of treating another compañera badly, nor do I think that ever happened." Gutiérrez Campos related that she was hesitant to use a feminist lens to analyze the dynamics of the guerrillas: "I would never say that [the guerrilleros] were *machistas*, demonizing the compañeros doesn't seem like a good idea . . . how am I going to label them with feminist terms when what they did was heroic." For her, criticizing the masculinist actions of the guerrilleros disrespected their memory. She continued: "I'm going to be very careful when I talk about my compañeros, for example some of then died during torture, others were disappeared, and others were in prison for many years."

I do not intend to criticize or disavow Gutiérrez Campos's account of her time in the Liga; her testimony does, however, evoke a sense of haunting that I infer as gendered. Clearly, Gutiérrez Campos is affected by the traumatic loss and violence inflicted by the state on former guerrilleros and her compañeros, and this shapes how she recounted her history of political activism in the Liga. It would seem, then, that respecting the memory of a (masculine) heroic revolutionary subject is critical to Gutiérrez Campos—and other guerrilleras—especially since the historical memory of the armed struggle in Mexico already inhabits a maligned and demonized position in the dominant narrative. However, Alejandra challenges this position by questioning the gendered constructs that emerged within leftist political organizations: "there couldn't be democracy with inequality even in the guerrilla groups, and wherever there was inequality, there could not be democracy. You want to democratize society, but you don't democratize your home, and then I realized that men and groups like the Church, the governments, are bothered more by a feminist than [a guerrillero] who is armed."

Although their narratives reveal conflicting accounts of the gender dynamics in the guerrillas, Prieto Stock, Balderas Silva, Alejandra, and Gutiérrez Campos all expressed political convictions that defied expectations of some of their *compañeros* as well as the gender norms dictated by the patriarchal Mexican state. As historian Adela Cedillo notes, "The fact that these women positioned themselves in a way that powerfully subverted gender norms represents women's emancipation and empowerment, which could be considered an empirical form of feminism, not a theoretical feminism."[36] In the foreword to *First National Assembly of Ex-Guerrilleras*, the organizers state: "We women integrated into the armed struggle, and in many ways we broke away from the role that society had assigned for us. We left behind our parents, our families, sometimes our children or the notion of having a comfortable life with a husband who would take care of us. We became involved in activities where we knew we could lose our lives. We knew we had to be brave and participate shoulder to shoulder with our male compañeros in the various tasks of the organizations."[37] The women not only contravened gender norms within the leftist armed movements, they represented a threat to the national, patriarchal order of the Mexican state. Hence, *Flor en Otomí* positions its protagonist as a guerrillera killed by the Mexican army and makes central the complex and unknown gender history and politics of the historical trauma of the Dirty War. The cultural texts and testimonies intervene into the dominant framings of the historical memory of the armed insurgencies; however, this model of historical memory conveys the ways in which loss is embedded in how the women remember the past and where absence constantly haunts the form and content of these cultural productions. The nuanced and at times contradicting testimonies and cultural texts illuminate the legacy of a gendered haunting of the revolutionary past on the Latin American imaginary.

Gendered haunting also occurs when the state attempts to erase any trace of the guerrilleras' involvement in these armed struggles. In *Flor en Otomí*, the state authorities literally eradicate Prieto Stock's existence from official records. As Ayari Prieto Stock, Dení's sister, recounts, the Mexican government had identified Prieto Stock as an "adulta desconocida" (Jane Doe/unidentified woman) on her death certificate, and her body was not returned to her family but instead placed in a mass grave. The death certificate denies Prieto Stock any political or historical relevancy. The legal document expunges all evidence of her subjectivity, except for her gender, which is denoted by the feminine pronoun. The inclusion of her gender on her death certificate as an identifying feature of her personhood exemplifies the state's attempt to disavow gendered participation in resistance movements in 1970s Mexico, since guerrilleras defied the norms of the patriarchal state. Even in death, the state regulates control over dissenting, gendered bodies by not only executing the power to determine who is to live or die, but also deciding whether or not their bodies are returned to the families, disappeared or released. State's control over their bodies even in death effectively denied ghosts a "hospitable memory," and the absence of the guerrilleras' presence in this history contributes to the gendered haunting.

The tonal atmosphere of a gendered haunting is established within the first few minutes of *Flor en Otomí*. Returning to the film's opening sequence, Riley includes the *Excelsior* newspaper article that lists Prieto Stock as one of the deceased "extremists" killed in the raid. The following scene takes place in the present day as a vehicle heads toward the safe house in Nepantla. Ayari's woman's voice recounts the history of the media coverage of the ambush. The camera is fixed ahead on the open highway on a clear, sunny day, as Ayari relays the shock on reading her sister's full name as listed among one of the deceased in the *Excelsior* article. The scene then cuts to Ayari's image as she continues her testimony, her face portraying the impact of reliving this trauma. Ayari describes the last conversation she had with her sister: "The time came, Dení stood up, looked at my parents and said: 'I'll be back later. Come with me to the door,' she said. They were picking her up and she had to go out to the gate at a certain time. Surprisingly, surprisingly, our parents didn't stand up. When my sister turned to them and said, 'I'll be back later,' that was the last time they saw her."

The conflation of the film's three narrative arcs in this sequence not only contributes to this "hazy feeling" of haunting, it also invokes the violence of the past—the site of Prieto Stock's death in the safe house—onto the temporal plane of the present by relying on the present tense to refer to the past. Ayari's evocation and repetition of her sister's final words—"I'll be back later"—suspends the narrative of the film in the temporal present of 1970s Mexico City, holding the spectators captive in this moment of frozen time. The final words furthermore imply a return, as Dení promises her family that she will be back "later." Of course, the promise went unfulfilled since she became one of the many victims killed by the Mexican state. By commencing the film in this manner, Riley introduces the haunting nature of Mexico's Dirty War to the audience and creates an anticipatory tone to the film as we await the return of Prieto Stock and other ghosts of this era. The spectral elements evoked in Prieto Stock's final words are indicative of Derrida's concept of hauntology as articulated in *Specters of Marx*: "everything begins by the apparition of a specter. More precisely by the waiting for this apparition."[38] At the start of *Flor en Otomí*, we spectators are held captive and made uneasy by the impossibility of awaiting Prieto Stock's return. Furthermore, her final words, "I'll be back later," serve as the film's introduction as it "begins by the apparition of a specter," the specter of Prieto Stock and other victims of the Dirty War. The opening sequence sets the tone of the film as Riley—and the spectators—must contend with the unrecognized legacy of these (gendered) specters.

Gender, Haunting, and Argentina's Armed Struggle

The haunting created by the guerrilleras' apparition is further evident in Marta Diana's 1996 *Mujeres guerrilleras*, where she investigates the disappearance of her childhood friend Adriana Lesgart and that of other former Argentine Montoneras. As Marta Diana immerses herself in her research for *Mujeres guerrilleras*, retracing the steps that led to Adriana's decision to join the Montoneros, she grapples with the inevitable absences in this history. The gaps and uncertainties, however, are clearly gendered; little information is available on the history of Argentinean women who joined the armed struggle in the early 1970s. Argentinean feminist historians Karin Grammático, Andrea Andújar, and Débora D'Antonio assert that while there has been an increase of scholarship produced on Argentinean history of the 1960s and 1970s since the early 2000s, there is still very little critical interrogation of the gender politics of this era.[39]

Diana's *Mujeres guerrilleras* is a testament to the gaps and fissures that result from the lack of gender scholarship on Argentina's armed struggle. Diana's text is pathbreaking as it is one of the only texts to center exclusively on the history and testimonies of former Argentine guerrilleras; yet as she tries to reconstruct the history of Adriana and other guerrilleras' militancy in the Montoneros, she encounters more questions, uncertainties, and silences.[40] She notes during her interviews with the women that "it seems that I am submerged each time into a sea of pain, hatred, indignation and impotence, where one floats by as best one can, to the border, many times, of failure."[41] However, it is precisely by immersing ourselves in the gray areas of "indignation and impotence" that we encounter the gendered specters of the armed struggles who may emerge and reclaim their histories of political agency and, perhaps, attain a kind of justice.

Although the legacy of the Latin American armed struggle in contemporary political and academic discourses is polemical and often fraught in nature, these particular political and scholarly debates often center on a masculine subject of the guerrilla. As Ileana Rodríguez contends, the subjectivity of the guerrillero is always already masculine, and the subject positionality is therefore a "masculine I . . . [aimed] at narrating a collective subject that does not include women."[42]

Despite the predominance of the masculine "I"/subject in the discourses on Argentina's armed struggle, most of the women Diana interviews in *Mujeres guerrilleras* expressed a desire to reclaim and reposition themselves as protagonists of the movements. Indeed, the former guerrilleras I interviewed in Buenos Aires in 2014 similarly asserted themselves as politically aware and driven young women who consciously decided to join these groups with little regret. There is a parallel in the personal interviews I conducted in 2014 to the interviews included in *Mujeres guerrilleras* that evince the urgency in rescripting the narratives of the armed struggle so that they validate the guerrilleras' experiences. In my interview with Liliana Forchetti in 2014, a former member of the ERP in Tucumán, Argentina, and a former political prisoner, she recounted: "Look, I was young, they were my ideals and I think the most wonderful time of my life, no, I say that even with all that had to happen after all. . . . I think it was my attempt I made for change, beyond the defeat, I say it was worth a try . . . to me it was wonderful and I also met the nicest people." Forchetti historicized her testimony during a time in which her youth, political consciousness, and idealism converge and inspired her to dedicate herself to the ERP. Despite the repression and years of incarceration she and many others endured as a result of her political activity, Forchetti denoted that this signified for her "the most wonderful time of [her] life." Similarly, in *Mujeres guerrilleras*, Diana interviewed Nelida Augier, who asserted that "we aimed to represent the community. Even still, I feel proud for having participated in that generation of Argentines. . . . But above all I will not remain silent, because I was a militant in the PRT and I was one of the founders of the ERP." In another interview Diana conducted, former Montonera "Negrita" reflected on an idyllic era of their youth: "For me, it was a beautiful experience to be a militant. . . . I do not regret the struggle that we endured because our reasons were just." Another guerrillera, Mariana, revealed in an interview with Diana that she joined the guerrilla because she believed in "a better society, more just and free, where 'new' men and women could live in another way. And it's only by understanding that dream [of a better society] that one can understand the decision to join the guerrilla, which was very difficult and resulted in the loss of many lives."[43]

Mariana and other guerrilleras frequently refer to the concept of "the new man and new woman" in their testimonies. This notion of "the new man" illuminates another important facet of the gendered history of Latin America's armed insurgencies. As Rodríguez examines in her text on Central American guerrillas, the ideal subject of the revolution is the "warrior/guerrilla-*guerrillero*," a "new man" who is closely linked to the masculinity of the guerrilla warrior and the "I" of Che.[44] Rodriguez's scholarship importantly points to the masculinization of the subject-positionality of the "new man," even though many guerrilleras discuss the importance of creating both a "new man" and a "new woman." Thus, *Mujeres guerrilleras* and the oral histories I conducted in Argentina reveal a critical tension that emerges in relation to the concept of the "new man" and the guerrilleras' reaffirmation of their political subjectivity: while many former guerrilleras assert their political positionality and pride for having participated in this history of revolutionary struggle, there seems to be no place for the creation of a "new woman" in the left's dominant narrative on the armed insurgency. That is, the absence of acknowledging or interrogating the gendered history and politics of Argentina's armed organizations contributes to the haunting of its revolutionary past in the present. The current debates on the armed struggle center the hetero-masculine/I and "new man" as the subject of the discourse on the armed struggle. This, in turn, unsettles the public imaginary on Argentina's revolutionary past as gendered specters of the armed struggle have no recourse to seek justice.

The interviews in *Mujeres guerrilleras* allude to this masculinization of the "new man" and gender inequality within the structure of the armed organizations. To some guerrilleras, gender equality was subsumed under the general political platform of a socialist revolution. As "La Gringa" explained to Diana, "the topic of women was not discussed back then as it is discussed today, and in that moment women were not separated from what we considered the overall social struggle."[45] It is critical to historicize the interviews and oral histories because these women are reflecting on the gender dynamics of their experiences of the armed struggle nearly twenty years after participating in the organizations. Several of the women I interviewed in 2012 and 2014 used a feminist lens to speak of the gender dynamics of the 1960s and 1970s, and several noted that the issue of gender equality was not its own separate agenda. As Forchetti explained to me in 2014: "The gender issue becomes central years later . . . in the '70s. . . . We did not discuss gender, feminism . . . we focused on imperialism, dependency, class struggles, the transformation of our society, and what the transformation of our society would entail for our struggle, a transformation of this patriarchal situation that is tied to the capitalist system, but I'm saying, we were looking at it [gender equality] through that lens, we did not specifically consider the situation of women, no." Thus, while some former guerrilleras specifically mentioned the concept of creating both a "new man" and a "new woman," the overall goal of combatting capitalism and attaining social justice and equality was at the core of their revolutionary objective. As Argentine scholar Isabella Cosse points out, feminist historians centering on the history of Argentine leftist organizations reveal that gender equality "took a back seat to the more important strategic goal of seizing political power."[46] In this vein, some former guerrilleras asserted that gender discrimination was not part of their personal experience in the guerrilla. When I asked Mirta Sgro about the gender dynamics of her time in the ERP, she told me: "I always considered it to be a time where I least noticed gender differences, the [ERP] was an opportunity for me in all aspects, as a person, as a woman, as a mother, for me, it was an experience that never limited me, but instead, it allowed us to fulfill our ideals at that time." She did say, however, that she knows of other former guerrilleras who experienced gender bias within their organizations. Sgro added that while she personally never had any problems with the compañeros of ERP, she recalled that divisions did exist, particularly when it came to assigning labor according to gender.

To many guerrilleras, however, gender division of labor did not necessarily mean that they were actively discriminated against by the guerrilleros in their organizations. Forchetti discussed this further with me: "It's true that we [women] were the ones who performed most household chores, but because, because the private realm was not just relegated to the home, I mean, our home life and private life were an integral part of the communal whole." For the Montoneros and the ERP, the political was indeed personal, especially for the guerrilleros who lived in safe houses with other members of the organization. As Forchetti noted, there was an integration of the (feminine) private sphere with the (masculine) political sphere, with no distinct separation between the two worlds. For many of the women, then, their identities as politically active women, mothers, and partners were integral to their overall subjectivity as guerrilleras and their "communal whole."

It is precisely this blurring of the private/public and feminine/masculine binarism that seemed to trouble Marta Diana in her conversations with former guerrilleras. While *Mujeres guerrilleras* is a text that attempts to re-subjectivize and validate the histories of women who participated in the armed struggle, Diana at times seems unable to reconcile the traditional gender norms associated with women (as mothers and caretakers) with their positions as armed combatants. This is most evident when Diana discovers that Adriana had participated in the assassination attempt of Juan Gelman for his alleged defection from the Montoneros' cause. Diana's memory of her childhood friend as "reserved," "sensible," and "sweet" does not align with this particular image of Adriana, armed with a machine gun, engaging in an assassination attempt. The anecdote—and other narratives—contradict Diana's own ideas about political militancy and feminine behavior, and she is therefore haunted by these images of Adriana as "violent" or "rebellious." Understanding that Diana will never have the complete account of this story, she is "left with a gap" and with the following unanswered questions: "Did her commitment to an ideology change [Adriana] that much?" "What would Adriana have told me about this incident if we had been able to meet up?"[47] This "gap" to which Diana refers is indicative of the inevitable absence in documenting women's involvement in the armed insurgencies, as many of the women are no longer here to provide their narratives; furthermore, this sense of unease Diana experiences alludes to tensions that are derived from guerrilleras who disrupt gendered expectations of women engaging in armed activity.

Diana's discomfort uncovers the gendered notion that guerrilla warfare and violence pertains to the masculine-public realm, illuminating internal contradictions within the structuring of the armed groups. While former guerrilleras such as Sgro and Forchetti attest to gender equality in their organizations, they also reveal that women were sometimes prohibited from participating in certain dangerous operations. As Cosse states, "while the incorporation of women in guerrilla training camps expressed a commitment to gender equality, it also fueled fears of those who valued the contribution of women but—heeding Che Guevara's advice—believed they were better suited to the rearguard."[48] Being positioned in the "rearguard" meant that guerrilleras were sometimes not involved in armed activities, and these ideals are rooted in a masculinist logic that ordered the guerrillas. Pilar Calveiro states that "militarization is based on a masculine logic" and that this revolutionary masculinity relies on "the use of violence and aptitudes that were socially created for men."[49] Thus, the revolutionary guerrilla subject is always assumed to be male, and women who inhabited this role destabilized not only traditional gender expectations posited by Argentine society, but also challenged the allotted roles for women within leftist armed political organizations.

Perhaps what is most troubling to Diana, however, is the question of motherhood and armed militancy, as the latter evokes a subject position of violence, and the former connotes nurturing and affection. In *Mujeres guerrilleras*, Diana appears supportive of the political ideology of the Montoneros and the ERP; however, she clearly disagrees with the decision to take up arms. This particular criticism of the armed struggle is gendered as she opines that motherhood and armed militancy are irreconcilable. For Diana, woman-as-guerrillera and woman-as-mother are mutually exclusive subject positionalities and she appears unable to reconcile Adriana-as-mother with Adriana-as-guerrillera. After her interview with former Montonera Mercedes, the topic of militancy and motherhood arose; Diana and Mercedes disagreed on whether a guerrillera was right for leaving her child in her friends' and her husband's care in order to join the armed struggle. Diana believed that her commitment as a mother superseded her obligation to the armed struggle, a belief that I argue reifies gendered notions of biologically predetermined roles for woman-as-mother and cultural expectations of woman-as-nurturer.

The above refers to another tension that appears in *Mujeres guerrilleras*; as Diana strives to represent the political subjectivities of the guerrilleras, she seemingly places more importance on the guerrilleras' roles as mothers and reaffirms traditional expectations of motherhood. In a sense, this evokes a similar tension that appears in *Flor en Otomí*, as Riley devotes a significant portion of the film to Prieto Stock's feminine features and romantic relationships. Both Diana and Riley's cultural productions, I would argue, seem disturbed by a central contradiction between feminine gender expressions and maternal expectations on the one hand, and, on the other hand, women's participation in dangerous and sometimes violent operations in the armed struggle.

Rather than disavowing Diana's perspective here, however, I would like to center on the tension her text elicits as it challenges us to contend with traditional notions of motherhood. This furthermore what Diana calls a "hueco" (gap) in the scholarship conducted on the nuanced and often contradictory gender history of the armed struggle. The question of gender, motherhood, and armed insurgency requires more investigation and conversation.[50] Returning again to Diana and Mercedes's conversation about the guerrillera who left her daughter behind with friends, Mercedes argues that this represented "another level of consciousness" and that the girl's mother was "acting like a revolutionary, and she was also fighting for her daughter and she was not abandoning her."[51] Similarly, Mirta Sgro expressed to me in our interview that her identity as a guerrillera in the ERP did not contradict her identity as a mother. She said that the guerrilleros had carefully considered and discussed the topic of having children while active in the resistance, and she came to a conscious, informed decision. She explained: "Personally at that time, for me, militancy was absolutely about inclusiveness, it was my life . . . the children . . . for me, they had to be at the center of this life. . . . I felt my militant life . . . was the life I had chosen and in that life, I wanted to have children. And also for me, we were working so that they [our children] could live in a completely different world." Thus, guerrilleras in the 1970s were women who not only challenged gender norms by participating in political organizations, they furthermore defied social codes of conduct as proper woman—most significantly, as proper mothers—by using arms to attain their revolutionary goals. Even for leftist sympathizers like Diana, political ideologies based on non-violence are best suited for mothers. However, armed combat belongs to the realm of men, and thus, as mothers and women, armed guerrilleras ultimately defied strict gender and social codes of conduct. The question of violence, especially politically motivated violence, is irreconcilable with proper codes of Argentine femininity and motherhood.

Oftentimes dominant narratives and debates on the Argentine guerrillas tend to reduce the multifaceted, heterogeneous aspects of the history of the armed struggle to this question of violence and the taking up of arms. This reductionist lens fails to critically explore the narratives of women's experiences in this history and invariably elides their important, multiperspectival accounts on their time in the armed insurgencies. That particular lens can provide a myopic and reductionist account of the history of armed struggle. As many guerrilleras stated in *Mujeres guerrilleras*, the question of taking up arms represented only a small component in the overall historical narrative of their political activism.

The cultural memory of the history of the armed struggle has centered on a narrative of criminalization that has deeply affected the lives of many former guerrilleros. Returning again to my interview with Gutiérrez Campos, I am still struck by the haunting and opaque feeling of loss that she communicated during the day we spent together. After the trip to the former detention center, Oblatos prison, she offered to show me around the neighborhood in which she grew up and where she was politicized as a young adult. After treating me to an ice cream, Gutiérrez Campos and I strolled around the plaza near her childhood home, near the barrio where she would reunite with other future guerrillas. She continued to share with me memories of her youth and activism and even showed me the area of town where agents of the state murdered her young partner, Prados Rosas. The palimpsest of trauma, loss, and impunity in these spatial locations of the city deepen the sense of haunting that emerges in cultural representations of Mexico's and Argentina's revolutionary movements of the 1970s.

The legacy of this revolutionary past is apparent in very real ways that affect former guerrilleras' lives today. For example, Gutiérrez Campos told me that it took years for the Mexican state to expunge her criminal record. The criminalization of political activists during this period affected their ability to perform tasks such as apply for a job, purchase property, and so on. Therefore, not only did Gutiérrez Campos and other former guerrilleras experience the devastating loss of friends and compañeros, but they had to witness and contend with the impunity that the perpetrators enjoyed for years. Furthermore, she personally had to grapple with the real effects this trauma had on her daily life and the many social interactions after her release from prison. As a survivor, Gutiérrez Campos still struggles with the daily difficulties and stigma attached to former guerrillas in a culture that does not want to recognize its history of state and gendered violence. As the following chapter shows, the gendered haunting that comes from the trauma of surviving state-sanctioned violence has shaped the way women have articulated their experiences of loss and resistance in interviews I conducted in Mexico and Argentina. The final chapter uncovers the feminist theory and knowledge that can be found in the oral histories of women participants of revolutionary groups of the Dirty War era, where many of the women transformed traumatic experiences into a site of collective solidarity and action.

CHAPTER FOUR

Gendered Memories, Collective Subjectivity, and Solidarity Practices in Women's Oral Histories

> Memory is embodied and sensual, that is, conjured through the senses; it links the deeply private with social, even official, practices. Sometimes memory is difficult to evoke, yet it's highly efficient; it's always operating in conjunction with other memories "all of them pulsing, regularly, in order."
> —Diana Taylor, *Archive and the Repertoire*

> We survived.... We have never stopped fighting. We have never stopped marching.... I have to continue, and why? ... And for what reason? So that this may be known, that justice may be done so that this may never happen again.
> —Ana Ignacia Rodríguez Márquez, member of the 1968 Mexico City student movement

"I was born, raised, abducted, and reappeared, all in La Plata" (Yo soy nacida, criada, secuestrada, reaparecida y todo en La Plata), Nilda Eloy stated at the commencement of our interview, conducted on July 22, 2009, in La Plata, Argentina. It was a politically assertive way of responding to the interview's opening question, "where were you born?" My May 2010 interview with former political prisoner of the 1960s Mexico City student movement, Ana Ignacia Rodríguez Márquez, began similarly: "My name is Ana Ignacia Rodríguez Márquez and

I'm known as la Nacha from the movement, precisely because the armed forces, the authorities, gave us an alias in order to criminalize our movement. But la Nacha comes from my name Ignacia and so they gave me 'la Nacha' as a nickname, as an alias . . . because they tried to criminalize us, and our movement."

At the start of the interviews, both Eloy and Rodríguez Márquez, along with the thirteen other women I interviewed in Argentina and Mexico between 2009 and 2014, situated their personal narratives within Argentina's and Mexico's histories of political repression and state-sponsored violence. I met Nilda Eloy after I attended a weekly meeting of the AEDD in Buenos Aires in the summer of 2009. An active member of the AEDD and other La Plata human rights organizations, Eloy was a survivor of six different clandestine centers and concentration camps that operated in the Buenos Aires region during the military dictatorship. Eloy poetically and powerfully connected her place of birth to the history of her disappearance and reappearance during the Argentinean dictatorship. As a *reaparecida* (reappeared person), Eloy survived one of Argentina's most harrowing forms of state terrorism: mass disappearance of Argentineans deemed by the dictatorship to be political subversives.[1] Eloy's very survival and subjectivity as a reappeared person exposes the dictatorship's intent to criminalize, exterminate, and disappear unwanted bodies and ideologies from the nation. In a similar vein, Rodríguez Márquez began our interview by referring to the Mexican state's criminalization of the student movement. Rodríguez Márquez was a witness and survivor of the October 2, 1968, massacre in Mexico City. Originally from Taxco, Rodríguez Márquez became an active participant in the student movement once she moved to Mexico City to study law at the National Autonomous University of Mexico (UNAM, Universidad Nacional Autónomo de México). Days after the massacre, she was arrested and sentenced to sixteen years in prison, where she served two years and was released in 1970 due to international human rights pressure from Germany. In the above passage, she appropriated the once-denigrating alias assigned to her by the Mexican officials, Nacha, and infused it with new, politicized meaning that linked her name to her activism during the movement.

Eloy's and Rodríguez Márquez's opening statements challenge the master narratives constructed both by the Argentinean and Mexican states that have criminalized women's participation in socialist movements. The Mexican and Argentine states instituted policies that sanctioned the use of extralegal violence against men and women deemed a threat to national security. As mentioned in the introduction to this book, the states justified their repressive policies by relying on a discourse of criminalization that positioned political activists as subversives who threatened the nation's welfare. The narrative of criminalization pervaded the national imaginary for decades and is linked to the Two Devils theory, which establishes a false equivalency between the violence committed by the Argentinean and Mexican governments and the guerrilla groups. In the decades after the Dirty Wars, Argentina—and to a lesser degree, Mexico—adopted a human rights narrative that emphasized teleological progress and legitimated the contemporary neoliberal government while the government distanced itself from the nation's recent history of state-sponsored crimes. Official state narratives have deeply affected the national consciousness, which not only continues to read these former members of leftist political groups as terrorists and criminals, but this emphasis on historical progress also alludes to state-sponsored *olvido*, or forgetting, of their recent histories of violence.

The women's interviews also challenge another master narrative set forth by leftist, political organizations that have ignored the gendered hierarchies within these groups, as well as the gendered dynamics of state violence. For many years in post-dictatorship Argentina, state-backed human rights organizations focused on a gender-neutral victim of human rights violations in order to denounce crimes of the state. When specific cases of gender-based violence were addressed in official human rights accounts, many of the women were portrayed as apolitical victims of a despotic military regime. For Mexican women survivors of state violence, their stories were largely ignored by the state (along with some of their male compañeros), and in the rare occasion that human rights violations were acknowledged by the state, the former leaders (mostly male) of leftist organizations spoke for the collective group. Many women were joining leftist political groups in 1970s Latin America in record numbers; women comprised between 20 percent and 30 percent of Southern Cone socialist militant groups in that period, resulting in a demographic shift that allowed women to participate more actively in politics.[2] In many Argentinean and Mexican leftist political groups of the time, gender equality was espoused but not always practiced, and many women in these groups encountered sexism and a gendered hierarchy. Although more recent scholarship has focused on the gender dynamics of armed and unarmed leftist political organizations that were active during the Dirty Wars, there is still a need to explore the transnational dimensions of women's experiences of gender discrimination in order to unearth parallel experiences of ingrained sexism in the organizations.[3] To this end, the women's memories of activism and resistance deepen our understanding of the Dirty Wars and the solidarity practices evoked in their testimonies reflect their efforts to combat state-sanctioned olvido.

This chapter centers on interviews I conducted with twelve women, all of whom were survivors of state trauma and members of different leftist political organizations during Argentina's and Mexico's Dirty Wars. The interviews examined here contest dominant narratives that have positioned women's stories on the periphery. The interviewees' memories of state violence intervene into dominant narratives that have excluded them or have situated them as apolitical victims of state terror. In their oral histories, the women rescript and recuperate an historical memory that centers their experiences in the revolutionary movements during the Dirty Wars. Their memories often require a return to their experiences of past traumas, and this repeated return to the past disrupts the state's emphasis on teleological progress. The structure of trauma is cyclical, and as Dori Laub asserts, trauma "is an event that has no beginning, no ending, no before, no during and no after."[4] The very act of speaking out against past crimes and their survival is a constant reminder of the legacy of state terrorism. The nonlinear progression of the interviews creates an alternative structure to the chronology of their narratives, irrupting the dominant, mainstream narratives that have produced hegemonic knowledges on the Dirty Wars. To this end, the women's oral history memory projects serve as critical "disruptive archival" sources that create a feminist epistemological shift by producing new knowledge on the gendered history of the Dirty War.

Moreover, the very nature of trauma inevitably creates gaps in memory production and knowledge formation precisely because the traumatic experience can never be encountered again. Surviving harrowing acts of state trauma, coupled with the passage of time, can lead to gaps in memory, distortions, or inaccuracies in the oral histories. Traumatic experiences, in turn, shape how language is produced when one is speaking—or not speaking—of the past in the present.[5] The lapses, however, point to what I call the transformative possibilities of trauma in women's oral histories of solidarity and resistance. It is the very structure of trauma that allows us to intervene in these women's gaps and silences and interrogate the meanings that are produced there. The interviews' disjointed, nonlinear narrative structure is caused by the retelling of traumatic memories and often results in gaps and lapses in their memories. The oral histories are critical disruptive archives that evince the importance of not only what the oral histories relate in their content, but how these memories are expressed. This, in turn, creates a form of embodied knowledge that implicates us, the listener and researcher, in the formation of this knowledge.[6] As a mediator of cultural texts (the interviews), I am cognizant of the ways in which I intervene in this construction of knowledge by writing about the silences and embodied expressions in the interviews that are produced by trauma. Building on Maylei Blackwell's and Diana Taylor's conceptualization of embodied knowledge as that which does not "fit into the realm of documentary evidence" and eludes the archive, this chapter considers how the interviews relay the transformative possibilities of trauma and solidarity as they rescript the master narratives that set forth active forgetting, or olvido, of women's histories of resistance.[7] The embodied memories, the disruptive archives, contribute to formation of new feminist knowledge on women's histories of resistance in Latin America.

The women's memories of individual and collective historical traumas recuperate their positions as protagonists of this history and reveal the radical politics of solidarity. Borrowing from oral historian Alessandro Portelli's concept of "history telling," which looks at the "connection between biography and history, [and] between individual experience and the transformation of society," I argue that the women's narratives of trauma and survival evince the radical possibilities of Latin American oral history telling and its importance in unearthing feminist perspectives of the Dirty War.[8] In each interview I conducted, the women clearly asserted their political agency in revolutionary movements, while also denouncing the normalization of state terrorism and olvido. Here, then, oral history serves as an essential feminist methodological tool to create a space for archiving gendered memories of resistance and solidarity and as oral historian Daniel James notes, "enables us to approach the issues of agency and subjective intervention in history."[9] The oral histories of trauma, solidarity, and resistance subvert dominant discourses that have erased their histories; in their radical act of oral history telling, the women create new memory projects and situate themselves as agents of social change. Furthermore, they importantly situate themselves as active producers of knowledge on the gendered histories of the Dirty War.

Latin American Women's Oral Histories

The oral histories in this chapter center on women's memories of political repression and activism during Argentina's and Mexico's Dirty Wars. Almost all the interviews relay a sense of urgency and in the case of the Mexican women I interviewed, their narratives exhibit a desire to document histories of activism in a national memory that has actively excluded them. In July 2012 I interviewed Alejandra, a former guerrillera of Guadalajara's Liga and People's Union in the early 1970s. She informed me that it was important for her to share her story and speak out against Mexican state violence precisely because so little is known about the history of the guerrillas. Similarly, Rodríguez Márquez told me that she "never refused doing an interview," despite the risks that speaking of past traumas could incur psychologically and physiologically. Even in Argentina, where survivor testimony of the dictatorship is more accessible to the general public, the women I interviewed stated that there is still more that must be shared regarding the cultural memory of gendered trauma and state violence. In the summer of 2009, I interviewed Marta Díaz, a former political prisoner from Rosario, Argentina, who was detained by the armed forces in 1979 and sentenced to prison for her participation in the Armed Revolutionary Forces (FAR, Fuerzas Armadas Revolucionarias). During our interview, she stated: "This history is incomplete. There's this part, and another, and it is unknown. We complete the history together, in order to have a more complete picture of this history. And it will never be complete, it will never be complete. State terrorism concealed it, so there are things we will never find out (*pause*)."

Díaz's words point to the challenges and possibilities of oral history as a feminist methodological tool. As some historians have argued, the passage of time can distort memories or produce inaccuracies in their accounts, particularly when the memories recount histories of trauma. However, as Latin American oral historians Gerardo Necoechea García and Andrés Torres Montenegro state, oral histories should not necessarily be studied as "credible sources," but rather, their "fissures" and "contradictions . . . should be studied hermeneutically."[10] These histories will always be incomplete, as Díaz tells us, because the nature of trauma does not allow for the survivor to return to the moment in the past and recount it as it happened, thus producing gaps and silences in the narrative. The gap in her testimony—evident in the ellipses and pause after her statement—exhibits the effect of state trauma and its ability to conceal an "unknown" history, a part of history that will always be controlled by the state. While the factual basis of oral sources has long been debated, many of the interviews document empirical historical facts that are not widely known and contribute to the growing literature on the Dirty Wars. This is particularly important in the Mexican Dirty War context, as the scarcity of knowledge and literature on this historical period reflects the success of the master narratives in submerging non-hegemonic histories of state violence.

This chapter does not attempt to revisit the debates over the legitimacy of oral history as a methodological approach when centering on documenting histories of revolutionary struggle and state terror. However, I would like to echo previous scholars' emphasis on the possibilities of oral history, particularly from a feminist perspective, as the women's voices reveal the importance of using a gendered lens to examine what has *not* been disclosed in other histories of Latin American state violence. In an important sense, oral histories provide us with intimate portraits of individual and collective experiences, and often voice histories from below that have been excluded from official historiography. For Latin Americanists, particularly historians, oral history has been an invaluable research method that has unearthed histories of resistance and political action in the latter twentieth century.[11] The tradition of Latin American oral historiography has strong ties to the Latin American *testimonio*, a literary genre that made its mark internationally with the publication of Rigoberta Menchu's testimonial text in 1983. While indeed its own genre, the testimonio and Latin American oral historiography both center on recuperating narratives from below, with special attention to marginalized subjectivities and histories of political, racial, gendered, and indigenous resistance to state power.[12] In this chapter, I rely on the term "oral history" rather than "testimonio" because the former term captures the dialogic relationship between interviewer and interviewee and importantly centers on the embodied knowledge evinced in the aural processes of disseminating information.

As Argentinean historian Pablo Pozzi notes, the tradition of oral history in Latin America that started in the 1950s has continued to encompass academics and activists invested in the recuperation of historical memory in the Americas.[13] Latin American historians Necoechea Gracia and Patricia Pensado Leglise's text on the histories of leftist militancy in Latin America demonstrates this growing body of scholarship on oral historiography and its specific focus on the forgotten histories of revolutionary struggle during Latin America's Dirty Wars. The pathbreaking work by scholars and academic organizations has demonstrated the importance of utilizing oral history when researching histories of resistance to Latin American state repression. This body of work furthermore reflects the growing attention that Latin American cultural anthropologists and oral historians have placed on women's subjectivities. Hence, this chapter contributes to an expanding body of literature by adding a feminist and cultural studies lens to women's oral narratives of leftist militancy in Latin America.

What's more, my approach to the interviews relied on a feminist framework and this chapter builds on the critical scholarship by Latin American, US, and UK feminist oral historians, among them Joan Sangster, Elizabeth Jelin, Daniel James, Ana María Araujo, and Janine Comes da Silva. Since the early 1970s, oral history has been a critical methodology used by feminist scholars to validate women's lived experiences and to challenge official "truths" and knowledge in traditional historiography. Over the past few decades, however, poststructuralist theory has emphasized the textual form and linguistic structure of the oral source, which some feminist scholars have argued has diminished feminist oral history's "radical edge" by questioning the relationship between experience and representation, thus reducing women's agency.[14] For Latin American feminist scholars in particular, oral history plays a key role in recognizing women's political agency and resistance to authoritarian regimes. To that end, as Alejandra

Oberti notes, this methodology "offers new ways to understand the past and redefine the tools we use to analyze the recent past in order to develop a critical memory" by centering specifically on "what cannot be so easily represented."[15]

Of course, my engagement with the interviews is based on my own subjective analysis of the women's testimonies. While much of my analysis in this chapter is based on the textual transcriptions of the interviews, it is critical to center on the embodied memories of the interviews. I approach oral histories as critical cultural texts that provide us with important, if incomplete, histories of politically active women in resistance movements in Mexico and Argentina. Oftentimes narratives of survival and trauma illuminate competing or contradictory experiences in their political organizations, and it is imperative that we examine these interviews as cultural products that are informed, shaped, and influenced by their positionality, perspective, and location.

This chapter engages deeply with the gaps, contradictions, and silences that can emerge in the oral narratives of the women and how the women perceive themselves as active historical subjects of social change. While the textual transcripts do not necessarily relay the gestures, pauses, sighs, tears, and other embodied memories that were shared during the interviews, it is also critical to be cognizant of the affective dimension of oral history-telling. Thus, as already noted, it was essential to pay attention to not just what women's histories revealed but to how their histories were told. In addition, the process of giving testimony reflected the speaker's subjectivity, and how they saw themselves as agents of social change. In this chapter, I closely examine the complex structure of the women's oral histories, particularly in how these memories are articulated; the oral history memory projects convey how loss is embedded in remembrance and how absence constantly haunts speech, producing gaps, lapses, and contradictions in these oral histories. It is precisely *within* these gaps and contradictions that this chapter explores the new feminist knowledge on Latin America's Dirty Wars and histories of women's political militancy.

In Díaz's statement quoted above, she alludes to the transformative possibility of trauma and solidarity as she and other survivors work to "complete this history together." For the women I interviewed, invoking a collective subjectivity of oral history telling allowed the possibility of speaking out against their histories of gendered state trauma and combatted the legacy of silence and impunity that is deeply etched into the national consciousness. The plural narrative voice is a dominant thread throughout many of the women's oral histories, and the recuperation of the political history of their individual narrative is an essential part of their history telling. As Blackwell and other feminist oral historians note, "re-membering is a vital act in creating political subjectivity" and is couched within a political framework that calls on a collective memory of surviving state violence.[16] The women's oral histories illustrate this relationship between individual and collective memory and the meaning that is made from surviving shared histories of gendered state violence.

Representing Gendered State Violence: The Individual and the Collective Subject

At the start of the 2012 documentary film, *Campo de batalla, cuerpo de mujer,* a survivor of the Argentinean dictatorship Sylvia Nybroe declares, "Nobody has ever sat down with and told me, 'Hey, tell me what happened,' ... And nobody has ever stayed to listen to what I had to say."[17] As Nybroe and the women I interviewed mentioned in their testimonies, what happens if no one listens or even wants to listen to the histories of gender-based violence? How does this silence and lack of an empathetic listener affect the ways in which gendered memories of trauma are represented, if represented at all? The role of the listener is critical, and the absence of an engaged listener contributes to another layer of trauma, the dimension of olvido, or forgetting. Oral histories based on trauma invariably call on the listener, an active participant in the formation of memories of resistance to state-sponsored terrorism.

In Argentina, gender-based repression was a central component to systemic torture in the carceral spaces. In the summer of 2009, I interviewed Margarita Cruz, survivor of the Escuelita de Famaillá clandestine detention center in Tucumán, Argentina. Cruz was abducted from her home in 1975 during the constitutional government of Isabel Martínez de Perón, one year before the coup d'état of 1976. She was detained in the Escuelita de Famaillá, which instructed military officials in torture. The abduction and repression of many political dissidents in the Tucumán province was committed during a counter-resistance operation by the government in 1974 called the Independence Operation (Operativo Independencia). Her interview debunks the narrative that state violence only occurred during the years of the dictatorship. During our interview, she discussed the ways in which men and women were treated in the centers: "We don't distinguish between men and women who were in the clandestine centers. But, yes I believe that the subjectivity of women, that the repression manifested differently and had different consequences. For that reason yes, it wasn't the same, from the perspective of gender." Cruz's statement reflected a tension between retaining the collective, politicized subject of testimony in order to denounce state-sanctioned crimes, and on the other hand, illuminating personal experiences of state repression based on gender. While bearing witness to histories of collective trauma and violence was an arduous task, articulating one's experiences of sexual violence was often avoided.

As Cruz and other women shared with me, it took them many years before they could speak out against state terrorism, and even so they typically did not mention, or only obliquely referenced, their individual experiences of sexual violence. For many of the women, their oral histories highlighted, as Joan Sangster asserts, the "collective scripts of a social group" wherein very few divulged the histories of "women's vulnerability to violence."[18] Yet some scholars, such as Elizabeth Jelin, posit that Latin American women survivors of state violence "emphasize their vulnerability as sexual beings and the affective and nurturing bonds that developed among them."[19] The women I interviewed rejected being labeled as vulnerable "sexual beings" and instead addressed systemic, state-sponsored violence from a place of political solidarity. Other scholars such as John Beverley claim that women do not "produce textually an essentialized 'woman's experience'" in their testimonies and that, by definition, testimony refers to a collective struggle.[20] However, this collective struggle is, by default, a masculine subject and can erase the very gendered experiences of violence and the national imaginaries which position and remember these histories of gendered state violence. In essence, the frameworks either portray women as sexualized, vulnerable beings subjected to state violence, or women's experiences of sexual violence are submerged under a gender-neutral target of state repression.

While the women rely on the collective subject of testimony in the various iterations of their traumatic memories, the gendered memories are sometimes glossed over or avoided altogether. The memories of trauma produce a tension between the need to retell individual experiences of gender-based violence while also referring to a plural, collective subjectivity of the survivors of historical traumas. While turning to a collective memory is crucial for the women's formation of their political subjectivities, examining narratives within the collective subject of testimony can overlook the gendered context of the memories that inform us about structural Latin American gender-based state violence. Oftentimes, women's individual histories of gendered state violence were expressed in silent moments, in pauses, and other embodied gestures that conveyed the difficulty of articulating traumatic memories. Thus, we must cautiously and conscientiously approach the topic of gendered violence in women's oral histories, carefully unpacking what is stated, what is alluded to, and the meaning that is ascribed by the women to their gendered memories.

What do testimonial silences indicate about the legacy of systematic gendered state violence in the post–Dirty War era? If, as Ximena Bunster-Burotto,

Jean Franco, and other feminist scholars have articulated, Latin American state violence was a means to castigate subversive men and women who deviated from proper gender norms, how are memories of gendered trauma relayed in oral histories, if they are mentioned at all? How do women survivors represent themselves in oral histories "in a discursive system in which women are unrepresentable as subjects"?[21] How do survivors piece together the fragments of such shattering, intimate forms of violence, especially when such a topic was discursively, culturally, and legally ignored for years? And most importantly, how do we engage with and read these oral histories without—as Diana Taylor cautions—re-traumatizing or making a spectacle of the horrendous, brutal acts of violence that women endured and without making the women appear as passive victims of sexual violence?

In order to best address the intersecting and, at times, contradictory expressions of gender violence, I turn to my 2014 interview with Liliana Forchetti. Forchetti was a former PRT member and former political prisoner of the Villa Urquiza prison in Argentina's Tucumán province. At the time of our interview, she was participating in a Buenos Aires human rights trial that exclusively centered on gender-based crimes committed at the Villa Urquiza detention center during the dictatorship. Due to the years of amnesty in Argentina, these trials did not resume until 2003; sexual crimes were not prosecuted as separate charges from other forms of torture until later, and Forchetti participated in the Villa Urquiza Case in 2012. When I asked why gender-based state crimes were not presented as separate charges in earlier human rights tribunals, she responded:

> All this ... (*pause*) concerning interrogation and torture, in the case of the women, in my case especially concerning rape (*pause*).... One could not have talked about that in the, (*pause*), first official testimonies, because there were thousands of other things that took priority, I'm talking about the disappeared, the names of the compañeros, what happened there, all of it because for many years, what we witnesses said that we had survived did not seem to (*pause*), it did not carry enough weight.... Through our testimonies (*pause*) ... they begin to (*pause*) it's as if society begins to be astonished. We have been saying from the beginning, I mean, we drew the complaint while still in prison, but we did not have enough reach. With rape, it was the same, I mean, we mentioned it, but compared to the thirty thousand disappeared, and also the issue is that, you know, people did not want to hear about it either, as one should always take care of what one said, how one said it, to whom, and the impact it caused. And of course at the judicial level, there was no acknowledgment of it because for them, rape was nothing (*exasperated chuckle*).

Forchetti's answer illuminates the gender politics involved when relying on the pluralized voice of testimony. In effect, the testimonial voice here, particularly in the years after the end of the dictatorship, assumed a collective, gender-neutral subject of testimony. This was done strategically, as she informed me, because there were "thousands of other things that took priority," such as searching for the disappeared and accounting for the compañeros with whom they were incarcerated. As explored in chapter 1, the gender politics of human rights emerges in Argentina's case, as sexual crimes committed during the dictatorship were not prioritized or judicially acknowledged at first; once they were, women's political agency was dismissed while their status as passive victims was highlighted. Argentina's CONADEP and its publication of *Nunca más* did not explicitly refer to sexual violence as one of the multiple forms of torture sanctioned by the state. Within the context of Argentina's transitional justice, this was the strategic approach of the plaintiffs and victims of state violence when denouncing the crimes committed during the regime. As human rights lawyer Ana Laura Zavala Guillén asserts, "the perception of sexual violence as a just cause, even for women, appeared relatively late" in the tribunals in Argentina.[22]

Forchetti's passage also highlights the intersecting modes of silence—discursive, social, and legal—that have developed in relation to gender violence committed during the Dirty Wars and how forms of silence have shaped women's oral histories. This passage evinces a critical component of testimony: the role of the active, receptive listener.[23] Cruz also mentioned in her interview that she encountered silence and apathy, even from her family, after her release from the Escuelita de Famaillá center: "The family did not want (*pause*) . . . the family did not want to hear what happened to us . . . they never asked what happened, where you were, no, no. That was like nothing, not wanting to think, not even think about this particular situation. . . . 'Well, they're alive, and we don't talk about that, that's it, it's over.' . . . They were terrified, but above all, they never asked, not just our own families, but society as a whole did not want to know what happened in those places." Cruz and Forchetti both relay how silence operated in conjunction with the state's master narrative that intended to erase and forget the crimes of the state. Out of fear and terror, many family members and friends preferred to ignore the harrowing details of what the survivors endured, choosing silence over listening to the survivors.

For survivors of sexual violence, there was even less acknowledgment of this form of state terrorism. This violence is intricately tied to gendered notions of shame and propriety (see chapter 2). Furthermore, while Forchetti states that she and other women denounced their sexual violations "from the beginning," sexual crimes were not as urgent as denouncing the thirty thousand desaparecidos. In other words, "sexual violence was considered taboo within the mechanisms of transitional justice" in many social frameworks.[24] Many women experienced and feared rejection from their communities and families after their sexual violations, which piled onto the trauma itself feelings of shame. Therefore, many women kept silent about their gendered trauma. Silence, then, is a projected goal of the Argentinean and Mexican states. Indeed, the cultural, political, and social silence resulting from state terrorism produced the phenomenon of social amnesia, or olvido.

While Forchetti is speaking of her survival of sexual violence decades after the fact, she relies on the collective subjectivity of her compañeros to guide her oral narrative. In one way, her oral history corroborates Zavala Guillén's assertions that women's narratives of sexual trauma were not considered as urgent as denouncing other forms of state torture, particularly in Argentina's first junta trials that commenced in 1984. Because sexual violence was not acknowledged in a juridical sense, women kept silent for decades on the topic. Forchetti's interview exposes the tension between prioritizing certain human rights crimes and denouncing the systematic use of rape and other sexual crimes committed during the dictatorship. For her, years of silence on the topic of gendered state violence impelled her to participate in recent trials that center specifically on sexual crimes committed during the dictatorship; however, in the first years after the dictatorship, she and other survivors focused on other human rights causes. Forchetti's passage directly refers to the social ideologies of the post-dictatorship era that espoused silence when centering on the topic of systemic gender violence. As she recalls, "the issue is that, you know, people did not want to hear about it either."

Despite the apparent ease with which Forchetti discussed her history of surviving state repression, the performative details of this passage of her oral history capture the complexities associated with speaking about gendered state trauma. When broaching the topic of the culture of silence that ignored the normalization of rape during the dictatorship, her voice slowed, and her use of the term "issue" instead of "rape" reflected the cursory way in which postdictatorship Argentina approached the subject: an "issue" that did not situate easily within their narrative of progress and democracy. Furthermore, Forchetti gestured toward me as she said "you know," which illustrated the dialogic and performative aspects of memory and oral history and the embodied expressions that occurred off-tape. In this manner, Forchetti was involving me as a sympathetic listener when discussing the legacy of discursive, legal, and cultural silence, which were the official responses to gender violence.

However, when she discussed the judicial system's refusal to acknowledge sexual crimes committed by the state, her voice became more assertive and deliberate as she explained incredulously that, for the courts, "rape wasn't anything [*exasperated chuckle*]." Forchetti's incredulous laugh at the end of this passage expressed her disbelief at the justice system's disavowal of rape as a human rights violation in the early years after the dictatorship, despite her attempts to speak of her experiences of being sexually violated by the state. Here, then, Forchetti converted the legacy of juridical and social silence on sexual state violence into a transformative act of resistance against years of impunity.

While Forchetti spoke with relative ease about her experiences of sexual violence, it was critical to be attentive to her particular context as perhaps influencing what she disclosed in her oral history, as well as *how* she articulated her history. At the time of our interview in 2014, she was participating in the Villa Urquiza tribunal, which focused on gender-based human rights crimes committed at the detention center. The tribunal offers official state acknowledgment of the history of gendered forms of human rights violations. Other women, however, were more reticent to discuss the topic even as their narratives allowed them to rearticulate the very political subjectivities that the state attempted to destroy through the violent act of sexual and psychological torture. For many women, silence was also invoked as a way of surviving and processing their histories of state-sponsored, gender-based terrorism.

In my interview with Eloy in La Plata, she refrained from discussing her personal experiences of sexual violence, yet she informed me that the systematic use of rape in the detention centers was a common form of domination and torture against women who transgressed their roles: "For women it was worse, just by the simple fact of being women. It was very difficult at first, as rape is the least denounced crime in everyday society. It [rape] is the norm . . . it was habitual." She stated that when asked in court about the Law of Due Obedience and whether the officers were merely following orders from above, she retorted, "I answered them that I understood that one of the practices that occurred in the camps that demonstrated the falsity of this claims was rape. Because I understood that no man has an erection just because his boss commands him to. It is absolutely a voluntary act."[25] At this point Eloy paused momentarily, glancing down at her hands before continuing: "And that voluntary, degrading act against women was a habitual practice and though one has to understand that it doesn't come up often in testimonies, one has to know how to read between the lines because in general it takes a lot for women to denounce [the crime of rape]."

Eloy discussed the problematic silences produced in response to sexual violence against women. She noted that rape was not merely one of the numerous crimes committed during the dictatorship, but rather, its prevalence in "everyday" societies was symptomatic of patriarchy's violent control over women's bodies. This appears in Eloy's powerful declaration against the officers who were granted amnesty due to the Law of Due Obedience; in one succinct statement—"no man has an erection just because his boss commands him to"—Eloy undermined the validity of this law while simultaneously exposing its gendered underpinnings. Eloy's testimony revealed how the dictatorship institutionalized sexual torture in order to punish "subversives." Additionally, her account criticized the amnesty law, which merely highlighted the legacy of dictatorship-era violence against women.

While this passage powerfully criticizes Argentina's systematic forms of violence against women, her testimony also reflected pauses and embodied gestures when she turned to her personal experiences. For instance, after denouncing the use of rape as a systematic form of dehumanization, she took a long pause before remarking on the difficulty rape survivors encounter when attempting to speak of their trauma, including her own:

> When this military officer of the Infierno [camp] became known, I remember that they told me that they were going to take my testimony separately and I was walking with my lawyer and she asked me, "Are you sure?" [And I replied:] "Do you know how many times he raped me? And you're going to discourage me from pressing charges? No." "Well, I had to ask." And yes. Yes, yes. That is what I did. Because in those testimonies I had never said I had been raped. I had always been vague. And I would say in those testimonies that for two months I had been the only woman for the whole Infierno camp. I would not say anything more than that. . . . I had not even noticed that I had not said anything about that. It was my way of saying that. Often, in the testimonies of compañeras, you have to read between the lines. Because obviously it is very difficult for us *(pause)* . . . so, it is, it is *(pause)* . . . very, very difficult for us, but in everyday life, and not only here, everywhere, the crime of rape is one that is the least denounced. And, women are so aware of this that it might seem that we are the ones that provoke that crime, because it is not part of our belief that we can say no. And that this no must be respected. But well, it is the same everywhere.

In the above passage, Eloy discusses her individual trauma of rape, however, she evades clearly stating that she was raped in various camps during her detention. Eloy's statement—"I would say in those testimonies that for two months I had been the only woman for the whole Infierno camp"—was the closest she could come in that moment to revealing that she had been raped. Only later did she realize that she had merely alluded to her violations. She then reverted back to the collective subject and to her compañeras who had also suffered the trauma of rape in the camp. As Eloy discussed her experiences in the camp, her body language reflected the pain of recounting the memory. With eyes downcast, she avoided eye contact until she resumed the collective narrative voice where she spoke with pain and anger when she related the moment she told her lawyer that the former official of the Infierno had repeatedly raped her, fueling her commitment to denounce him in court.

We must approach with caution this powerful moment of her testimony, because it is critical not to analyze these passages of her testimony as indicative of her vulnerability as the only woman in the Infierno camp. Rather, I read this passage as a testament to her determination to denounce the institutionalized forms of state violence whereby politically active women were subjected to repeated rape as a form of degradation, where the "destruction of the body after rape was a message of extreme hatred."[26] Such "extreme hatred" evokes the state's apprehension of politically active women; in our interview, Marta Díaz shared the following with me: "For them [the officers] it was an insult that women had the capacity to be politically active. That's why I think in some way this also caused them a lot of anxiety. It was much more of an issue, because women had to care for the children, why did you have to study, you shouldn't study, you shouldn't ask questions . . . you could not think politically. . . . I think that's what I saw in the [human rights] trials. They [the officers] did not look us in the face."

Eloy, Forchetti, and Díaz each alluded to deep-seated feelings of shame surrounding the discourse of rape and the silence that accompanies their survival. Their testimonies illuminate the prevalence of gender-based violence against politically dissenting women, and, as Díaz's passage indicates, their memories capture the cultural and discursive silences that are embedded in Argentina. The avoidance of the topic of gender—especially in terms of personal experiences of sexual violence—is tied to the complexity of survivor guilt and institutionalized, cultural notions of shame related to rape. Avoidance also reveals the women's rejection of being passive victims of sexual violence. The narrative voice uses the plural in order to invoke the collective survival voice for human rights purposes.

While sexual state violence was not as prevalent during Mexico's Dirty War, many survivors relate that gender-based violence was one of the many forms of torture used by state agents. It is noteworthy, however, that the women I interviewed in Mexico did not directly refer to experiences of sexual violence, except for Rodríguez Márquez. Similar to the Argentinean women's accounts of sexual violence, Rodríguez Márquez expressed the importance of solidarity among men and women activists in her oral narrative. Rodríguez Márquez's testimony was predicated on this collective subject, a sign of her belief that solidarity helped her survive the psychological torture she had endured during her two-year incarceration in Mexico City's Lecumberri Prison. Rodríguez Márquez's narrative shed light on the gendered hierarchies of the political prisoner experience in Mexico's post-1968 years. Rodríguez Márquez related that being detained in the holding cells called the Separos de Tlaxcuaque, "were the most difficult days of my life." Many women were sexually assaulted and subjected to other forms of torture in that traumatic space. Although Rodríguez Márquez was not sexually assaulted, she recounted how many guards took female inmates out of the cells at night to rape them, and how the guards repeatedly threatened her with this violence. She recalled her terror: "I couldn't sleep. You couldn't . . . the holding cells were very difficult because there were only bars, and so they could see everything you did. . . . So it was a horrible night, so frightening and I thought, they are going to do something to me, they're going to harm me or something."

The prison guards used gender-based psychological torture on Rodríguez Márquez while she was in the holding cells. During this time, she was forced to witness the torture of others, instilling both fear and a sense of powerlessness because of her inability to assist her fellow prisoners. Ultimately she was released, but with a harrowing warning that reinforced the state's power and control: "Well at the end they finally let me out, but they had already marked me . . . they threatened me, they told me, 'Go home because the next time it will result in your death.'" In Poniatowska's *La noche de Tlatelolco*, Rodríguez Márquez's cellmate and compañera of the movement, Roberta Avendaño Martínez, declared in her testimony that many women detained after October 2 were subjected to brutal torture, with burning cigarettes and other instruments applied to their breasts and genitals, while other women were raped on the usually false promise of being released if they submitted.

While the guerrilleras I interviewed in Mexico did not openly mention having suffered sexual violence, the Mexican agents employed brutal tactics of gender-based torture and repression, particularly against women who joined the guerrillas. As journalist Laura Castellanos writes in *Mexico armado*, prison guards subjected imprisoned guerrilleras to *el chocho*, in which they would wake the women up in the middle of the night, strip them naked while dumping buckets of cold water over their bodies, all the while threatening them with rape. Castellanos notes that gender-based humiliation and torture were integral forms of repression used by the Mexican antiguerrilla task force, the White Brigade (Brigada Blanca), and many of the same tactics were utilized in the Southern Cone dictatorships.[27]

Gender-based torture of guerrilleros was common in Mexico's clandestine centers, yet there is little literature published on this particular topic in the history of the nation's Dirty War. In our interview, Alejandra of the Liga in Guadalajara noted that she did not experience gender violence herself, but she did refer to the 2007 collection of testimonies, *First National Assembly of Ex-Guerrilleras*, self-published by former guerrillera María de la Luz Aguilar Terrés. Alejandra told me to "go check out the book—it says women were tortured more, because in addition to being a guerrilla fighter, you're also a woman." She then shared the story of compañera and former guerrillera Marta Alicia Camacho Loaiza, whose harrowing narrative of survival I mentioned in chapter 1. Camacho Loaiza endured beatings to her pregnant body and witnessed the sexual brutalization and murder of her husband, Jose Manuel Alapizco Lizarraga, by agents of the White Brigade. This part of Alejandra's interview highlights the similar tactics of state violence used in both Argentina and Mexico, and importantly, it evinces that the Mexican state denied having committed systemic, gender-based violence during the Dirty War. Furthermore, Alejandra involved me in her narrative as she asked me if I had read about this history in Aguilar Terrés's book, which is difficult to find. In fact, a member of the Comité '68 gifted me his copy of the text, and it bears noting how obscure much of the literature is on gender issues and Mexico's Dirty War more generally. It further reveals the limited amount of information documenting the extensive mechanisms of gendered repression that the Mexican state instituted during the Dirty War.

I would like to momentarily turn to Taylor's *Disappearing Acts*, in which she questions whether her research on Argentinean dictatorship-era sexual violence is reproducing the violence in her description of gendered torture, or perhaps "trafficking in obscenity."[28] I decided to strategically incorporate the passages on violence from the women's oral histories despite the risk of "falling into the trap" of replicating such spectacles of violence. These testimonies unearth histories of Mexican gendered state violence that have been erased from official discourses on the Dirty War and also document genealogies of hemispheric repression in Latin America. What is pertinent here is that that the women I interviewed are asking us—both directly and indirectly—to bear witness to the years of trauma, violence, and silence that they have endured and continue to endure by listening to the histories of (gendered) survival that have often been erased from the dominant history. Their articulations of surviving state-sanctioned gender and sexual violence are meant to unsettle us, and they serve as critical disruptive archives to the dominant narratives on the Latin American Dirty Wars. These disruptive archives, however, are not to be read as sensationalized spectacles of sexualized violence; instead, these archives transform memories of terror into political projects seeking accountability for the past. Such memories, "operating in conjunction with other memories," as Diana Taylor says in the first epigraph to this chapter, take on the collective voice and contribute to new knowledge formation on the Dirty Wars that is dangerously sliding into oblivion. The pluralized voice of oral history in the women's testimonies is an essential form of solidarity building with other survivors of state violence. Perhaps this is why gendered perspectives on the revolutionary movements' era are not foregrounded in their testimonies.

Memory and the Gender Politics of Leftist Revolutionary Movements

In my interviews, the topic of gender was not explicitly addressed until I asked the women to reflect on the dynamics between the men and women of their political organizations. As previously noted, the women indicated that what was fundamental to their political subjectivities was the solidarity formed with other activists during their moments of repression and with other survivors upon their release from captivity. Many times they would state that they did not center on questions of gender because they did not want to divide the solidarity groups along gender lines. Latin American oral historian Pensado Leglise encountered a similar experience in her research on oral histories with women who participated in leftist movements in Latin America during the 1960s. In her research on leftist Latin American activist women, Pensado Leglise notes that the women did not voluntarily raise the topic of gender and that their oral histories centered on a gender-neutral subject who resisted and survived state terrorism.[29]

The global feminist movement, anti-imperialist, and decolonization movements of the 1960s and 1970s profoundly shaped many women's political perspectives in Latin America, and women were joining organizations in large numbers in both urban and rural settings. For most of the women I interviewed, their militancy in political groups signified a critical shift in the way they perceived themselves as agents of social transformation in the public sphere. As Rodríguez Márquez stated about joining the Mexico City '68 student movement, "for me, I was breaking away from all those structures, with all those norms that they were controlling... [the movement] wanted the participation of women." Rodríguez Márquez shared that she and many other young women crossed the threshold from the private to public sphere, which was typically dominated by men. Women in the student movement joined brigades, and the organizations helped inform local communities of their political rights: "What was most important about the movement of '68 to me, what gave the most vital force to the movement, were the brigades. So, we started to join various brigades." Rodríguez Márquez noted that the brigades were critical for disseminating information about the movement. "I remember when we would get on the buses . . . we would explain to them [the locals] what was happening, we would go to factories, to public plazas, and—very important—we would go to public markets and the people would support us."

Although many of the revolutionary organizations touted an ideology based on equality, gender equality was not always practiced within the groups. Yet some of the women I interviewed found it difficult to talk openly about the gendered hierarchies of their political organizations. To them, the revolutionary organizations were predicated on gender equality and social justice, and so they emphasized these tenets in their oral histories. Only a few of the women I interviewed openly criticized the gendered hierarchization of their organizations, among them Rodríguez Márquez and former guerrillera Alejandra. The integral role of women in the Mexican student movement was obfuscated from the history of the massacre and, as Rodríguez Márquez commented before our interview and to the Mexican periodical, *La Jornada* in 2002, "The discrimination against women in '68—seriously!—was enormous. Our participation was pivotal (. . .). And in spite of that, only the men speak about the movement."[30]

As chapter 3 closely examines the gender dynamics that emerged in armed insurgent groups in both nations, I would like to assess not what the women indicate about gender arrangements in the organizations but how memories of the gender divisions are expressed in their testimonies. In her study of women's oral histories in armed organizations in 1970s Southern Cone, Alejandra Oberti asserts that the role of the feminist oral historian is to "recover their more subtle gestures, what cannot be so easily represented."[31] It is critical to examine how the social ideology of the revolutionary organizations based on gender equality shaped the memories of the women I interviewed. What do the gaps and contradictions in the women's memories of their revolutionary movements say about dominant narratives of these political organizations, and how does the weight—or guilt—of trauma and survival inform their testimonies?

While Rodríguez Márquez and a few other women criticized the paternalism and gender divisions that existed in their revolutionary organizations, the majority of the women I interviewed stated that they personally did not experience gender discrimination in their political organizations. If anything, as Mirta Sgro of Argentina's ERP told me, it was a time "where I least noticed any gender differences." However, in acknowledging gender discrimination in their organizations, the women stated that it had happened to other compañeras, as Sgro claims in her interview. In some interviews, the women noted that displays of gender difference were tied to paternalistic overprotection. Silvia Yáñez of Argentina's ERP stated that some of the guerrilleros were "very *machista*," but "they respected us very much, to the point where they would take care of us, well, you know, too much." For Yáñez and other women, the compañeros treated them in a respectful albeit paternalistic manner, wanting to restrict the women from engaging in dangerous armed actions.

Overall, many of the women evaded directly addressing any gendered tensions in their militant organizations, a pattern that also appears in Scheibe Wolff, Pedro, and Gomez da Silva's 2016 study, "'Gendered Memories': Women's Narratives from the Southern Cone." In their analysis, they found that many of the women in Latin American leftist organizations "claim[ed] they did not feel discrimination," which the scholars attribute to the women's positive memories of participating in political organizations that "recognize[ed] women as militants side by side with their male comrades."[32] Forchetti's testimony echoes this sentiment, as she told me that her participation in the ERP was "the most marvelous era of my life, even with everything that we had to go through later (*pause*)."

Forchetti's oral history reveals the relationship between trauma and the processes of oral history telling, particularly when it comes to how women remember (or do not remember) moments of gender discrimination. For Forchetti and others, the revelation of "even with everything that [they] had to go through later" alludes to having survived the devastating losses and crimes committed by the state during the Dirty Wars. The legacy of Dirty War–era trauma has shaped private and public discourses, and the guilt of survival is also reflected in their testimonies. At this part of her interview, Forchetti had difficulty stating the details of "everything that [they] had go through." The trauma was too overwhelming, marked by the pause at the end of her carefully oblique statement. While Forchetti eventually assessed the gender dynamics of her organizations, she noted that she was only able to do so "years later," after surviving traumatic experiences.

Many women, however, did not feel comfortable speaking critically of the compañeros who were killed, tortured, or disappeared. The traumatic losses incurred by the crimes of the state took precedence over denouncing any experiences of sexism in the revolutionary groups. This is exemplified in the interviews I conducted with compañeras of the Guadalajara Liga, Alejandra and Gutiérrez Campos. As noted in chapter 3, although Alejandra recalled fellow guerrilleros of the Liga subjecting her friend Bertha Lilia Gutiérrez Campos to gender discrimination, Gutiérrez Campos herself explicitly denied being discriminated against in that way. What was important to her, however, was *how* she spoke of her compañeros: "When I work on something related to gender, I'm going to be very careful when I talk about my compañeros. For example some of them died during torture, others were disappeared, and others were in prison for many years. I would never say that they were *machistas*, demonizing the compañeros doesn't seem like a good idea . . . how am I going to label *them* with feminist terms when what they did was heroic? In that sense, gender theory doesn't work for me." While both women claimed to be feminists, Gutiérrez Campos clearly stated that using a gender lens when speaking of her past experiences can "demoniz[e] the compañeros."

As discussed in chapter 3, the national narrative of the armed insurgencies in Argentina, and especially Mexico, portrayed the guerrillas as criminal, violent groups who terrorized the nations. For Gutiérrez Campos, it is important to recuperate and validate the histories of struggle and the "heroic" actions of her compañeros, as the dominant discourses on the guerrilleros have maligned and "demonized" the memory of their struggle. Clearly, Gutiérrez Campos and other women have been affected by the traumatic loss and violence inflicted by the state on former compañeros, which affects how they portray their histories of political activism in their organizations. The trauma she endured experiencing the violent loss of two romantic partners and witnessing the torture and disappearances of other compañeros directly shaped how she articulated her narrative. For Gutiérrez Campos, it became more important to denounce the crimes of the state and to recuperate the hidden history of her fallen compañeros than to decry the gender hierarchies of the organization.

The women's accounts challenge the master narratives of Mexico's Dirty War and illuminate how collective experiences of trauma are experienced and recounted in diverse ways. Their narratives resist the cultural memory that has portrayed their leftist groups as criminal organizations. The collective experience of trauma that the Liga and her compañeros endured is represented differently for both women; for Alejandra, as we've already seen in chapter 3, it remains critical to challenge the masculinist historiographical focus of the Mexican guerrillas, and her oral history offers an important feminist perspective on the Mexican armed insurgencies. Gutiérrez Campos, on the other hand, is committed to denouncing the crimes sanctioned by the Mexican state and, thus, her narrative centers on exposing the criminal actions of the state while simultaneously debunking the dominant narrative that positioned the Liga as a criminal group.

These testimonies remind feminist researchers to be cautious when engaging with women's testimonies of political resistance, trauma, and loss. The contradictory memories of gender that appear in Alejandra and Gutiérrez Campos's testimonies demonstrate how the passage of time and social frameworks shape how the women give their testimony. Both women articulate their own complex version of a historical memory on the gender dynamics of the Dirty War that has been elided and silenced. Rather than dismissing a testimony as inaccurate or un-feminist in their eschewing of gender theory, we must be attentive to how the women's narratives of trauma and survival are political testaments to resistance against state violence, impunity, and the erasure of their histories. The burden of surviving the loss of compañeros, who have been erased from the dominant narratives of the Dirty War, guides the trajectory of their interviews. For Gutiérrez Campos and other women, speaking of their past trauma transforms their memories into a political, radical act that decenters dominant narratives that have actively tried to disavow their histories of resistance.

Speaking Is Resisting: Survival and the Politics of Solidarity

Although the interviews examined thus far capture the diverse experiences of women involved in resistance struggles in Latin America, the narratives are ultimately a testament to what Chandra Mohanty has termed the "politics of solidarity" and the creation of transnational imagined communities that resist the legacy and impunity of state terror. While Mohanty's "politics of solidarity" refers to the transnational feminist organizing of women workers in anticapitalist and antiracist struggles, the solidarity practices of the women I interviewed reflect what I read as a transnational trend to combat the pervasive and destructive force of state-sanctioned olvido across the Americas. In this sense, it is important to center on the ways in which oral history and storytelling function as imagined sites of community, solidarity, and resistance to Latin American state violence and olvido. The notion of solidarity in this particular context refers more to the imagined communities of resistance that are created by women survivors of state violence across the Americas. While there indeed exist transnational Latin American human rights and feminist alliances, the women I interviewed for this book did not participate in transnational feminist organizations, and most of them did not know one another. However, their narratives embody the emergence of a transnational and hemispheric Latin American feminist ethos and imagined community. This is evident in the women's similar stories of resistance and survival of state terror in the past, and commitment to social justice in the present. The oral histories reveal the radical possibilities of a transnational Latin American feminist memory, as the women's oral histories of gendered state trauma challenge dominant narratives of apathy, oblivion, and impunity that have taken root in contemporary Latin American cultural discourses.

The construction of a hemispheric, transnational feminist theory of solidarity and resistance appears in even simple linguistic choices in the interviews. In my 2009 interview with Lelia Ferrarese of Rosario, Argentina's Museum of Memory, she turned to the plural speaking subject "we" when discussing her traumatic past. She described her release from Villa Devoto, where she was detained as a political prisoner, and she related the difficulty she encountered in speaking of her past trauma in post-dictatorship Argentina: "For me in the beginning, it took a lot for me to speak . . . we women there [in Villa Devoto] when we asked for something . . . it was in the plural, *nosotras*. Here, it is the return to the individual self. So I was lacking the word, *nosotras* . . . I lacked the protection of the compañeras around me." Ferrarese alluded to her past trauma as a dehumanized being in the Villa Devoto political prison and asserted that what helped her to survive were the networks of support and solidarity created in the prison. By referring to the collective, inclusive speaking subject "nosotras," Ferrarese aligned the various subjectivities of fellow political prisoners with her own subjectivity, which became critical for her survival after her release from prison. The simple use of "nosotras" evinces how critical this solidarity was in not only Ferrarese's survival but also how the narratives and words of the women survivors formulate an imagined space of transnational solidarity and resistance.

The solidarity efforts formed around shared experiences of trauma, as Ferrarese noted in her testimony, were not only necessary for their survival but also helped critically disrupt the state's intent on using trauma to silence and erase the cultural memory of women's resistance to state violence. As active producers of knowledge on the elided histories of the Dirty Wars, the women worked collaboratively to disseminate shared histories of trauma and resistance. Their very survival and their speaking out and sharing their oral histories of trauma and resistance, is, in essence, a radically subversive act that critically pushes against the master narratives which have condemned their stories to oblivion. These memories of their resistance and revolutionary ideals do not only serve as "a corrective" to "hegemonic masculinist history," as Mohanty reminds us, but rather these narratives and the practice of speaking out "leads to the formation of politicized consciousness and self-identity."[33] In essence, while the desired intent of the state's repressive mechanisms was to terrorize and traumatize people into silence, as well as to individualize and destroy the collaborative efforts of their leftist organizations, the women's oral histories of shared trauma led to the formation of solidarity networks that contribute to a transnational trend that challenges the state's narrative of olvido and impunity.

For many years, however, Mexican and Argentinean state terrorism had successfully traumatized many into silence. Survivors had to grapple with not only processing their own traumas inflicted by state repression, but they also had to contend with the guilt and trauma of survival. Rodríguez Márquez captured the difficulty this presented to her: "One of the things I always say when I'm interviewed is: when I awoke on the morning of October 3rd, I wondered, why did I not die yesterday? Why were we privileged and why were we not killed?" As I explore in chapter 2, forms of silence and shame are tied to survival. They indelibly mark the survivor, particularly because their social worlds believe they committed an act of betrayal in order to survive. Furthermore, as Cruz explained to me, many people believed that anyone targeted by the regime warranted such violence committed against them. She stated that many believed "por algo será" (for some reason), implying that for some *legitimate* reason she was detained, tortured, degraded, and then released by state authorities.

For these and other reasons, many survivors repressed memories of the state-sponsored trauma and rarely spoke about their experiences of state violence. Rodríguez Márquez stated that many of the women involved in the student movement were terrorized into silence after the Mexico City massacre: "there are many very brave women of '68, but anonymous ... there are many women who don't speak. Concerning October 2nd, they have never spoken, nor do they want to speak.... Many people were scared. And I understand them ... there are many women who were protagonists of that history, that form part of that memory and who have not spoken of it. They don't want to, and I respect that." Similarly, Eloy related that after her release from prison, she did not join any survivor groups nor did she speak of her experience to anyone. However, after hearing a presentation in 1999 by Spanish judge Carlos Castresana concerning his role in the indictment of former Chilean dictator Augusto Pinochet, she broke her silence: "Something happened to me that made me go [to Castresana's talk]. When he finished, I got up, I extended my hand to shake [his], and I started to cry. I had never cried in that way." A key, powerful effect of the legacy of Dirty War–era state violence was its ability to individualize and splinter any efforts of collaborative, solidarity efforts among survivors and other individuals (e.g., family members of survivors) affected by this violence. As Ferrarese noted, the "return to the individual self" after experiencing state trauma merely served to exacerbate the silence and isolation that many survivors endured.

In order to combat this divisive outcome of state-sanctioned trauma, the women I interviewed turned to survivor networks and committed themselves to providing their testimonies to various sources: human rights tribunals, journalists, researchers, filmmakers, and writers. The use of the collective narrative voice is an act of solidarity and is essential to the women's survival, facilitating their ability to repeatedly provide testimony. That is why many of the interviews rely on the memories of solidarity to propel their narratives. After breaking her sixteen-year silence in 1999, Eloy contended that speaking of her time in the concentration camps is an arduous, political act that inevitably conjures painful memories of her compañeros who did not survive: "The majority of testimonies have to do with talking about the compañeros that were with them . . . I always considered it an obligation, because many of those compañeros that are no longer with us, are the ones who made it possible for me to be here. Those that, with a word, a caress, allowed you, helped you, survive. That is the debt to them. I feel that deeply." Eloy alludes here to the Latin American tradition of testimonio as a form of collective resistance to impunity against state-sponsored violence; her words underscore the importance of solidarity in the act of testifying. Eloy's memories evoke the voices of her compañeros whose acts of solidarity assisted in her survival, and these acts of solidarity are expressed in the vacillation between the "I" and "you/we" speaking subject of her testimony. Perhaps Diana Taylor's examination of collective memory and trauma best describes the relationship between the singular speaking subject of testimony, "I," and the collective "you." As she explains, "'I' and 'you' are products of each other's experiences and memories, of historical trauma, of enacted space, of sociopolitical crisis." Eloy's blurring of the "I" and "you," then, is indicative of the political possibilities of oral history, as this "allows for a broader understanding of historical trauma, communal memory, and collective subjectivity."[34] Eloy and the other women I interviewed often relied on this collective subjectivity to help them articulate their histories of trauma, and this evinces the solidarity practices that are inherent to women's oral histories.

Furthermore, survivor-led human rights organizations that centered on the recuperation of Latin America's history of political repression and state violence represent an important expression of solidarity. While many types of human rights organizations formed in Argentina and Mexico, most of the women I interviewed belonged to survivor-run coalitions that had no ties to state organizations. When discussing her work with the Buenos Aires–based AEDD, Eloy stated that the organization represents "pieces of memory that we mix together, kneading small bits of memory . . . because these bits of memory represent our companions who did not survive." Eloy's political subjectivity is predicated on the innumerable memories she has of the compañeros she was incarcerated with and of those who did not survive. Yet her memories are "always operating in conjunction with other memories all of them pulsing, regularly, in order."[35] Since breaking her silence in 1999, Eloy joined the AEDD and found the strength to speak of her experiences by turning to the collective political subjectivity formed by AEDD members. Providing testimony is a laborious practice of solidarity in which uniting fragmented "pieces of memory" created by trauma unearth new knowledge on the histories of the Dirty Wars.

The solidarity efforts of the civic organizations are also reflected in the various political projects they undertake, such as the participation in human rights tribunals and organization of annual commemorative marches. Mexico City's Comité '68 has centered on political projects that recuperate the historical memory of the Dirty War. For example, the Comité engaged in *escrache* in front of the residences of former Mexican officials who participated in the repression against activists during the Dirty War.[36] Rodríguez Márquez described the importance of participating in such collective, public acts:

> We survived. And the fact that you're [Echeverría] sleeping and we yell, "Murderer!," that is to be alive. That is what being alive feels like. What's more, in Mexico, there had never been a former president who was condemned to house arrest. That is the achievement of the Comité. Then you have some people who say that we're a bunch of stubborn old people, and things like that, I don't know— but look, if it weren't for us, there wouldn't be a case against Echeverría seeking justice. We are always involved in that, constantly. . . . We have never stopped fighting. We have never stopped marching. . . . I have to continue, and why? Others ask us to leave it alone, that this is nothing but an act of vengeance . . . we do not want to forgive. It is known that Echeverría was a perpetrator of genocide. . . . The truth will be known. We do not want to forgive him, because he doesn't deserve to be forgiven. And not just him, but all the military officers who were involved and some of them are older, but they're strong, and they're still alive. We want punishment for those responsible. And for what reason? So that this may be known, that justice may be done so that this may never happen again.

Here, Rodríguez Márquez asserts that concentrating on achieving justice for past crimes is integral to the survival of the Comité members who unearth previously elided historical atrocities committed by the Mexican state. Rodríguez Márquez notes that contemporary Mexican discourses portray them as "stubborn old people," obsessively entrenched and haunted by the past and on a quest for vengeance. She and the other members of the Comité '68 continuously combat a national discourse that attempts to "get beyond its past" of the Tlatelolco massacre and other Dirty War–era acts of violence. In this instance, the committee's collective organizing around documenting the historical memory of the 1968 massacre led to the house arrest warrant and indictment of former president Echeverría, who served as Mexico's interior minister during the time of the 1968 massacre. As Rodríguez Márquez proudly states, the Comité '68 and other Mexican human rights organizations spearheaded this judicial process. However, this form of justice was limited. As Rodríguez Márquez noted, Echeverría is only one of many culpable figures involved in Dirty War violence and most of the "genocidas" live in amnesty. What's more, the charges against Echeverría were dropped in 2009, when he was exonerated of all charges tying him to the 1968 massacre. For these reasons, Rodríguez Márquez emphatically declares that "I have to continue" to rely on a politics of solidarity and collaborative efforts against impunity "so that this may be known, that justice may be done so that this may never happen again."

In a similar vein, Cruz explained that the AEDD's collective political subjectivity was essential in bringing former officials of the Argentinean dictatorship—*genocidas*—to trial: "Through our story, the only way to prove that the concentration camps existed is through the survivors—there is no other way. . . . The survivors know what happened in those places. . . . For that reason we say ex-detained-disappeared." Since the amnesty laws were repealed in 2003, many AEDD members have provided their testimonies in the human rights trials that are still ongoing. In 2006, Eloy and Jorge Julio López were key witnesses for the prosecution against Miguel Etchecolatz—former chief of the Buenos Aires police during the dictatorship. On the day he was due to finish his testimony, September 18, 2006, López was disappeared for the second time in his life. Today he remains disappeared, a harrowing testament to the violent vestiges of the dictatorship.

This act of violence was committed during the constitutional government of President Nestor Kirchner, and human rights organizations and activists, including the AEDD, denounced López's disappearance as a terrorist act that intended to silence and deter other survivors from coming forward to participate in human rights trials. The intimidating tactic of López's abduction and presumed murder did not hinder Eloy from providing her testimony in the future. On the contrary, Eloy invoked López's memory when providing her testimony at later dates, which are critical, radical acts of solidarity and resistance. Eloy described the moment of Etchecolatz's sentencing in 2006, right after López's disappearance:

> In the middle of the desperation we felt with Jorge's [López] absence, I was able to look at him [Etchecolatz], and I was looking at him—I don't know how to explain it, but, I was looking at him but, as if I had two images, what I had was the images of compañeros, of moments, as if it were a scene of a movie, the joy of hearing the verdict, the desperation we felt with Jorge's absence. . . . I was seated.

> I could not move for the activity around me. I could not move. I was staring at Etchecolatz the moments before [the guilty verdict].

Eloy's depiction of the moment of his conviction was indeed like a scene of a film, where the elation of those around her in the courtroom was juxtaposed against her immobile stance, her gaze fixed firmly on Etchecolatz, one of thousands of military officials who had lived comfortably in amnesty for years but now was sentenced to life in prison. Eloy converted her individual loss and mourning into collective action in her future endeavors. As she related to me, she continued to provide her testimony and she called on the many ghosts of her past to constitute a collective subject of testimony so that justice could be achieved.

Thus, returning to past traumas in the women's oral histories is a radical act of political subversion and solidarity that contests the cultures of amnesty and apathy in post-dictatorship Argentina and post–Dirty War Mexico. The women I interviewed, the "stubborn old people," inserted themselves into the dominant narratives by forming solidarity networks and memory projects that hold the states accountable to the crimes committed during the Dirty War era. The circularity of trauma, its temporal nonlinearity, inserts the past onto the terrain of the present, unsettling the nations' narratives attempts to "move past" their histories of violence. The return to past traumas furthermore exposes that state terrorism continues in the present, as demonstrated by the case of the disappeared Jorge Julio López. The oral histories, these disruptive archives, reveal memories that are shaped by experiences of survival, trauma, and a radical politics of solidarity that recuperates the historical memories of those affected by state violence.

EPILOGUE

The Legacy of State-Sanctioned Violence and Specters of the Dirty War's Radical Women

> They want to annihilate me. They won't be able to do that with me. I won't let them break me. This is something I told myself since the beginning. This is something that continues to be present.
>
> —Lelia Ferrarese

> I think all aspects of a society should be recuperated, no? Because a society of the 1970s, the Dirty War, what they call the Dirty War . . . in truth, it was simply an abuse, no? . . . They believe that we were defeated, but no, no. The great revolution is the revolution of ideas, and those still exist, no? So in that way, they did not defeat us. They just abused, destroyed, and killed young people, and for that reason, this should be known. And one cannot live in a society that only talks of victories. . . . In my life, my issue was with authoritarianism . . . my problem is that I was always critical, and I still am. . . . I am a relentless old lady.
>
> —Alejandra

On the morning of March 29, 2010, fifty-one-year-old Silvia Suppo was murdered in front of her business in downtown Rosario, Argentina. Suppo's death came shortly after she provided testimony for the prosecution in a 2009 human rights trial in Santa Fe, Argentina. Suppo, a former detainee and torture survivor of the Argentinean dictatorship, revealed how military officers detained her in 1977 when she was just seventeen years old. In her testimony, she denounced the systemic forms of gender violence she endured at La Casita detention center—including rape, impregnation, and forced abortion by her torturers—and she exposed sexual terrorism as one of the key repressive mechanisms used by the masculinist, dictatorial state. Her testimony was essential in convicting Victor Brusa, a civil servant of the dictatorship who assisted with the interrogations of the detained-disappeared in the camps. The conviction was a landmark case, as Brusa was the first Argentinean federal judge to be charged with crimes against humanity for his role in the dictatorship. Four months after the trial ended, Suppo was found murdered in front of her business. Two young men were arrested and sentenced for the crime, which police described as a robbery gone wrong; however, her family, human rights activists, and other survivors have maintained that her murder was politically motivated. Women's human rights organizations in Argentina believe that Suppo's audacity to speak out about the dictatorship's use of systemic gender violence was what led to her murder in 2010.

A public act of gender terrorism, Suppo's murder illustrated the enduring culture of fear that was fomented during the Dirty War era. She was stabbed twelve times in front of her workplace in the morning, which sent a clear message to other survivors who were involved in human rights trials: speaking out against the dictatorship can lead to your death. Her case is similar to the 2006 disappearance of Jorge Julio López (see ch. 4). Both López's and Suppo's disappearances during Argentina's era of democracy signal to us that denouncing the state crimes of the past can have horrifying consequences.

Speaking out against the legacy of state terrorism in Latin America has had dangerous and devastating results, and we must interrogate the vestiges of Dirty War violence in contemporary Mexico and Argentina. Contemporary acts of violence do not only send a clear sign to survivors, they serve as a reminder to the public that the systems of power of the Dirty War era still influence the political culture and historical memory of the country. The Dirty War–era forms of violence continue to haunt the present in Argentina and Mexico and have now taken shape in new, modernized iterations of Dirty War violence. In Argentina, these terrorizing acts have also taken shape in economic forms of violence, which is most notable in the 2001 economic collapse. Political economists have termed this crash a "crisis of neoliberalism" with links to Dirty War–era economic policies, which included a structural adjustment program that resulted in extreme privatization, deregulation, and an increase of the national debt. While the origins of the collapse are multifaceted, it is clear that the business-oriented economic model that was implemented during the dictatorship was strengthened during former president Carlos Menem's tenure. While still president, Menem pardoned six senior military officers of the dictatorship, including Jorge Rafael Videla and Emilio Massera, setting into motion an era of amnesty and impunity for those involved in the military dictatorship.[1] President Kirchner abolished the amnesty laws in 2003, however, a ruling by the Argentinean Supreme Court in 2017, known as the 2x1 Law (Ley del 2x1), ruled in favor of reducing the sentences of human rights convicts, which harkened to the previous era of impunity.

While Argentina has had a nonlinear path toward achieving restorative justice, Mexico has not indicted or prosecuted any former heads of state or military officials who participated in Dirty War–era crimes. Although the 2001 FEMOSPP report named the Mexican officials responsible for the political genocide sanctioned by the state, more recent Mexican heads of state have stalled any official judicial processes. Clearly, it is evident that there is a national interest in keeping the history of state-sanctioned terrorism, disappearance, torture, and mass killings in the deep recesses of Mexican history. What's more, in March 2015, the Mexican government quietly classified the archives on the Dirty War. The classification of archival materials connected to the torture, disappearance, abduction, and incarceration of political dissidents during the Dirty War marks a critical moment for those invested in transnational Latin American cultural studies and human rights. The action not only underscores the power and legacy of authoritarianism that the Mexican government has showcased from the PRI era of the Dirty War, but it further limits and excludes access to certain forms of knowledge that was once available to the public.

With no official acknowledgment of these state crimes until 2001, the Mexican state continued to carry out violent acts that have echoed Dirty War terror tactics. The Mexican state has endorsed various forms of gendered and racialized violence against its citizens. Since the early 1990s, hundreds of young, poor factory working women have been brutally murdered and sexually assaulted in Ciudad Juárez, along the United States–Mexico border. These gender-based murders, *feminicidios*, evoke the gender violence normalized during the Dirty War. Indeed, as Rosa-Linda Fregoso notes in *Terrorizing Women*, some of the former officers who worked for the PRI during the Dirty War era have become Chihuahua state officials, the very state where the impunity of rampant feminicidios have taken hold. She claims that "the pervasive specter of civil wars and Latin America's Dirty Wars must also be factored into the architecture of feminicide, for the sexual degradation and dehumanization of feminicidal violence echo the repressed history of regimes of punishment designed for women under military regimes." Jean Franco adds that "the dirty wars turned the degradation of women into a routine occurrence," which commands us to interrogate how the new neoliberal Latin American states have relied on Dirty War–era terror tactics in order to reaffirm a new neoliberal order.[2]

This legacy of gendered, state-sponsored violence has coalesced with neoliberal politics in exceedingly violent and horrific ways in contemporary Mexico. In 2008, former President Felipe Calderón declared a war on drugs, which led to violent clashes between drug cartels and the government. The increased militarization of the state has resulted in thirty thousand disappearances and fifty thousand deaths; what's more, due to the hypermasculine performative nature of both the armed forces and the cartels, members of both organizations have committed rape and other forms of sexual violence.[3] The war on drugs has further marginalized Mexico's already vulnerable populations—the indigenous, women, rural communities—and now these groups are at the behest of the violent, modern neoliberal militarized narco state. What's more, as Jean Franco notes, the demise of Mexico's agrarian economy and rising unemployment and poverty lines has led many young men to join the cartels, which provide them with a sense of economic security while reinscribing a hypermasculine, violent gender performativity.

Speaking out or documenting Mexico's current humanitarian crisis has had devastating consequences. Since 2000, approximately 140 journalists have been murdered and more than two dozen journalists have been disappeared; Mexico is currently one of the most dangerous countries in the world for journalists. While many of these journalists were reporting on cartel violence, some were verifying the link between state Dirty War violence and the drug war. Since journalist Laura Castellanos published *Mexico armado* in 2007, she has been subjected to increasing intimidation tactics by the state. According to the periodical *Article 19*, each time she presents her research she is subjected to another harassing and intimidating incident.[4] Despite making a formal complaint of the incident to the Special Prosecutor's Office for the Attention of Crimes Committed against Freedom of Expression in Mexico, Castellanos states that her lack of faith in the Mexican justice system stems is due in large part to the fact that 65 percent of all reported crimes against journalists were committed by state agents.

Read alongside each other, these harrowing examples of contemporary state-sponsored aggression can effectively paralyze and numb us into inaction and apathy. Indeed, as many of the women I interviewed mentioned, many people were terrorized into silence and complacency with the violence of the nascent Latin American neoliberal, authoritarian state. Despite the real terror and violence that many survivors of the Dirty War face, many women I interviewed contended that they felt a moral imperative to denounce state violence of the past and present. During our interview, Forchetti mentioned Suppo's murder and the fear and terror it had sewn in the human rights community. When I ask her why she continued to provide her testimony in human rights trials despite the danger she could face, she paused for a moment and then declared, "Well look, one has a commitment to one's society, and it's one I will not abandon. I draw strength from my own context, and for me, it continues to be a necessity in my life, it is part of who I am. This is who I am, I would not be me if I didn't continue to do this, whatever it costs, you see?" For her and other women I interviewed, the experiences they endured have formed "part of who [they] are" and they have transformed these dehumanizing, shattering moments into a Latin American feminist radical politics that demands accountability and justice for past and present crimes of the state.

By tracing the genealogy of a transnational Latin American feminist memory in the cultural productions and women's testimonies, this book shows the radical possibilities for achieving gender justice for crimes of the state. In my conversations with various survivors of Latin America's historical traumas, they express the limits that are found in conventional, dominant narratives of the Dirty War. They also denote the vexing limitations formal justice—trials, prosecutions, universal human rights discourse, and truth commissions—represents in contemporary Mexico and Argentina. Many survivors emphasize that while restorative justice is symbolically important, these legal proceedings and universal human rights discourse do not represent true justice, a "comprehensive justice" that survivors would like to establish. This comprehensive justice would entail investigating the past and assuming historical memory projects that many survivors are involved with in the present. In this manner, the survivors are indeed considered by many, as Alejandra articulates "relentless old [people]" stuck in the past, or as Nelly Richard notes, "irritating remnants of a world that has disappeared."[5] In order to truly achieve radical feminist forms of justice, we must return to this "world that has disappeared" and recuperate the momentum of the movement that the Mexican and Argentinean authoritarian regimes violently decimated.

In a sense, this book is an attempt to delve into this disappeared world, to engage with the hauntings, lapses, and gaps of the past, and to excavate the bones of so many of Latin America's forgotten youths. Yet it is within these gaps and excavation of bones that we can create alternative Latin American feminist epistemologies of the Dirty War era. Thus, the narrative thread that unites each chapter of *Disruptive Archives* is a Latin American feminist theory of justice that is articulated in these cultural texts and words of these women. The words of the women survivors of state violence fuse past with present and generate new knowledge and theory on effectively challenging and dismantling the violent legacy of the Dirty War era. The theory and knowledge their words produce not only command us to reckon with an elided past, but they make us acknowledge the legacy and continued presence that gendered forms of violence and terrorism have on the contemporary landscapes. The narratives examined in this project posit a critical space of Latin American feminist justice and solidarity that has been abnegated by Mexican and Argentinean officials for decades. The survivors remain involved in historical memory projects searching for justice and denouncing the crimes committed during the Argentine and Mexican political genocide, and they also are engaged with political projects that seek social and economic justice for various disenfranchised communities in Mexico and Argentina. In the epigraphs above, Ferrarese's and Alejandra's words work against these histories of masculinist forms of state violence that had literally and symbolically tried to "annihilate" and "destroy" them, and whose modern variances have continued to do so. Their memories and their acts of speaking out, giving their testimony, and documenting their stories work to subvert these dominant, masculinist forms of knowledge on the Dirty War that have actively attempted to erase them from the archive.

Disruptive Archives illuminates the critical ways in which women's testimonies dialogically relate the possibility of a transnational Latin American feminist praxis, as survivors remain engaged in oppositional movements that demand justice for state-sponsored violence and systemic forms of oppression in the past and the present. It is their specters, their words, their narratives, and their various iterations of gendered resistance and resilience that encourage us to dismantle hegemonic, masculinist forms of knowledge on Latin American social movements. The words and memories of these radical women of the Dirty War era command our attention and demand that their histories of gendered resistance disrupt and challenge the neoliberal present in Mexico and Argentina.

Notes

Introduction

The quotation in the chapter title is from Chilean writer Roberto Bolaño's acceptance speech for the 1999 Rómulo Gallegos award.

1. When I wrote about "Alejandra's" history of activism and participation in the armed insurgencies in Guadalajara, she asked that I use a pseudonym. Due to the active role of the United States in counterinsurgency campaigns against so-called communist agitators during Mexico's Dirty War, Alejandra has remained critical of US interventionism in Mexico. For these reasons, she requested that I use "Alejandra" instead of her real name when publishing her narrative in a US-based publication.

2. For further historical context on Guadalajara's FER and the rise of the urban guerrillas, see Castellanos, *Mexico armado*, and Calderón, "From Books to Bullets."

3. Comité '68 is a civic organization founded by former members of the 1968 student movement's National Strike Council (CNH). The organization has centered on recuperating the historical memory of Dirty War era repression, such as the Tlatelolco Massacre, the 1971 Corpus Christi Massacre, and the counterinsurgency task force campaign that resulted in the deaths and disappearance of hundreds of political dissidents.

4. The Southern Cone Dirty Wars, as well as the gendered nature of state violence that characterized these histories of state terrorism, are already well covered by the scholarship. See Jelin, *State Repression*; Taylor, *Disappearing Acts*; Vezzetti, *Pasado y presente*.

5. Brown, "Most We Can Hope for," 453.

6. A large body of scholarship closely examines US interventionism in Latin America during the Cold War era, particularly as it relates to the US role in sponsoring Operation Condor in the Southern Cone; for example, see McSherry, *Predatory States*; Zanchetta, "Between Cold War Imperatives and State-Sponsored Terrorism"; Martorell, *Operación Cóndor, el vuelo de la muerte*. Padilla and Walker, "In the Archives," and Castellanos, *Mexico armado*, reveal the history of US interference in Mexico, such as its support and financial and military assistance, to establish the White Brigade antiterrorist task force, which was responsible for the torture and murders of dissidents during the Dirty War.

7. See Aviña, *Specters of Revolution*; Keller, *Mexico's Cold War*; Padilla and Walker, "In the Archives"; Calderón and Cedillo, *Challenging Authoritarianism*.

8. See Adela Cedillo's blog post, "Mujeres, guerrilla y terror," and Rayas, "Subjugating the Nation."

9. Calderón and Cedillo, *Challenging Authoritarianism*, 4.

10. Keller, *Mexico's Cold War*, 168.

11. The government responded violently to political protests, such as the repression of 1965 doctor's strike at the National Autonomous University in Mexico City (UNAM), claiming they were infiltrated by communist agitators. See Keller, *Mexico's Cold War*, 169.

12. See Castellanos, *Mexico armado*; Keller, *Mexico's Cold War*.

13. For more on the historical context leading to the military coup of 1976, see Romero, *History of Argentina in the Twentieth Century*.

14. It is also important to note here that the military dictatorship was supported by Argentina's middle and upper classes, as their personal interests had been previously threatened by the burgeoning working-class movements and thus the dictatorship promised to protect their private interests. See Vezzetti, *Pasado y presente*; Feitlowitz, *Lexicon of Terror*.

15. Vezzetti, *Pasado y presente*, 47–48.

16. Duhalde, *El estado terrorista Argentino*, 67.

17. Franco. *Cruel Modernity*, 15.

18. See Taylor, *Disappearing Acts*; Jelin, *State Repression*; Franco, *Cruel Modernity*; Bunster-Burotto, "Surviving Beyond Fear."

19. Sutton, "Poner el cuerpo," 130.

20. Cedillo, "Mujeres, guerrilla y terror." See also Cohen and Frazier, "Talking Back to '68," 57.

21. Castellanos, *Mexico armado*, 138.

22. For more background on the Agrupación Evita, the women's front of the Montoneros armed organization, see Grammático, "Populist Continuities in 'Revolutionary' Peronism?"

23. McClintock, "No Longer in a Future Heaven," 104.

24. See Taylor, *Disappearing Acts*; Franco, *Cruel Modernity*; Sutton, *Surviving State Terror*.

25. Taylor, *Disappearing Acts*, 9.

26. Bunster-Burotto, "Surviving Beyond Fear," 109.
27. Cedillo, "Mujeres, guerrilla y terror."
28. Gelman and la Madrid, *Ni el Flaco Perdón de Dios*, 107.
29. Barbara Sutton. *Surviving State Terror*, 10.
30. For additional information on the historical context behind the rise of guerrilla movements in Argentina, please see Calveiro, *Politica y/o violencia*, and Di Tella, *Montoneros, una historia* (documentary); for the history of Mexico's armed movements, see Aviña, *Specters of Revolution*, and Castellanos, *Mexico armado*.
31. Mendoza García, "Reconstructing the Collective Memory," 130.
32. Castellanos, *Mexico armado*, 225.
33. CONADEP, *Nunca más*, 1. Much has been written about the damage caused by the entrenchment of the Two Devils theory in collective and individual consciousness; while much more has been produced in relation to the Two Devils Theory in the Southern Cone nations, recently, more attention has been placed recently on this similar narrative in the Mexican context. See Bayer, "Pequeño recordatorio," and Calderón and Cedillo, *Challenging Authoritarianism in Mexico*.
34. Enloe, *Bananas, Beaches, and Bases*, 42.
35. Jelin, *State Repression*, 88.
36. Sutton, "Poner el cuerpo," 130.
37. Aguilar Terrés, *Memoria*, 25.
38. Castellanos, *Mexico armado*, 18.
39. Mohanty, *Feminism without Borders*, 78.
40. Taylor, *Archive and the Repertoire*, 20.
41. Franco, *Cruel Modernity*, 11. Bolaño, *Savage Detectives*, xvii.
42. Bueno-Hansen and Falcón, "Indigenous/Campesina Embodied Knowledge," 57–58.
43. Blackwell, *Chicana Power!*, 40.
44. Silvia Yáñez was one of the few survivors of the Monte Chingolo massacre in the army barracks of Monte Chingolo in Buenos Aires on December 23–24, 1975. The People's Revolutionary Army (ERP) had planned to take the arsenal from Army Battalion 601, but they were intercepted by the military who had infiltrated the ERP and knew of their plans. Although Yáñez survived the military's brutal attack, she witnessed the massacre of many of her compañeros that night.
45. Taylor, *Archive and the Repertoire*, 20.
46. Ellingson, *Embodiment in Qualitative Research*, 5.

Chapter 1. Critical Latin American Feminist Perspectives and the Limits and Possibilities of Human Rights Reports

1. For more on the debates surrounding the creation of FEMOSPP, see Rangel, "Gobernando el pasado."
2. Huyssen, "International Human Rights," 607–8.
3. Collins et al., "New Directions," 303.

4. Bueno-Hansen, *Feminist and Human Rights Struggles*, 11–12.
5. Fregoso and Bejarano, *Terrorizing Women*, 21.
6. Collins et al., "New Directions," 307.
7. Hayner, *Unspeakable Truths*, 7.
8. Balardini quoted in Valente, "Argentina." Bueno-Hansen, *Feminist and Human Rights Struggles*, 53.
9. Ross, *Bearing Witness*, 65.
10. Katherine Franke notes in "Gendered Subjects of Transitional Justice" that even gender-sensitive states and tribunals recognize women as victims of sexual assault, not agents of social change and they ignore the gender-based violence men experience.
11. Franke, "Gendered Subjects of Transitional Justice."
12. Enloe, *Bananas, Beaches, and Bases*, 13.
13. Theidon, "Justice in Transition," 436.
14. CONADEP, *Nunca más*, 307. All translations from the original Spanish texts are mine.
15. Brown, "Most We Can Hope For," 453.
16. CONADEP, *Nunca más*, 305.
17. Hundreds of women gave birth while illegally detained in various clandestine centers in Argentina and the babies born in captivity were placed in families of the regime's sympathizers.
18. Calvo later cofounded the Association of Ex-Detained Disappeared in Buenos Aires, where she remained an activist until her death in 2010.
19. Calvo quoted in Gelman and la Madrid, *Ni el flaco perdón de Dios*, 99.
20. Ibid., 107.
21. Ibid., 110, 115.
22. Richard, *Cultural Residues*, 19.
23. Strejilevich, *Single, Numberless Death*, 3.
24. Ibid., 24.
25. Ibid., 64, 61.
26. Ibid., 41.
27. Ross, *Bearing Witness*, 71.
28. Strejilevich, *Single, Numberless Death*, 14.
29. Franco, *Cruel Modernity*, 15.
30. Strejilevich, *Single, Numberless Death*, 69.
31. Ibid., 15.
32. Ibid., 87–88.
33. Quezada and Rangel, "Neither Truth nor Justice," 60.
34. Flaherty, *Hotel Mexico*, 42. Flaherty also notes that the creation of the CNDH was mandated under PRI president Salinas de Gortari, so that Mexico could participate in NAFTA and prove its commitment to human rights concerns.
35. For a detailed analysis of what was edited out of the original report, see the introduction to vol. 10 of Comité '68, *Mexico*. One of the central criticisms of the cen-

soring of the original report was the minimizing of the armed forces' role in extralegal killings and disappearances of political dissidents.

36. Both original and edited versions of the report were still available on the National Security Archive website as of February 2020; see https://nsarchive.gwu.edu.
37. Flaherty, *Hotel Mexico*, 42.
38. Doyle, "Official Report."
39. FEMOSPP, *Informe Histórico*, 441.
40. Carey and Gaspar, "Carrying on the Struggle."
41. Aguayo Quezada and Treviño Rangel, "Neither Truth nor Justice."
42. The prosecutors insisted on using the charge of genocide against former president Luis Echeverria, when political genocide had no legal basis or influence within the Mexican legal system. Turn to the Human Rights Watch report on the special prosecutor's findings for more detailed information on how the charges of genocide reflected the inexperience of the lawyers in the office, see Human Rights Watch, "Justice in Jeopardy."
43. Ironically, the government's decision to ratify the Convention on the Non-Applicability of Statutory Limitations to War Crimes and Crimes against Humanity in 2002 inadvertently provided amnesty for perpetrators. This convention lifted the statute of limitations on crimes committed by the state, yet this would only apply to crimes committed 2002 and onward. For more detailed findings on the conflicts of interests and other legal obstacles that impeded the prosecution of the perpetrators, see Human Rights Watch, "Justice in Jeopardy," as well as Rangel, "Gobernando el pasado."
44. Gräbner, "Beyond Innocence," 167.
45. Aguilar Terrés, *Memoria*, 76.
46. FEMOSPP, *Informe Histórico*, 579.
47. Poniatowska, *La noche de Tlatelolco*, 14, 15.
48. Cohen and Frazier, "Talking Back to '68," 156.
49. Poniatowska, *La noche de Tlatelolco*, 30.
50. For a more in-depth historical contextualization of the student movement, see Zermeño, *Mexico*; Monsivais, *El '68*; Carey, *Plaza of Sacrifices*.
51. Poniatowska, *La noche de Tlatelolco*, 89, 23, 87.
52. Ibid., 94.
53. Ibid., 100.
54. Ibid., 144.
55. Ibid.

Chapter 2. Sexual Necropolitics, Survival, and the Gender of Betrayal

1. Mbembé, "Necropolitics," 39.
2. For instance, while Argentinean extermination camps such as the Infierno in La Plata had very different functions from that of Mexico City's Lecumberri prison, both carceral spaces reflected a necropolitical logic of the nation states through the constant presence of death and subjugation of its prisoners.

3. Wright, "Necropolitics, Narcopolitics, and Femicide," 726.

4. Agamben, *Homo Sacer*, 139. "Bare life" is Agamben's biopolitical term that refers to a body at the moment of birth and the implicit connection to the sovereign state as a political subject: "birth immediately becomes nation such that there can be no interval of separation between the two terms" (128).

5. There exists, however, the misconception that sexual dehumanization was only subjected to incarcerated women prisoners, yet many testimonies refer to the sexual violence male prisoners endured. Oftentimes male prisoners were derided with homophobic taunts and subjected to various forms of sexual violence with the intent to emasculate them. Military officers considered male prisoners to be weak, effeminate, and unable to withstand physical pain, an apparent reflection of their nonexistent masculinity.

6. See Bartra, *La jaula de la melancolía*.

7. Kaminsky, "Marco Bechis' *Garage Olimpo*."

8. Maranghello, *Breve historia*, 268.

9. This and all subsequent quotations from the film are from Bechis, *Garage Olimpo*.

10. For more information on the "vuelos de la muerte" (death flights), see Robben, *Political Violence and Trauma in Argentina*.

11. Agamben, *Homo Sacer*, 139.

12. Weheliye, *Habeas Viscus*, 45.

13. Spillers quoted in ibid., 67.

14. I do not intend to conflate the experiences of subjugated, dehumanized, sexualized bodies in the Argentinean case with the experiences of dehumanization, sexualization, and racialization in the case of enslaved women. I do not want to deracinate the theoretical production of black feminist scholarship; however, I believe that the theoretical production of black feminist scholarship on the sexualization of bare life proves fruitful for my analysis of the eroticization and dehumanization of the captive body in the Argentinean concentration camp.

15. See Lagarde, *Los cautiveros de las mujeres*.

16. Weheliye, *Habeas Viscus*, 108.

17. Mia Mask quoted in Kaminsky, "Marco Bechis' *Garage Olimpo*."

18. Kaminsky, "Marco Bechis' *Garage Olimpo*."

19. Mbembé, "Necropolitics," 39.

20. Calveiro, *Poder y desaparición*, 53.

21. Covino, *Amending the Abject Body*, 17.

22. Calveiro, *Poder y desaparición*, 53.

23. Ibid., 24.

24. Agamben, *Homo Sacer*, 170.

25. Weheliye, *Habeas Viscus*, 2.

26. Longoni, *Traiciones*, 141, 151.

27. J. Revueltas, *El apando*.

28. Elía and Hernández, "*El apando* o del encierro en el encierro."

29. Durán, "Apuntes Sobre el Grotesco," 90.
30. Elena Poniatowska quoted in A. Revueltas and Cherón, *Conversaciones*, 142.
31. For a more detailed genealogy of the establishment of the Lecumberri Penal system in Mexico City, see Zolov, *Iconic Mexico*.
32. J. Revueltas, *El apando*, 26.
33. Ibid., 25.
34. Ibid., 27.
35. Durán, "Apuntes Sobre el Grotesco," 97.
36. J. Revueltas, *El apando*, 26.
37. Ibid., 31, 31–32.
38. Ibid., 31.
39. Ibid., 32.
40. For an excellent analysis of the novella's homophobic and homoerotic context, see Manzo-Robledo, "Erotismo y homofobia."
41. Manzo-Robledo, "Erotismo y homofobia," 358.
42. J. Revueltas, *El apando*, 35, 34, 37, 35.
43. Ibid., 26.
44. McClintock, "No Longer in a Future Heaven," 90.
45. J. Revueltas, *El apando*, 39.
46. McClintock, "No Longer in a Future Heaven," 90.
47. J. Revueltas, *El apando*, 28, 44.
48. Ibid., 30.
49. McClintock, "No Longer in a Future Heaven," 90.
50. Kandiyoti, "Identity and Its Discontents," 376; McClintock, "No Longer in a Future Heaven," 90.
51. J. Revueltas, *El apando*, 47.
52. Paz, "Sons of La Malinche."
53. Ibid., 25.
54. Cosse, "Infidelities," 445.
55. As Cosse notes, the Montoneros trained guerrillas to take cyanide in order to evade giving in to torture and providing the regime with information. To the Montoneros and other revolutionary groups, suicide was preferable to betraying the cause through rendering information, or worse, one's body to the enemy.
56. Valdés, *Diary*, 78.
57. Gelman and La Madrid, *Ni el flaco perdón de Dios*, 113.
58. Di Tella, *Montoneros*.
59. Longoni, *Traiciones*, 97.
60. Ibid., 148–47.
61. Lewin and Wornat, *Putas y guerrilleras*, 17, 30.
62. Álvarez, *Campo de batalla*.
63. Longoni, *Traiciones*, 151.
64. Lewin and Wornat, *Putas y guerrileras*, 31.

65. Aguilar Terrés, *Memoria*, 148.
66. Cosse, "Infidelities," 445.
67. Aguilar Terrés, *Memoria*, 147.

Chapter 3. "Ghosts of Another Era"

The chapter epigraph is quoted in Aguilar Terrés, *Memoria*, 30.

1. "No son las calles / lo que duele / son los muertos / nuestros muertos / los que no me dejan / dormir / ni vivir / y a veces ni morir."
2. Riley, *Flor en Otomí*.
3. This notion of haunting and ghosts is tied to trauma and memory. As Dominick LaCapra notes in *Writing History, Writing Trauma*, trauma refers to being possessed and held captive by the repetition of a past event. For more on the difference between trauma and haunting, see María del Pilar Blanco and Esther Pereen's edited volume, *The Spectralities Reader*.
4. Gordon, *Ghostly Matters*, xvi, 19, xvi.
5. Derrida, *Specters of Marx*, 175.
6. See Ulloa Bornemann, *Surviving Mexico's Dirty War*; Vezzetti, *Sobre la violencia revolucionaria*; Magdaleno Cárdenas, "Los otros muertos."
7. Beverley, "Rethinking the Armed Struggle," 50.
8. Rodríguez, *Women, Guerrillas, and Love*, 50.
9. Franco, *Cruel Modernity*, 120.
10. It is critical to point out the numerous differences among the guerrillas that operated in Argentina and Mexico in various areas of each nation starting in the late 1950s and ending in the early 1980s (e.g., the rise of rural guerrilla movements such as the Party of the Poor in the Mexican countryside and the student-lead urban guerrilla group in Guadalajara, the Revolutionary Student Front, which had very distinct historical-social contexts).
11. "Flor en Otomí" refers to the translation of Prieto Stock's first name, which means "flower" in the Otomí language, spoken by the indigenous Otomí community from central Mexico.
12. Barthes, *Camera Lucida*, 76.
13. Nichols, "Voice of Documentary," 18.
14. This and all subsequent quotations from the film are from Riley, *Flor en Otomí*.
15. Luisa Riley, interview by Viviana MacManus, Mexico City, July 2012.
16. Mulvey, *Death 24x a Second*, 11, 10.
17. Elisa Benavides Guevara, one of the surviving members of the Nepantla raid, discusses the clandestine life she shared with Prieto Stock in the safe house. Although she and the other individuals interviewed in the film are never identified, Benavides Guevara is a prominent and well-known figure in Mexico's human rights community, and for many years she has advocated for indigenous rights in Chiapas.
18. Mulvey, *Death 24x a Second*, 60.

19. Ibid.
20. Diana, *Mujeres Guerrilleras*, 13.
21. For more on this history, see Tomás Eloy Martínez, *La pasión según Trelew*.
22. Diana, *Mujeres guerrilleras*, 14.
23. Ibid., 415, 408.
24. Avelar, *Untimely Present*, 2–3.
25. Diana, *Mujeres guerrilleras*, 13.
26. Ibid., 11.
27. Gordon, *Ghostly Matters*, 63.
28. Diana, *Mujeres guerrilleras*, 167.
29. Jelin, *State Repression*, 5.
30. Diana, *Mujeres guerrilleras*, 168.
31. Derrida, *Specters of Marx*, 4.
32. See Michael Langán, "Argentine President Menem's First Pardons."
33. Beverley, "Rethinking the Armed Struggle," 50.
34. Hesford and Kozol, *Haunting Violations*, 2.
35. *Flor* also discusses the impact her political decisions had upon her family members and also alluded to how Prieto Stock's political involvement seemed to fulfill her father's own personal political ambitions.
36. Cedillo, "Mujeres, guerrilla y terror."
37. Aguilar Terrés, *Memoria*, 18.
38. Derrida, *Specters of Marx*, 4.
39. See Andrea Andújar et al., *De minifaldas*, for excellent feminist analyses of the history of women's militancy and political activism during 1970s Argentina.
40. Another critical, seminal text on women's political agency during 1970s Argentina is Viviana Beguán, *Nosotras, presas políticas*.
41. Diana, *Mujeres guerrilleras*, 16.
42. Rodríguez, *Women, Guerrillas, Love*, xvii. For more on the difficulties posed by studying the Latin American armed struggle, see Beverley, "Rethinking the Armed Struggle"; Vezzetti, *Pasado y presente*; Sarlo, "Cuando la política era joven."
43. Diana, *Mujeres guerrilleras*, 87, 178, 146.
44. Rodríguez, *Women, Guerrillas, Love*, 42.
45. Diana, *Mujeres guerrilleras*, 182.
46. Cosse, "Infidelities," 416.
47. Diana, *Mujeres guerrilleras*, 407.
48. Cosse, "Infidelities," 434.
49. Lazzara, Olivera-Williams, and Szurmuk Pilar, "Violencia, memoria, justicia," 343.
50. Many excellent scholarly works deal with the question of motherhood, gender, and sexual politics of Argentina's armed insurgencies. Most of the works, however, are by South American feminist scholars and only available in the original Spanish. See, for example, Andujar et al., *De minifaldas*; Grammático, *Mujeres montoneras*;

Cosse, "Infidelities." There is very little literature available on Mexican guerrilleras and motherhood; however, the 1986 short film *Una isla rodeada de agua* (dir. María Nova) centers on this premise, as does the 2008 documentary *Trazando Aleida* (dir. Christiane Burkhard).

51. Diana, *Mujeres guerrilleras*, 127.

Chapter 4. Gendered Memories, Collective Subjectivity, and Solidarity Practices in Women's Oral Histories

1. For more on Argentina's phenomenon of the *reaparecidos* and the shame associated with surviving state violence, see Parks, *Reappeared*.

2. Scheibe Wolff, Pedro, and Gomez da Silva, "'Gendered' Memories," 64.

3. See ibid. and Cohen and Frazier, "Talking Back to '68."

4. Laub and Felman, *Testimony*, 69.

5. For more on the relationship between trauma and testimony, see Caruth, *Unclaimed Experience*; Jelin, *State Repression*; Laub and Felman, *Testimony*.

6. Taylor, *Archive and the Repertoire*, 191.

7. Blackwell, *Chicana Power!*, 10.

8. Portelli, *Battle of Valle Giulia*, 6.

9. James, *Doña María's Story*, 36.

10. Necoechea Gracia and Torres Montenegro, *Caminos de historia y memoria*, 113.

11. For more specifically on the genre of Latin American oral history scholarship, see James, *Doña María's Story*; Camarena, Morales Lersch, and Necoechea Gracia, *Métodos y Técnicas de Historia Oral*; Benmayor, Cardenal de la Nuez, and Domínguez Prats, *Memory, Subjectivities, and Representation*; Pozzi et al., *Oral History in Latin America*.

12. For more on the genealogy of the Latin American *testimonio*, see Beverley, *Testimonio*; Gugelberger, *Real Thing*.

13. Pozzi, "Oral History in Latin America," 2.

14. See, for example, Gluck, "Has Feminist Oral History Lost Its Radical/Subversive Edge?"; Sangster, "Telling Our Stories."

15. Scheibe Wolff, Pedro, and Gomez da Silva, "'Gendered' Memories," 60.

16. Blackwell, *Chicana Power!*, 11.

17. Álvarez, *Campo de batalla*.

18. Sangster, "Telling Our Stories," 8–9.

19. Jelin, *State Repression*, 84.

20. Beverley, "Margin at the Center," 41.

21. Taylor, *Archive and the Repertoire*, 89.

22. Zavala Guillén, "Argentinean Transitional Process," 59.

23. Laub and Felman iterate the importance of an active listener to histories of trauma in order to process or work through the trauma.

24. Zavala Guillén, "Argentinean Transitional Process," 58.

25. Eloy is referring to the amnesty law, Law of Due Obedience, instated in 1987 and repealed in 2006; this amnesty law stated that military official working during

the years of the dictatorship could not be charged with crimes against humanity since they were merely complying with their superiors' orders.

26. Franco, *Cruel Modernity*, 82.
27. Castellanos, *Mexico armado*, 250, 268.
28. Taylor, *Disappearing Acts*, 25.
29. See Pensado Leglise, "Memorias de la experiencia politica."
30. Petrich, "Entrevista."
31. Scheibe Wolff, Pedro, and Gomez da Silva, "'Gendered' Memories," 60.
32. Ibid., 64.
33. Mohanty, *Feminism without Borders*, 78.
34. Taylor, *Archive and the Repertoire*, 191, 211.
35. Ibid., 82.
36. *Escrache* refers to public demonstrations and performative, political acts outside the residences of former military and army officials in Argentina, Chile, Mexico, and other Latin American nations. They are organized by various human rights groups in order to call attention to the various forms of amnesty and leniency granted to the perpetrators of human rights abuse.

Epilogue

1. For more on the economic collapse of 2001, see Teubal, "Economic Groups"; Veigel, *Dictatorship, Democracy, and Globalization*; McIntosh, "Debt, Dollars, Democracy and Dictatorships."
2. Fregoso and Bejarano, *Terrorizing Women*, 12–13. Franco, *Cruel Modernity*, 224.
3. Franco, *Cruel Modernity*, 219, and Achterling, "University Researchers Preview Testimony."
4. Reyes, "Violence against Journalists."
5. Richard, *Cultural Residues*, 16.

Bibliography

Selected Interviews

Aguilar Terrés, Luz. Mexico City, July 17, 2012.
"Alejandra." Guadalajara, Mexico, July 13, 2012.
Balderas Silva, Maricela. Glen Burnie, Maryland, August 13, 2013.
Cruz, Margarita. Buenos Aires, Argentina, July 13, 2009.
Díaz, Marta. Rosario, Argentina, August 3, 2009.
Eloy, Nilda. La Plata, Argentina, July 22, 2009.
Ferrarese, Lelia. Rosario, Argentina, August 3, 2009.
Forchetti, Liliana. Buenos Aires, June 19, 2014.
Gutiérrez Campos, Bertha Lilia. Guadalajara, Mexico, July 14, 2012.
Riley, Luisa. Mexico City, Mexico, July 17, 2012.
Rodríguez Márquez, Ana Ignacia. Mexico City, Mexico, May 22, 2010.
Sgro, Mirta. Buenos Aires, Argentina, June 9, 2014.
Yáñez, Silvia. Tigre, Argentina, June 12, 2014.

Works Cited

Achterling, Michael. "University Researchers Preview Testimony on Mexico's Disappeared." *Minnesota Daily*, October 5, 2017. http://www.mndaily.com/article/2017/10/university-researchers-preview-testimony-on-mexican-disappearances.
Agamben, Giorgio. *Homo Sacer: Sovereign Power and Bare Life*. Translated by Daniel Heller-Roazen. Stanford, CA: Stanford University Press, 1998.

Aguayo Quezada, Sergio, and Javier Treviño Rangel. "Neither Truth nor Justice: Mexico's De Facto Amnesty." *Latin American Perspectives* 33, no. 2 (March 2006): 56–68. https://doi.org/10.1177/0094582X05286085.

Aguilar Terrés, María de la Luz, ed. *Memoria del Primer Encuentro Nacional de Mujeres Exguerrilleras: Análisis y reflexión sobre la participación de las mujeres en el movimiento armado socialista*. Mexico, DF: [author], 2007.

Álvarez, Fernando, dir. *Campo de Batalla, Cuerpo de Mujer*. Buenos Aires: Perro en la Luna, 2012.

Andujar, Andrea, Débora D'Antonio, Fernanda Gil Lozano, Karin Grammático, and María Laura Rosa. *De minifaldas, militancias y revoluciones*. Buenos Aires: Luxemburg, 2009.

Arizmendi, Martha Elía, and Angélica Beatriz Hernández. "*El apando* o del encierro en el encierro." *La colmena* 76 (October–December 2012). http://web.uaemex.mx/plin/colmena/Colmena_76/Aguijon/5_El_apando_o_del_encierro.pdf.

Avelar, Idelbar. *The Untimely Present: Postdictatorial Latin American Fiction and the Task of Mourning*. Durham, NC: Duke University Press, 1999.

Aviña, Alexander. *Specters of Revolution: Peasant Guerrillas and the Cold War Mexican Countryside*. New York: Oxford University Press, 2014.

Barthes, Roland. *Camera Lucida: Reflections on Photography*. New York: Hill and Wang, 1981.

Bartra, Roger. *La jaula de la melancolía*. Mexico, DF: Grijalbo, 1987.

Bayer, Osvaldo. "Pequeño recordatorio para un país sin memoria." *Página/12*, no date. https://www.pagina12.com.ar/2001/01-03/01-03-22/suplex01.htm. Accessed May 2011.

Bechis, Marco, dir. *Garage Olimpo*. Argentina: Classic Paradis Films, 1999.

Beguán, Viviana, coord. *Nosotras, presas políticas: 1974–1983*. Buenos Aires: Nuestra América, 2006.

Benmayor, Rina, María Eugenia Cardenal de la Nuez, and Pilar Domínguez Prats, eds. *Memory, Subjectivities, and Representation: Approaches to Oral History in Latin America, Portugal, and Spain*. New York: Palgrave Macmillan, 2015.

Beverley, John. "The Margin at the Center: On *Testimonio* (1989)." In *The Real Thing: Testimonial Discourse and Latin America*, edited by Georg M. Gugelberger, 23–41. Durham, NC: Duke University Press, 1996.

———. "Rethinking the Armed Struggle in Latin America." *Boundary 2: An International Journal of Literature and Culture* 36, no. 1 (2009): 47–59.

Blackwell, Maylei. *Chicana Power! Contested Histories of Feminism in the Chicano Movement*. Austin: University of Texas Press, 2011.

Blanco, María del Pilar, and Esther Pereen, eds. *The Spectralities Reader: Ghosts and Haunting in Contemporary Cultural Theory*. New York: Bloomsbury, 2013.

Bolaño, Roberto. *The Savage Detectives*. Translated by Natasha Wimmer. New York: Farrar, Straus and Giroux, 2007.

Bonnasso, Miguel. *Recuerdo de la muerte*. Buenos Aires: Editorial Planeta, 1998.

Brown, Wendy. "'The Most We Can Hope For . . .': Human Rights and the Politics of Fatalism." *South Atlantic Quarterly* 103, no. 2/3 (2004): 451–62.
Bueno-Hansen, Pascha. *Feminist and Human Rights Struggles in Peru*. Urbana: University of Illinois Press, 2015.
Bueno-Hansen, Pascha, and Sylvanna M. Falcón. "Indigenous/Campesina Embodied Knowledge, Human Rights Awards, and Lessons for Transnational Feminist Solidarity." In *Decolonizing Feminism: Transnational Feminism and Globalization*, edited by Margaret A. McLaren, 57–80. New York: Rowman & Littlefield International, 2018.
Bunster-Burotto, Ximena. "Surviving Beyond Fear: Women and Torture in Latin America." In *Surviving Beyond Fear: Women, Children and Human Rights in Latin America*, edited by Marjorie Agosín, 98–125. New York: White Pine Press, 1993.
Burkhard, Christiane. *Trazando Aleida*. (*Tracing Aleida: The Story of a Search*.) Documentary. 2008. 88 min.
Calderón, Fernando Herrera. "From Books to Bullets: Youth Radicalism and Urban Guerrillas in Guadalajara." In Calderón and Cedillo, *Challenging Authoritarianism*, 105–28.
Calderón, Fernando Herrera, and Adela Cedillo, eds. *Challenging Authoritarianism in Mexico: Revolutionary Struggles and the Dirty War, 1964–1982*. New York: Routledge, 2012.
Calveiro, Pilar, *Poder y desaparición: los campos de concentración en Argentina*. Buenos Aires: Ediciones Colihue, 1998.
———. *Politica y/o violencia*. Buenos Aires: Siglo XXI, 2013.
Camarena, Mario Ocampo, Teresa Morales Lersch, and Gerardo Necoechea Gracia. *Métodos y técnicas de historia oral*. Mexico, DF: Instituto Nacional de Antropología y Historia, Universidad Autónoma de México, 1990.
Carey, Elaine. *Plaza of Sacrifices: Gender, Power, and Terror in 1968 Mexico*. Albuquerque: University of New Mexico Press, 2005.
Carey, Elaine, and José Agustín Román Gaspar. "Carrying on the Struggle: El Comité '68." North American Congress on Latin America, May 1, 2008. https://nacla.org/article/carrying-struggle-el-comit%C3%A9–68.
Caruth, Cathy. *Unclaimed Experience: Trauma, Narrative, and History*. 20th anniv. ed. Baltimore, MD: Johns Hopkins University Press, 2016.
Castellanos, Laura. *Mexico armado: 1943–1981*. México, DF: Ediciones Era, 2007.
Cedillo, Adela. "Mujeres, guerrilla y terror de estado en la época de la revoltura en México." *La Guerra sucia en México* (blog), May 9, 2010. http://guerrasuciamexicana.blogspot.com/2010/03/mujeres-guerrilla-y-terror-de-estado.html.
Cohen, Deborah, and Lessie Jo Frazier. "Talking Back to '68: Gendered Narratives, Participatory Spaces, and Political Cultures." In *Gender and Sexuality in 1968: Transformative Politics in the Cultural Imagination*, edited by Deborah Cohen and Lessie Jo Frazier, 145–72. New York: Palgrave MacMillan 2009.
Collins, Dana, Sylvanna Falcón, Sharmila Lodhia, and Molly Talcott. "New Directions in Human Rights." *International Feminist Journal of Politics* 12, nos. 3–4 (December 2010): 298–319.

Comité '68 Pro Libertadores Democráticas. *México: Genocidio y Delitos de Lesa Humanidad, Documentos Fundamentales (1968–2008)*. México, DF: Comité '68 Pro Libertadores Democráticas, 2008.

CONADEP (Comisón Nacional sobre la Desaparición de Personas). *Nunca más: Informe de la Comisión Nacional sobre la Desaparición de Personas*. Buenos Aires: Editorial Universitaria de Buenos Aires, 1984.

Cosse, Isabella. "Infidelities: Morality, Revolution, and Sexuality in Left-Wing Guerrilla Organizations in 1960s and 1970s Argentina." *Journal of the History of Sexuality* 23, no. 3 (2014): 415–50.

Covino, Deborah Caslav. *Amending the Abject Body: Makeovers in Medicine and Culture*. Albany: State University of New York Press, 2004.

Derrida, Jacques. *Specters of Marx: The State of the Debt, the Work of Mourning, and the New International*. Translated by Peggy Kamuf. New York: Routledge, 1994.

Diana, Marta. *Mujeres guerrilleras: La militancia de los setenta en el testimonio de sus protagonistas femeninas*. Buenos Aires: Planeta, 1996.

Di Tella, Andrés, dir. *Montoneros, una historia*. Produced by Roberto Barandalla. Buenos Aires: Cine Ojo, 1998. 90 min.

Doyle, Kate. "Official Report Released on Mexico's 'Dirty War.'" *National Security Archive*, November 21, 2006. http://nsarchive.gwu.edu/NSAEBB/NSAEBB209/index.htm#informe.

Duhalde, Eduardo Luis. *El estado terrorista argentino*. Buenos Aires: Editorial Universitaria de Buenos Aires, 1999.

Durán, Javier. "Apuntes Sobre el Grotesco en Tres Novelas de José Revueltas." *Chasqui* 28, no. 2 (November 1999): 89–102.

Elía, Martha and Angélica Beatriz Hernández. "*El apando* o del encierro en el encierro." *La colmena* 76 (October–December 2012). http://web.uaemex.mx/plin/colmena/Colmena_76/Aguijon/5_El_apando_o_del_encierro.pdf.

Ellingson, Laura L. *Embodiment in Qualitative Research*. New York: Routledge, 2017.

Eloy Martínez, Tomás. *La pasión según Trelew*. Buenos Aires: Punto de Lectura Argentina, 2007.

Enloe, Cynthia. *Bananas, Beaches, and Bases: Making Feminist Sense of International Politics*. Los Angeles: University of California Press, 1990.

Feitlowitz, Marguerite. *A Lexicon of Terror: Argentina and the Legacies of Torture*. New York: Oxford University Press, 1998.

FEMOSPP (Fiscalía Especial para Movimientos Sociales y Políticos del Pasado; Special Prosecutor for Social and Political Movements of the Past). *Informe Histórico a la Sociedad Mexicana*. Mexico: Procuradía General de la República, November 2006.

Flaherty, George F. *Hotel Mexico: Dwelling on the '68 Movement*. Oakland: University of California Press, 2016.

Franco, Jean. *Cruel Modernity*. Durham, NC: Duke University Press, 2013.

Franke, Katherine M. "Gendered Subjects of Transitional Justice." *Columbia Journal of Gender and Law* 15, no. 3 (2006): 813–28.

Fregoso, Rosa-Linda, and Cynthia Bejarano, eds. *Terrorizing Women: Feminicide in the Américas*. Durham, NC: Duke University Press, 2010.

Gelman, Juan, and Mara la Madrid, eds. *Ni el flaco perdón de Dios: Hijos de desaparecidos*. Buenos Aires: Editorial Planeta, 1997.

Gluck, Sherna Berger. "Has Feminist Oral History Lost Its Radical/Subversive Edge?" *Oral History* 39 (January 2011): 63–72.

Gordon, Avery. *Ghostly Matters: Haunting and the Sociological Imagination*. Minneapolis: University of Minnesota Press, 1997.

Gräbner, Cornelia. "Beyond Innocence: Mexican Guerrilla Groups, State Terrorism, and Emergent Civil Society in Montemayor, Mendoza, and Glockner." *A Contracorriente: A Journal on Social History and Literature in Latin America* 11, no. 3 (spring 2014): 164–94.

Grammático, Karin. *Mujeres montoneras: Una historia de la Agrupación Evita, 1973–1974*. Buenos Aires: Luxemburg, 2012.

———. "Populist Continuities in 'Revolutionary' Peronism? A Comparative Analysis of the Gender Discourses of the First Peronism (1946–1955) and the Montoneros." In *Gender and Populism in Latin America: Passionate Politics*, edited by Karen Kampwirth, 122–39. University Park: Pennsylvania State University Press, 2010.

Gugelberger, Georg M., ed. *The Real Thing: Testimonial Discourse and Latin America*. Durham, NC: Duke University Press, 1996.

Hayner, Priscilla B. *Unspeakable Truths: Transitional Justice and the Challenge of Truth Commissions*. New York: Routledge, 2011.

Hesford, Wendy, and Wendy Kozol, eds. *Haunting Violations: Feminist Criticism and the Crisis of the "Real."* Urbana: University of Illinois Press, 2001.

Human Rights Watch. "Justice in Jeopardy: Why Mexico's First Real Effort to Address Past Abuses Risks Becoming Its Latest Failure." *Human Rights Watch* 15, no. 4 (B) (July 2003). 33 pp. https://www.hrw.org/reports/2003/mexico0703/mexico0703.pdf.

Huyssen, Andreas. "International Human Rights and the Politics of Memory: Limits and Challenges." *Criticism* 53, no. 4 (fall 2011): 607–24.

James, Daniel. *Doña María's Story: Life History, Memory, and Political Identity*. Durham, NC: Duke University Press, 2000.

Jelin, Elizabeth. *State Repression and the Labors of Memory*. Translated by Judy Rein and Marcial Godoy-Anativia. Minneapolis: University of Minnesota Press, 2003.

Kaminsky, Amy. "Marco Bechis' *Garage Olimpo*: Cinema of Witness." *Jump Cut: A Review of Contemporary Media* 48 (winter 2006). https://www.ejumpcut.org/archive/jc48.2006/GarageOlimpo/text.html

Kandiyoti, Deniz. "Identity and Its Discontents: Women and the Nation." In *Colonial Discourse and Postcolonial Theory: A Reader*, edited by Patrick Williams and Laura Chrismas, 376–91. London: Harvester Wheatsheaf, 1993.

Keller, Renata. *Mexico's Cold War: Cuba, the United States, and the Legacy of the Mexican Revolution*. New York: Cambridge University Press, 2015.

LaCapra, Dominick. *Writing History, Writing Trauma*. Ithaca, NY: Cornell University Press, 1998.

Lagarde, Marcela. *Los cautiveros de las mujeres: madresposas, monjas, putas, presas y locas*. México, DF: Universidad Nacional Autónoma de México, 1990.

Langán, Michael. "Argentine President Menem's First Pardons: A Comparative Analysis of Coverage by Buenos Aires' Leading Dailies." *Canadian Journal of Latin American and Caribbean Studies* 16, no. 31 (1991): 145–56.

Laub, Dori, and Shoshanna Felman. *Testimony: Crisis of Witnessing in Literature, Psychoanalysis, and History*. New York: Routledge, 1992.

Lazzara, Michael J., María Rosa Olivera-Williams, and Monica Szurmuk. "Violencia, memoria, justicia: Una entrevista a Pilar Calveiro." *A Contracorriente: A Journal on Social History and Literature in Latin America* 10, no. 2 (2013): 324–46.

Lewin, Miriam, and Olga Wornat. *Putas y guerrilleras*. Buenos Aires: Grupo Editorial Planeta, 2014.

Longoni, Ana. *Traiciones: La figura del traidor en los relatos acerca de los sobrevivientes de la repression*. Buenos Aires: Grupo Editorial Norma, 2007.

Magdaleno Cardenas, María de los Ángeles. "Los otros muertos." *Históricas: Boletín del Instituto de Investigaciones Históricas, UNAM* 99 (January–April 2014): 2–14.

Manzo-Robledo, Francisco. "Erotismo y homofobia en 'El Apando' (1969) de José Revueltas." *Mexican Studies/Estudios mexicanos* 16, no. 2 (summer 2000): 347–66.

Maranghello, Cesar. *Breve historia del cine argentino*. Buenos Aires: Laertes, 2003.

Martorell, Francisco. *Operación Cóndor, el vuelo de la muerte: La coordinación represiva en el Cono Sur*. Santiago: Lom, 1999.

Mbembé, Achille. "Necropolitics." Translated by Libby Meintjes. *Public Culture* 15, no. 1 (winter 2003): 11–40.

McClintock, Anne. "'No Longer in a Future Heaven': Women and Nationalism in South Africa." *Transition* 51 (1991): 104–23.

McIntosh, David. "Debt, Dollars, Democracy and Dictatorships: Argentina and the Diminishing Logic of Post-Global Markets." *Public* 27: Shop (spring 2003): 117–29.

McSherry, J. Patrice. *Predatory States: Operation Condor and Covert War in Latin America*. New York: Rowman and Littlefield, 2005.

Mendoza García, Jorge. "Reconstructing the Collective Memory of Mexico's Dirty War Ideologization, Clandestine Detention, and Torture." Translated by Victoria J. Furio. *Latin American Perspectives* 43, no. 6 (November 2016): 124–40.

Mohanty, Chandra T. *Feminism without Borders: Decolonizing Theory, Practicing Solidarity*. Durham, NC: Duke University Press, 2003.

Monsiváis, Carlos. *El '68, la tradición de la Resistencia*. México, DF: Ediciones Era, 2008.

Mulvey, Laura. *Death 24x a Second: Stillness and the Moving Image*. London: Reaktion Books, 2006.

Necoechea Gracia, Gerardo, and Antonio Torres Montenegro, eds. *Caminos de historia y memoria en América Latina*. Buenos Aires: Imago Mundi, 2011.

Nichols, Bill. "The Voice of Documentary." *Film Quarterly* 36, no. 3 (1983): 17–30.

Nova, María, dir. *Una isla rodeada de agua*. Talachas and Women Make Movies. 1986. 28 min.

Padilla, Tanalís, and Louise E. Walker. "In the Archives: History and Politics." *Journal of Iberian and Latin American Research* 19, no. 1 (2013): 1–10.
Parks, Rebekah. *The Reappeared: Argentine Former Political Prisoners*. New Brunswick: NJ: Rutgers University Press, 2014.
Paz, Octavio. "The Sons of La Malinche." In *The Mexico Reader*, edited by Gilbert Joseph and Timothy Henderson, 20–27. Durham, NC: Duke University Press, 2002.
Pensado Leglise, Patricia. "Memorias de la experiencia politica de cinco latinoamericanas de izquierda." In *Caminos de historia y memoria en América latina*, edited by Gerardo Necoechea Gracia and Antonio Torres Montenegro, 217–28. Buenos Aires: Imago Mundi, 2011.
Petrich, Blanche. "Entrevista: Ana Ignacia Rodríguez, La Nacha." *La Jornada*, July 22, 2002. http://www.jornada.unam.mx/2002/07/22/009n1pol.php?printver=0.
Poniatowska, Elena. *La noche de Tlatlelolco: testimonios de historia oral*. México, DF: Era, 2004. Published in English as *Massacre in Mexico* (New York: Viking, 1975), translated by Helen R. Lane.
Portelli, Alessandro. *The Battle of Valle Giulia: Oral History and the Art of Dialogue*. Madison: University of Wisconsin Press, 1997.
Pozzi, Pablo. "Oral History in Latin America." In "Oral History in Latin America/Historia Oral en América Latina," edited by Pablo Pozzi, Alexander Freund, Gerardo Necoechea, and Robson Laverdi, 7 pp. Special issue, *Oral History Forum/Forum d'histoire orale* 32 (2012). http://www.oralhistoryforum.ca/index.php/ohf/article/view/442.
Pozzi, Pablo, Alexander Freund, Gerardo Necoechea, and Robson Laverdi, eds. "Oral History in Latin America/Historia Oral en América Latina." Special issue, *Oral History Forum/Forum d'histoire orale* 32 (2012). http://www.oralhistoryforum.ca/index.php/ohf/issue/view/42.
Quezada, Aguaya, and Javier Treviño Rangel. "Neither Truth nor Justice: Mexico's De Facto Amnesty." *Latin American Perspectives* 33 no. 2 (March 2006): 56–68.
Rayas, Lucía. "Subjugating the Nation: Women and the Guerrilla Experience." In Calderón and Cedillo, *Challenging Authoritarianism*, 167–81.
Revueltas, Andrea, and Felipe Cherón, eds. *Conversaciones con José Revueltas*. México, DF: Ediciones Era, 2001.
Revueltas, José. *El apando*. México, DF: Alias Editorial, 1985.
Reyes, Paola. "Violence against Journalists in Mexico: An Interview with Laura Castellanos." *Nacla*, June 7, 2010. https://nacla.org/news/2010/6/7/violence-against-journalists-mexico-interview-laura-castellanos.
Richard, Nelly. *Cultural Residues: Chile in Transition*. Translated by Alan West-Durán and Theodore Quester. Minneapolis: University of Minnesota Press, 2004.
Riley, Luisa, dir. *Flor en Otomí*. México, DF: Icarus Films, 2012. Documentary. 78 min.
Robben, Antonius C. G. M. *Political Violence and Trauma in Argentina*. Philadelphia: University of Pennsylvania Press, 2005.
Rodríguez, Ileana. *Women, Guerrillas, and Love: Understanding War in Central America*. Minneapolis: University of Minnesota Press, 1996.

Romero, Luis Alberto. *A History of Argentina in the Twentieth Century.* Buenos Aires: Fondo de Cultura Económica de Argentina, 1994.

Ross, Fiona C. *Bearing Witness: Women and Truth and Reconciliation Commission in South Africa.* Sterling, VA: Pluto, 2003.

Sangster, Joan. "Telling Our Stories: Feminist Debates and the Use of Oral History." *Women's History Review* 3, no. 1 (1994): 5–28.

Sarlo, Beatriz. "Cuando la política era joven." *Punto de vista* 20, no. 58 (August 1997): 15–19.

Scheibe Wolff, Cristina, Joana María Pedro, and Janine Gomez da Silva. "'Gendered' Memories: Women's Narratives from the Southern Cone." In *Memory, Subjectivities, and Representation,* edited by Rina Benmayor, María Eugenia Cardenal de la Nuez, and Pilar Domínguez Prats, 57–73. New York: Palgrave MacMillan, 2016.

Strejilevich, Nora. *A Single, Numberless Death.* Translated by Cristina de la Torre with the collaboration of the author. Charlottesville: University of Virginia Press, 2002. Originally published as *Una sola muerte numerosa* (Miami: North-South Center Press, 1997).

Sutton, Barbara. "Poner el cuerpo: Women's Embodiment and Political Resistance in Argentina." *Latin American Politics and Society* 49, no. 3 (fall 2007): 129–62.

———. *Surviving State Terror: Women's Testimonies of Repression and Resistance in Argentina.* New York: New York University Press, 2018.

Taylor, Diana. *The Archive and the Repertoire.* Durham, NC: Duke University Press, 2003.

———. *Disappearing Acts: Spectacles of Gender and Nationalism in Argentina's "Dirty War."* Durham, NC: Duke University Press, 1997.

Teubal, Miguel. "Economic Groups and the Rise and Collapse of Neoliberalism in Argentina." In *Big Business and Economic Development,* edited by Alex Fernández Jilberto and Barbara Hogenboon, 167–90. London: Routledge, 2008.

Theidon, Kimberly. "Justice in Transition: The Micropolitics of Reconciliation in Postwar Peru." *Journal of Conflict Resolution* 50, no. 3 (2006): 433–57.

Treviño Rangel, Javier. "Gobernando el pasado: El proceso de justicia transicional en México, 2001–2006." *Foro internacional* 54, no. 1 (January–March 2014): 31–75.

Ulloa Bornemann, Alberto. *Surviving Mexico's Dirty War: A Political Prisoner's Memoir.* Edited and translated by Arthur Schmidt and Aurora Camacho de Schmidt. Philadelphia: Temple University Press, 2007.

Valdés, Hernán. *Diary of a Chilean Concentration Camp.* Translated by Jo Labanyi. London: Victor Gollancz, 1975.

Valente, Marcela. "Argentina: Shedding Light on Dictatorship's Sex Crimes." Inter Press Service News Agency, June 28, 2011. http://www.ipsnews.net/2011/06/argentina-shedding-light-on-dictatorships-sex-crimes/.

Veigel, Klaus Friedrich. *Dictatorship, Democracy, and Globalization: Argentina and the Cost of Paralysis.* University Park: Pennsylvania State University Press, 2009.

Vezzetti, Hugo. *Pasado y presente: Guerra, dictadura y sociedad en la Argentina.* México, DF: Siglo veintiuno editores, 2002.

———. *Sobre la violencia revolucionaria.* Buenos Aires: Siglo XXI, 2009.
Weheliye, Alexander G. *Habeas Viscus: Racializing Assemblages, Biopolitics, and Black Feminist Theories of the Human.* Durham, NC: Duke University Press, 2014.
Wright, Melissa W. "Necropolitics, Narcopolitics, and Femicide: Gendered Violence on the Mexico-U.S. Border." *Signs* 3, no. 36 (March 2011): 707–31.
Zanchetta, Barbara. "Between Cold War Imperatives and State-Sponsored Terrorism: The United States and 'Operation Condor.'" *Studies in Conflict and Terrorism* 39, no. 12 (2016): 1084–102.
Zavala Guillén, Ana Laura. "Argentinean Transitional Process: Women Behind." *Journal of Peace, Conflict and Development* 20 (2013): 52–60.
Zermeño, Sergio. *México: Una democracia utópica.* México, DF: Siglo Veintiuno editores, 2003.
Zolov, Eric. *Iconic Mexico: An Encyclopedia from Acapulco to Zócalo.* Santa Barbara, CA: ABC-CLIO, 2015.

Index

Agamben, Giorgio, 63–64, 68–69, 75
Agrupación, Evita, 9, 105
Aguayo, Sergio, 50
Agustín Lanusse, Alejandro, 113
Alapisco Lizarraga, José Manuel, 52, 150
"Alejandra," 1–2, 22, 58, 122–23, 137–38, 150, 152–55, 162, 166–67, 169n1
Alfonsín, Raúl, 26, 31–32, 53
Almorzando con Mirtha Legrand, 96
Álvarez Garín, Raúl, 54–55
Amnesty International, 32, 49
amnesty laws, 160, 164, 178n25
Andújar, Andrea, 126
anticapitalism, 3, 9
anticommunism, 1–2, 5, 7, 12
anti-imperialism, 8, 151
Armed Revolutionary Forces (FAR), 138
Article 19, 165
Association of Ex-Detained Disappeared (AEDD), 21, 31, 134, 158–60
Augier, Nelida, 127
Avelar, Idelbar, 115
Avendaño Martínez, Roberta, 149
Aviña, Alexander, 103
Aztecs, 91

Balardini, Lorena, 33
Balderas Silva, Maricela, 50, 121
Barbara and Dick, 67
Barthes, Roland, 107, 111
Battle of Chile, The (1975), 106
Bazin, André, 111
Bechis, Marco, 61–62, 64–78, 84, 89, 92–96
Bejarano, Cynthia, 28
Benavides Guevara, Elisa, 109, 176n17
Beverley, John, 103, 117, 142
Blackwell, Maylei, 21, 136, 140
Bolaño, Roberto, 20
Bolivia, 103
Bonasso, Miguel, 78, 95
Brazil, 8
Brigada Blanca. *See* White Brigade (Brigada Blanca)
Brown, Wendy, 4, 36
Brusa, Victor, 163
Bueno-Hansen, Pascha, 20, 28, 33
Buenos Aires, Argentina, 21, 31–35, 41, 75–78, 112, 134, 143. *See also* El Olimpo
Bunster-Burotto, Ximena, 10, 142

Cabañas, Lucío, 6, 9

Calderón, Fernando, 6, 103, 165
Calveiro, Pilar, 71, 74, 130
Calvo de Laborde, Adriana, 10, 35–41, 43, 58, 94, 172n18
Camacho Loaiza, Martha Alicia, 52, 150
Campo de batalla, cuerpo de mujer (2012), 141
Campo Militar No. 1, 82
Carazo, Mercedes "Lucy," 95–96, 130–31
carceral state, 60–98, 141, 173n2. *See also* women prisoners
Cárdenas, Alejandra, 97–100, 103
Carey, Elaine, 49
Carrillo Prieto, Ignacio, 47
Castellanos, Laura, 18, 103, 149, 165
Castresana, Carlos, 157
Castro, Fidel, 5
Cedillo, Adela, 6, 9, 103, 123
Center for Legal and Social Studies (Buenos Aires), 33
Central Intelligence Agency (CIA), 22; and military aid, 5, 170n6
children, 52–53
Children for Identity and Justice Against Forgetting and Silence (HIJOS), 38
Chile, 6–8, 65, 93, 106, 157
Christianity, 33, 52, 97
church (institution), 2, 123
Ciudad Juárez, Mexico, 164
Cohen, Deborah, 9, 55
Cold War, The, 2, 4, 63. *See also* Southern Cone dictatorships
Collins, Dana, 27
Comes da Silva, Janine, 139
Comité '68. *See* Committee for Democratic Liberties (Comité '68)
Committee for Democratic Liberties (Comité '68), 1, 21, 49, 150, 159–60, 169n3
Communist Party (Los Angeles, CA), 22
Córdoba, Argentina, 105, 116
Corpus Christi massacre, 6
Cortez, Hernán, 91
Cosse, Isabella, 93, 128, 130
coup d'état, 7, 141
Covino, Deborah, 72
Cruz, Margarita, 20–21, 32, 94, 97, 141–42, 144–46, 157, 160
Cuban Revolution (1959), 5, 8, 22

Cuenca Díaz, Hermenegildo, 12
Cultural Residues (2004). *See* Nelly Richard
cultural studies, 21, 102–3, 136, 139
cultural texts/productions. *See* film; literary fiction; oral history; photography; poetry; *testimonio*

Daleo, Graciela, 96
D'Antonio, Débora, 126
da Silva, Gomez, 153
decolonization, 8, 151
de la Luz Aguilar Terrés, María, 150
de los Angeles Magdelano Cárdenas, María, 103
democracy, 2, 9, 27–28, 37, 58, 123
Derrida, Jaques, 102, 125
Diana, Marta, 101–2, 104–32
Díaz, Marta, 138–40, 148
Díaz Ordaz, Gustavo, 6, 12, 49
Dirty War: as contested term, 5–6; scholarship on, 5–8, 29, 48, 60, 63, 103, 107, 126, 131, 136–40, 150–56
disruptive archives (term), 17–20, 161
Di Tella, Andrés, 94–96
domesticity, 9–11
Doyle, Kate, 47
drugs. *See* narco-trafficking
Durán, Javier, 84

Echeverría, Luis, 6–7, 12–13, 49–52, 159–60, 173n42
El apando (1969). *See* José Revueltas
El Club Atlético center, 41, 45, 66
El fin de la historia. *See* Liliana Heker
Ellingson, Laura L., 22–23
El Olimpo, 61, 70, 74–78. *See also* Marco Bechis
Eloy, Nilda, 21, 133–34, 146–48, 157–61
embodied epistemology, 22, 136, 139–42, 167
embodied resistance, 9–11, 16, 28, 64, 71, 97, 124
Enloe, Cynthia, 15, 35
Escuelita de Famaillá center, 32, 141, 144
Espinoza, Eduardo Valle, 57
Etchecolatz, Miguel, 160–61
Eureka group, 49

Eurocentric, 20
Excelsior (newspaper), 108, 124

Falcón, Sylvanna M., 20, 23
fascism, 8
Federation of Students of Guadalajara (FEG), 1, 58
feminicide, 164
feminist literature, 8, 18–20, 32–44, 63–64, 103, 121, 126, 136–43, 150–55; and black feminist scholarship, 63, 69, 174n14
feminist movements, 2, 8–11, 18, 20, 31, 151–59, 166–67; historical erasure of, 11, 14–25, 34, 54–55, 98–135–61, 167. *See also* leftist revolutionary movements
Ferrarese, Lelia, 25, 156–58, 162, 167
film, 60–61, 64–78, 84, 89, 92–132, 141
Firmenich, Mario, 103
Flor en Otomí (2012). *See* Luisa Riley
Forchetti, Liliana, 32–34, 126–30, 143–46, 148, 153, 165–66
Foucault, Michel, 63
Fox Quesada, Vicente, 26, 46–50, 54
Franco, Jean, 8, 19, 44, 103, 143, 164–65
Franke, Katherine M., 34
Frazier, Lessie Jo, 9, 55
Fregoso, Rosa-Linda, 28, 164

Gallegos, Romulo, 20
Garage Olimpo (1999). *See* Marco Bechis
Gelman, Juan, 38–39, 129
gender-neutral framework, 17, 31
General Archive of the Nation (AGN), 46, 108, 115
Gonzales Carranza, Rosa María, 17
Gordon, Avery, 101, 116
Gracia, Necoechea, 139
Grammático, Karin, 126
Guadalajara, Mexico, 1–2, 99–100, 120, 122, 137
guerilla forces. *See* leftist revolutionary movements
Guerrero. *See* Party of the Poor (Guerrero)
Guevara, Che, 103, 130
Gutiérrez Campos, Bertha Lilia, 1, 21, 58, 99–101, 120–23, 132, 153–55

Guzmán, Patricio, 106

Habeas Viscus: Racializing Assemblages, Biopolitics, and Black Feminist Theories of the Human (2014). *See* Alexander Weheliye
Hayner, Priscilla B., 31
Heker, Liliana, 93, 95–97
Hesford, Wendy S., 118
historical memory (discourse), 11–25, 42, 99, 103, 106, 114, 135, 138–41. *See also* memory projects (discourse)
homosexuality, 84–90
human rights, 3–4, 13, 26–60, 164; activist reports, 38–60, 144, 147, 164, 173n42–43; organizations, 7, 15–16, 32, 47–49, 134, 155, 158–60, 163; state reports, 26–60, 144; tribunals, 31–37, 143–48, 157–60, 162–63, 166; universal standard, 27–31, 36–38, 41, 47–49, 54, 58, 166; violations of, 8, 14–17, 26–60, 82, 104–5, 113, 134, 143–48
Huyssen, Andreas, 27

imagined communities, 3–4
Independence Operation, 141
indexicality, 108–9
Infierno camp, 147–48
Institutional Revolutionary Party (PRI), 2, 4–8, 26, 47–53, 58, 121, 164; democratic image of, 5, 7–8, 12
Isabel, Margarita, 54–55

James, Daniel, 137, 139
Jelin, Elizabeth, 16, 116, 139, 142
Julio López, Jorge, 160–61, 163

Kaminsky, Amy, 65, 70
Keller, Renata, 6
Kirchner, Nestor, 160, 164
Kozol, Wendy, 118
Kristeva, Julia, 72
Kurlat, Marcelo, 95

La Casita detention center, 162
Lagarde, Marcela, 70
La Jornada, 152
La Madrid, Mara, 38–39

La Malinche, 64–65, 91–98
La noche de Tlatelolco (Massacre in Mexico) (1971). *See* Elena Poniatowska
La Plata, Argentina, 133–34
Laub, Dori, 136
Lecumberri Prison, 62, 81–82, 149
leftist revolutionary movements: in 1960s, 6–9, 48–50, 54–62, 84, 100, 133–39, 151; division of labor in, 128–29; formation of, 6, 9, 135, 176n10; male dominance in, 2–4, 9–19, 24, 57, 64, 78, 91–103, 122, 127–30, 135, 152–58. *See also* feminist movements
Leglise, Patricia Pensado. *See* Pensado Leglise, Patricia
Lesgart, Adriana, 104–5, 112–16, 125, 129–30
Lesgart, Liliana, 105, 116–17
Lesgart, María, 105
Lesgart, Rogelio, 105
Lesgart, Susana, 105, 112–16
Lewin, Miriam, 96
Liga. *See* 23rd of September Communist League (Liga)
literary fiction, 61, 64, 78–98
Longoni, Ana, 78, 96–97

Macías Loza, Enrique, 99
male prisoners, 174n5
malinchismo, 91–98
Manzo-Robledo, Francisco, 87
Maranghello, César, 65
María Araujo, Ana, 139
Márquez, Rodríguez, 16
Martínez de Perón, Isabel, 7, 141
Marx, Karl. *See* socialism/Marxism
Mask, Mia, 70
Massera, Emilio, 163
Mbembe, Achille, 63, 69
McClintock, Anne, 10
memory projects (discourse), 16–42, 98, 103–4, 117–18, 136–41, 167. *See also* historical memory
Menchu, Rigoberta, 139
Menem, Carlos, 38, 66, 117, 163
methodology, 20–23, 120–21, 138–40
Mexican Revolution (1910), 6, 81, 88
Mexico City, Mexico, 6, 21, 46, 80, 105, 151.

See also Lecumberri Prison; Tlatelolco massacre
Mohanty, Chandra T., 18, 155–56
Monte Chingolo massacre, 22
Montoneros, 7, 9, 93, 95, 105, 113–16, 125–30
Montoneros: Una historia (1994). *See* Andrés Di Tella
Mtintso, Thenjiwe, 34
Mujeres guerrilleras (1997). *See* Marta Diana
Mulvey, Laura, 68–70, 108, 111
Museum of Memory (Argentina), 156

narco-trafficking, 5, 80–81, 84–89, 165
National Action Party (PAN), 26, 35, 47, 50, 53
National Autonomous University of Mexico (UNAM), 134, 170n11
National Commission on Human Rights (CNDH) (Mexico), 26, 46, 172n34
National Commission on the Disappeared (CONADEP), 26–34, 40, 56, 59–60, 144
national identity, 8, 10–13, 16, 27, 52, 69, 88–93, 98, 142
nationalism(s), 6, 10, 15, 35, 69–70, 88
National Liberation Force (FLN), 101, 104–6, 109–11, 119–22
National Polytechnic Institute and the National University of Mexico (UNAM), 6
National Security Archive (Washington D.C.), 47
Navy School of Mechanics (ESMA), 94–97
Nazar Haro, Miguel, 10
Necoechea García, Gerardo, 138
necropolitics, 63–98. *See also* carceral state; women prisoners: rape/sexual violence
neoconservative, 103
neoliberalism, 3–5, 62–64, 66, 101–3, 112, 163–67; and progress, 115–17, 135
Nepantla safe house, 104–12, 122, 124–25
Ni el flaco perdón de Dios (1997), 29, 38–43, 58. *See also* Adriana Calvo de Laborde; Juan Gelman; Mara La Madrid
non-governmental organizations (NGOs), 32, 47
novels. *See* literary fiction
Nunca más (1984), 13, 27, 31–40, 44–45, 53, 57, 59, 144

Oberti, Alejandra, 140, 152
Oblatos prison, 132
Office of the Special Prosecutor for Social and Political Movements of the Past (FEMOSPP), 26–30, 34, 36–38, 45–54, 56, 59–60
olvido. See feminist movements: historical erasure
oral history, 138–61. *See also* historical memory (discourse); memory projects (discourse)

Party of the Poor (Guerrero), 9, 97, 99
Penal de Oblatos, 100
Pensado Leglise, Patricia, 139, 151
People's Revolutionary Armed Forces (FRAP), 1, 122
People's Revolutionary Army (ERP), 113, 126–31, 152–53
People's Union, 1–2, 17, 122, 137
Pernías, Antonio, 95
Peru, 34
photography, 107–13
Pinochet, Augusto, 157
poetry, 99–100
political exiles, 7
poner el cuerpo. See embodied resistance
Poniatowska, Elena, 29, 51, 53–60, 81, 149
Portelli, Alessandro, 137
Pozzi, Pablo, 139
Prado Rosas, Arnulfo, 120, 132
Prieto Argüelles, Carlos, 105
Prieto Stock, Ayari, 124–25
Prieto Stock, Dení, 104–13, 115, 117–25, 130
Process for National Reorganization (Proceso), 2, 4–5, 7, 14, 65

racializations, 63, 69, 93
Ramon Gaspar, Jose Agustin, 49
rape. See women prisoners: rape/sexual violence
Recuerdo de la muerte (1994). See Miguel Bonasso
Revueltas, José, 61–62, 64–67, 78–98
Richard, Nelly, 42, 166
Riley, Luisa, 101–2, 104–32
Río de la Plata, 67–68, 73, 76
Rodríguez, Ileana, 103, 126–27

Rodríguez Márquez, Ana Ignacia, 3, 49, 57, 59, 133–34, 137, 148–49, 151–60
Ross, Fiona, 34, 43

Sábato, Ernesto, 13
Saint Jean, Ibérico, 7
Sangster, Joan, 139, 142
Sarlo, Beatriz, 103, 117
Scheibe Wolff, Pedro, 153
Separos de Tlaxcuaque, 149
sexual violence. See women prisoners: rape/sexual violence
Sgro, Mirta, 21, 128, 130–31, 152
Silva, Juan, 94–95, 123
Single, Numberless Death, A (2002). See Nora Strejilevich
socialism/Marxism, 5, 7, 9, 12, 54, 81, 105, 125, 128, 135
Socialist Party, 105
South African Truth and Reconciliation Commission, 34
Southern Cone dictatorships, 3, 5–6, 8, 48, 63, 137–38, 141–64
Spillers, Hortense, 69
Stock, Evelyn, 105
Stock, Laura, 107, 110, 112, 119–21
Strejilevich, Nora, 38, 41–46
student movements. See leftist revolutionary movements; Student Revolutionary Front (FER); Tlatelolco massacre
Student Revolutionary Front (FER), 1–2, 58, 99, 120
Suppo, Silvia, 162–63, 165
Sutton, Barbara, 9, 11

Taylor, Diana, 10, 19, 70, 133, 136, 143, 150–51, 158
Tejas Verdes: Diario de campo (1974). See Hernán Valdés
Terrés, Aguilar, 150
Testa, Ana, 94–96
testimonio, 139, 158. *See also* oral history
Theidon, Kimberly, 35
Tlatelolco massacre, 6, 48–50, 54, 59, 62, 84, 134, 157, 159–60
Torres Montenegro, Andrés, 138
transnational politics, 8, 15, 20, 151, 155–56, 164, 166–68

Trelew massacre, 113
Treviño Rangel, Javier, 50
Trial of the Juntas (1985), 31–37
Tucumán, Argentina, 126, 141
23rd of September Communist League (Liga), 1–2, 50, 99, 120–23, 137, 150, 153
Two Devils theory, 12–13, 40, 135, 171n33

Ulloa Bornemann, Alberto, 103
United Nations World Conference on Human Rights (1993), 47
United States of America (USA): Central Intelligence Agency (CIA), 22; and military aid, 5, 170n6
Universal Declaration of Human Rights, 28. *See also* human rights: universal standard
University of Guadalajara, 1, 58, 120
University of La Plata, 35
University of Mexico (Mexico City), 6
Uruguay, 8

Valdés, Hernán, 93
Vásquez, Genaro, 6
Vezzetti, Hugo, 7, 103, 117

Videla, Jorge Rafael, 7, 12, 163
Villa Devoto prison, 156
Villa Urquiza prison, 32–33, 143, 146

Weheliye, Alexander, 63, 69, 75
White Brigade (Brigada Blanca), 1, 48, 149–50
woman (as social term), 17
women prisoners, 11, 43–44, 57, 61, 122–23, 132, 141–51, 156–59; and pregnancy, 35–37, 39–41, 53, 150, 162, 172n17; and rape/sexual violence, 43–46, 51, 53, 61–98, 142–51, 157, 162–65, 174n5
women's image, 9–16, 36, 43, 53, 60, 64, 70, 129–31, 142; and Madonna/whore dichotomy, 87–89; and nation/Motherland, 88–92. *See also* La Malinche
women's rights, 31, 37, 47–54. *See also* human rights
Worker's Revolutionary Party (PRT), 32, 127, 143
Wright, Melissa W., 63

Yáñez, Sylvia, 22, 153

Zavala Guillén, Ana Laura, 144

VIVIANA BEATRIZ MACMANUS is an assistant professor in the Department of Spanish and French Studies at Occidental College.

DISSIDENT FEMINISMS

Hear Our Truths: The Creative Potential of Black Girlhood   *Ruth Nicole Brown*
Muddying the Waters: Coauthoring Feminisms across Scholarship and Activism   *Richa Nagar*
Beyond Partition: Gender, Violence, and Representation in Postcolonial India   *Deepti Misri*
Feminist and Human Rights Struggles in Peru: Decolonizing Transitional Justice   *Pascha Bueno-Hansen*
Against Citizenship: The Violence of the Normative   *Amy L. Brandzel*
Dissident Friendships: Feminism, Imperialism, and Transnational Solidarity   *Edited by Elora Halim Chowdhury and Liz Philipose*
Politicizing Creative Economy: Activism and a Hunger Called Theater   *Dia Da Costa*
In a Classroom of Their Own: The Intersection of Race and Feminist Politics in All-Black Male Schools   *Keisha Lindsay*
Fashioning Postfeminism: Spectacular Femininity and Transnational Culture   *Simidele Dosekun*
Queer and Trans Migrations: Dynamics of Illegalization, Detention, and Deportation   *Edited by Eithne Luibhéid and Karma R. Chávez*
Disruptive Archives: Feminist Memories of Resistance in Latin America's Dirty Wars   *Viviana Beatriz MacManus*

The University of Illinois Press
is a founding member of the
Association of University Presses.

―――――――――――

University of Illinois Press
1325 South Oak Street
Champaign, IL 61820-6903
www.press.uillinois.edu